More Praise for

NEVER
SURRENDER

"An outstanding, gripping read by a popular historian. It blends colorful biographies, pungent anecdotes, and a solid grasp of the great strategic issues that weighed on decision-makers in 1940."

—Geoffrey Wawro, author of *A Mad Catastrophe: The Outbreak of World War I and the Collapse of the Habsburg Empire*

"Kelly successfully balances the big picture with stories of persons who range from Count Ciano, the foreign minister of Italy, to a British soldier waiting to be evacuated from Dunkirk."

—*Library Journal*

"Impressive in scope but attentive to detail . . . *Never Surrender* is a character-driven narrative of a crucial period in World War II history and of the men and women who shaped it."

—*The History of WWII Podcast*

ALSO BY JOHN KELLY

The Great Mortality:
An Intimate History of the Black Death,
the Most Devastating Plague of All Time

The Graves Are Walking:
The Great Famine and the Saga of the Irish People

Three on the Edge:
The Stories of Ordinary American Families
in Search of a Medical Miracle

NEVER
SURRENDER

Winston Churchill and Britain's Decision
to Fight Nazi Germany
in the Fateful Summer of 1940

John Kelly

SCRIBNER

New York London Toronto Sydney New Delhi

SCRIBNER
An Imprint of Simon & Schuster, Inc.
1230 Avenue of the Americas
New York, NY 10020

First Scribner trade paperback edition November 2016

SCRIBNER and design are registered trademarks of The Gale Group, Inc.,
used under license by Simon & Schuster, Inc., the publisher of this work.

For information about special discounts for bulk purchases, please contact
Simon & Schuster Special Sales at 1-866-506-1949 or business@simonandschuster.com.

The Simon & Schuster Speakers Bureau can bring authors to your live event.
For more information or to book an event, contact the Simon & Schuster
Speakers Bureau at 1-866-248-3049 or visit our website at www.simonspeakers.com.

Manufactured in the United States of America

1   3   5   7   9   10   8   6   4   2

Library of Congress Control Number: 2016303546

ISBN 978-1-4767-2797-4
ISBN 978-1-4767-2798-1 (pbk)
ISBN 978-1-4767-2799-8 (ebook)

For Jack Dawson Kelly

CONTENTS

NEVER
SURRENDER

CHAPTER ONE

NEVER AGAIN

London, July 18–19, 1919

The showers and cool temperatures predicted for July 19 arrived from Ireland a day early. By midafternoon on the eighteenth the air was heavy with the smell of rain, and the low, cheerless sky above Parliament had the look of trouble about it. In Kensington Gardens, transformed into a temporary billet for Allied and Empire troops, fifteen thousand soldiers sat in unheated tents, cursing the foul English weather in Italian, Polish, Portuguese, Serbian, and Japanese. At Albert Gate, where the Horse Guards had just finished a final drill for the next day's Victory Day Parade, a Guards colonel scanned the sky, then ordered a work crew to hurry and sweep up the horse droppings before the rain began. In Whitehall and Westminster, where the prestige of the British Empire was a perpetual preoccupation, there was concern about an international embarrassment should a heavy rain suppress turnout. Toward evening, with the sky still stubbornly overcast, almost the only outposts of hope remaining in the imperial capital were the War Office, which, despite the rain threat, had had a bust of Lord Kitchener moved down to the entrance for the parade, and the *Daily Mail*, which fearlessly predicted that "rain or no rain," the crowds would be huge; and so it proved.

Even before the lamplights were turned off at 5:00 a.m., people

1

were gathering along the six-mile parade route that ran in a rect-angle through central London. By 8:00 a.m. Trafalgar Square had become a throbbing mass of humanity. By 9:00 a.m. the swelling tide had spilled over into Whitehall; people stood six and seven deep. To provide more standing room, some merchants removed the glass panes from their display windows, but it was like putting a finger in a dike. Through the early morning hours, the throngs in central London swelled and swelled again. Veterans came on crutches and in wheelchairs; widows came in mourning black; the young, who had known nothing but war, came, eager to see what peace looked like; and the old came grieving for the Victorian world of their youth, when no one knew yet what a century of industrial revolution could do to the human body.

Not one in ten of the troopers assembled in the staging area at Albert Gate below Hyde Park had expected to be alive to see this day; some had begun to wonder whether their children would live to see it. Yet here it was, after a thousand savage dawns and three million Allied dead: victory, glorious victory. As the crowd looked on, the troops were briefed on the parade route. Big Ben chimed 10:00 a.m., church bells pealed from every point in the imperial capital, and the Americans, whom alphabetical order dictated come first, marched out of Albert Gate. Pine-tall and still fresh-faced after only a few months of heavy combat, the cocky Yanks were a reminder of what European soldiers had looked like before the machine gun and the artillery barrage found them. Rifles slung over the shoulder, arms swinging in unison, the Yanks disappeared into the crowd singing, "Over there, over there, send the word, send the word, the Yanks are coming, the Yanks are coming." The Belgians, who came next, were short and stumpy, and the state of their beards and mustaches did not speak highly of their personal hygiene. Still, unlike the Americans, the gallant little Belgians had been in the fight from the beginning, from August 1914, and the crowd was determined to find virtues in them, even if the virtues had to be invented. "There [is] something very citizen-like" about the Belgians, declared one spectator. The appearance of the French caused a frisson of excitement. Here was *le glorie* itself in an Adrian helmet and horizon-blue uniform. No army had emerged from the war with more prestige, and no Allied army, except the now-defunct Czarist Russian army, had paid so high a price for le glorie—1.3 million dead and 4.2 million wounded in a population of 40 million. Everywhere along the parade route, confetti and cheers showered down on the poilus, who had endured at Verdun, at the Marne—who had endured on battlefields even stones had found unendurable. Forty-five minutes of Serbians in brightly colored *sajkacas*—an indented cap that looked alarmingly like a collapsed birthday cake—Italians in jaunty, feathered alpine hats, and Japanese in faux European uniforms followed. Then the moment the crowd had been awaiting arrived. The British Expeditionary Force, given pride of place at the end of the parade, marched out of Albert Gate behind their commander, Field Marshal Sir Douglas Haig, a handsome blond cavalryman who, the *Manchester Guardian* would note the next day, looked even more handsome on a horse.

Anyone with an eye for such things could tell that the British contingent was composed of three different armies. The older men belonged to the prewar professional army, savaged during the encounter battles of 1914 and the early trench warfare of 1915; the younger men, to Kitchener's volunteer army, decimated in the battles of 1916 and 1917; and the youngest troops, many just boys really, belonged to the conscript army that, in its turn, had been badly mauled during the German offensive and Allied counteroffensives of 1918. On this Victory Day, the British death toll stood at seven hundred thousand for the home islands and more than a million for the empire as a whole, and grave details were still digging up the remains of Oxford boys on the

Somme, Canadian farmers at Passchendaele, and New Zealand and Australian sheepherders at Gallipoli. Not long before he was killed, the soldier-poet Wilfred Owen called the war a "carnage incomparable." For fifty-one months, the cream of the British Empire had been marched into the mud of northwestern France and Flanders and been slaughtered. There was no other word for it; but the truth was too unbearable, so as the casualty lists mounted, the human need to find meaning in death, especially young death, had, with some help from the British government, turned the great carnage into the "Great Sacrifice." Posters of a dead Tommy lying at the foot of the crucified Christ abounded, and rare was the school assembly that did not include a recitation of Rupert Brooke's poem "The Soldier":

> If I should die, think only this of me:
> That there's some corner of a foreign field
> That is for ever England.

Toward noon on Parade Day, a well-dressed, middle-aged woman emerged from the crowd in Whitehall, darted across the street, fell to her knees in front of the Cenotaph, and placed a bouquet of lilacs under the inscription at its base, "The Glorious Dead." Those spectators still on speaking terms with God offered up a prayer for the woman; those who were not just stared, transfixed by her grief. Then the blare of military music brought the crowd back to life, and the BEF marched by at parade pace under a blazing canopy of brightly colored regimental flags embroidered with the place-names that had become household words in Britain: First Battle of Ypres, Second Battle of Ypres, Third Battle of Ypres, First Battle of the Marne, Second Battle of the Marne, Somme, Loos, Vimy Ridge, Passchendaele, Gallipoli.

A year after the Victory Day Parade, the remains of six unidentified British soldiers were retrieved from the mud of a Flanders field and sent to a military facility in France, where a blindfolded Guards officer chose one set for internment in England. An hour later the remains were placed inside a casket, specifically designed for the occasion by the British Undertakers Association, and on Armistice Day 1920 the remains were interred at Westminster Abbey with full military honors. For King George V, the Westminster ceremony was the second memorial event of the day. Earlier that morning, he had unveiled a new cenotaph in Whitehall; the temporary plaster and wood model created for the Victory Day Parade had proved such a success that the government had decided to commission a permanent stone version. Soon thereafter, Manchester, Southampton, and Rochdale also had cenotaphs, and as the idea caught on around the empire, so, too, did Toronto, Auckland, and Hong Kong. In the early postwar years, human memorials to the "Great Sacrifice" also abounded. There were the legions of young women—part of Britain's 1.7 million "surplus women"—who gathered at the local cinema on weekends to dream about Ramón Novarro and Rudolph Valentino, now that all the boys they might have dreamed of had gone to a soldier's grave. There were the ubiquitous one-armed porters, one-eyed barristers, and one-legged butchers. Mercifully, the government kept the *grands mutilés*, the grotesquely disfigured of face and limbless of body, out of view in military hospitals.

Contrasting the pre- and postwar mood of Britain, the historian Arnold Toynbee noted that before 1914, "Westerners and . . . British Westerners above all, had felt that they were not as other men were or ever had been . . . Other civilizations had risen and fallen, come and gone but [the British] did not doubt that their own civilization was invulnerable." After 1918, vicars and public men continued to preach the same old verities in the same old ways, but the preaching had become reflexive, the way a body sometimes twitches after death. The young, having seen where patriotism leads, were throwing over God, King, and Country for pacifism, socialism, communism, trade unionism, internationalism, environmentalism, nudism, flapperism, Dadaism, anarchism, and any other ism they could get their hands on. And the intellectuals, having examined humanity from every imaginable angle, concluded that man's dark impulses would keep what one of them called the "death ship" of war afloat in perpetuity. The bookstores filled with titles that breathed despair—*The Dying Creeds, The Smoke of Our Burning, Life Against Death,* and *Can Civilization Be Saved?* And the old, bewildered by it all and heavy with sorrow, stood in half-empty churches, intoning that most melancholy of English hymns, "O God, Our Help in Ages Past."

> The busy tribes of flesh and blood,
> . . . Carried downwards by the flood
> And lost in the . . . years.

Initially, there were great hopes that the Treaty of Versailles, signed on June 28, 1919, would deliver a just and enduring peace to the world. But the French and, to a lesser extent, the British public found the treaty's terms insufficiently onerous, while the Germans, who had come to Versailles seeking mercy, left vowing retribution. The treaty stripped Germany of its colonies, its western border on the Rhine, and transferred several historically German regions to other nations. Asked how long the treaty would last, Field Marshal Ferdinand Foch, Supreme Commander of Allied Forces in the final year of the Great War, evoked the death ship: "This is not a peace. It is an armistice for twenty years."

Except for Adolf Hitler, Benito Mussolini, and a few other people the world had yet to hear from, Marshal Foch's view was not widely shared in the early postwar years. More than 37 million men, women, and children had been killed or wounded in the Great War. That number was nearly five times greater than the population of prewar Belgium (7.5 million), only 3 million less than the population of prewar France (40 million), and only 9 million less than the population of prewar Britain (46 million). Ruminating on the lessons of the Great Sacrifice, the *London Illustrated News* concluded that all the lessons came down to the same lesson: Never Again. "So vast is the cost of victory, no price can be too high to pay for avoiding the necessity of war."

During the 1920s, Never Again inspired a new international order based on collective security, disarmament, and the League of Nations. And for a time, the system seemed to work. The 1925 Pact of Locarno—signed by Germany, France, Britain, Belgium, and Italy—guaranteed the borders of Europe. Three years later the United States, Britain, Germany, Japan, Italy, and several other nations signed the Kellogg-Briand Pact, which renounced war as an instrument of national policy. Plans were also laid for the World Disarmament Conference. By the late 1920s, European civilization seemed to have emerged from the "brown fog" of despair, cleansed and renewed—like sun after rain. In Britain, unemployment, which had risen to two million after the war, fell to a million, and overseas investments rose to near-prewar levels. People forgot their troubles and lost themselves in a new dance craze, the Lindy Hop, or in new fads such as the crossword puzzle and a Chinese game called mah-jongg. Then, on October 29, 1929, Wall Street crashed. A week later the economist John Maynard Keynes reassured Britons that "there will be no serious direct consequences in London resulting from the Wall Street slump." He was wrong.

A good case can be made that 1931, the year Japan invaded

Manchuria and the Depression reached full force, marks the end of the post–World War One era and the beginning of the pre–World War Two era. On one side of the date lay the Locarno and Kellogg-Briand Pacts and the sunlit uplands of collective security and disarmament; on the other side, the howl of the approaching whirlwind. In 1932, Oswald Mosley founded the British Union Fascists, the unemployment rate in Britain rose to 2.5 million, and the streets of Europe filled with thousands of men, hardened by war, disillusioned by peace, impoverished by the slump, and possessing loyalties—to Nazism, Fascism, communism—that transcended national borders. In 1933, Hitler came to power and Germany and Japan walked out of the League of Nations and the World Disarmament Conference. Less noted but also significant, in 1933 the British Chiefs of Staff issued their first warning about a new European war. "Germany is not only starting to rearm, but . . . she will continue the process until within a few years hence she will again have to be reckoned a formidable military power. . . . It would therefore seem that anywhere in the next, say, three to five years, we may be faced with military demands for an intervention on the Continent." To deter the Germans, the chiefs recommended the creation of a British expeditionary force.

The politicians were horrified. The previous February, the Oxford Union had overwhelmingly carried this motion: "This house would not in any circumstances fight for King and Country." Then in October—the same month the Chiefs of Staff issued their warning—a Labour candidate running on a platform of unilateral disarmament won a by-election in the reliably Conservative London constituency of East Fulham. A quarter of a century later, in his memoir *The Gathering Storm*, Winston Churchill still sounded astonished by the East Fulham result.

In 1934, the Chiefs of Staff again unsettled the politicians by urging the creation of a British expeditionary force capable of fighting a Continental enemy. First and foremost, Never Again meant no British soldiers on European soil. Even the famously bellicose Churchill balked at such a prospect. The last time Britain sent an expeditionary force to the Continent, nearly seven hundred thousand men had not come back. Furthermore, Churchill, like many other politicians who kept current with advances in military technology, did not see the need for such a force. Airpower, not ground power, would dominate the battlefield of the future.

Gas bombs, chemical bombs, sky-darkening bomber streams: in the interwar years, the air threat was viewed in the same apocalyptic terms as the nuclear threat is today. "Our cities will be rendered uninhabitable by chemical bombs. . . . We are faced with the wipeout of civilization," declared an authority on aerial warfare. Films such as H. G. Wells's *Things to Come* put images to the warnings. For a score of weeks in hundreds of British theaters, fleets of bombers throbbed across the gray English sky; beneath their noteless drone cities exploded, people exploded, fire and black smoke flared from the holes where Parliament and St. Paul's had stood; civil defense workers tagged bodies in public parks, the underground collapsed on screaming passengers, and millions of refugees clogged the roads. A secret report compiled for the British government estimated that in the first two months of a new war bombing would produce 1.8 million casualties, including 600,000 dead.*

---

*In actual fact, between 1939 and 1945, 40,000 Britons died from bombing—a significant number, but far less than the predicted number. *Things to Come* also got a couple of other things wrong. Despite the round-the-clock Allied bombing campaign, German war production continued to rise, reaching a peak in 1944, the fifth year of the war. Not until a good part of the Luftwaffe had been destroyed in the Russian campaign and the bombers acquired fighter escorts capable of accompanying them to and from targets in Germany, did airpower begin to achieve the kind of results predicted by its prewar enthusiasts, and not until the atomic bomb did it become a decisive weapon.

As airpower came to dominate the rearmament debate, a tortoise-and-hare contest developed. The hare was Churchill, quick-thinking, quick-speaking, quick-acting; the tortoise, Stanley Baldwin, the leader of the Conservative Party and three-time prime minister. No one had ever called Stanley Baldwin quick at anything. At Cambridge, he was asked to resign from the debating society because he never spoke. The prime minister's chief attribute—indeed, his critics would say his only attribute—was likability. Baldwin, whose sagging English face gave him a certain resemblance to an amiable basset hound, was the most popular politician of the day. This fact in itself was a matter of no small wonder to his critics. As one historian has noted, Baldwin's "indolence was a miracle in his time and a legend in ours." The prime minister's idea of a busy day was to avoid official papers in the morning and his fellow politicians at lunch and to spend his afternoons writing personal letters. Yet, in the eyes of the public, Stanley Baldwin could do no wrong. The average Englishman liked it that Baldwin found hiking more pleasant than thinking, doing nothing more pleasant than doing almost anything, and found foreigners as incomprehensible and beastly as he did. "Wake me up when you are finished with that," Baldwin would say whenever foreign affairs were discussed at cabinet meetings.

On paper, Baldwin appeared badly overmatched by Churchill in the air debate. No one could imagine Stanley Baldwin saying anything as eloquent or clever as "I dread the day when the means of threatening the heart of the British Empire should pass into the hands of the present rulers in Germany." Nonetheless, Baldwin managed to hold his own—and, at some points in the debate, to more than hold his own. For this he owed no small debt to his second great attribute, luck. In the mid-1930s, Churchill was out of government and at the nadir of a long and checkered political career. To the public, he remained the Gallipoli man, the engineer of the ill-fated 1915 campaign that had produced little except three sunken battleships and misery and lamentation for mothers in Australia and New Zealand, whose sons had died in their thousands on the naked, sun-struck hills of Gallipoli. To the politicians, who knew Churchill more intimately, he was the witty, gifted, impulsive, erratic polymath who had two bad ideas for every good one and was unable to tell the difference between them. In a letter to a friend, Baldwin condensed Westminster and Whitehall's view of the pre–World War Two Churchill into a few wonderfully malicious sentences: "When Winston was born, lots of fairies swooped down on his cradle with gifts—imagination, industry, eloquence, ability—and then came a fairy who said, 'No one person has a right to so many gifts' and picked up Winston and gave him such a shake and twist that with all of these gifts he was denied judgment and wisdom. And that is why, while we delight in listening to him, we do not take his advice." Not long after Baldwin wrote this appraisal, Churchill reminded the British public of just how bad his judgment could be. During the abdication crisis of 1936, even friends were baffled by his support for Edward VIII, a man of limited intelligence who gave up the throne to marry Wallis Simpson, a twice-married American woman of limited character.

Baldwin's strong performance on the air debate also owed something to his instinctive understanding of what an antiwar electorate would tolerate in the way of defense. In the mid-1930s, when "the bomber will always get through" was the eleventh commandment of military doctrine, the RAF proposed to spend its entire budget on a bomber force. But the bomber was an offensive weapon, and Baldwin's political instincts told him that the 11.5 million Britons, half the national electorate, who had voted in the Peace Ballot of 1934–35, would find it as appalling as he did that "two thousand years after Our Lord was crucified,"

European children should be immolated by incendiary bombs. During the war, Baldwin would be widely criticized for allowing Germany to gain a lead in the air—not least by Churchill, who, on hearing the Germans had bombed an iron factory owned by Baldwin, remarked that that "was ungrateful of them." Nonetheless, and despite himself, Baldwin did bumble into one decision about airpower that, in retrospect, would prove farsighted. He pushed the RAF to pay more attention to the development of the fighter, not only because the fighter was much cheaper to build than the bomber—£5,000 to £10,000 per plane versus £50,000 for a bomber—but also because its defensive character made the fighter an acceptable weapon to an antiwar public. In the summer of 1940, when Britain's survival hung on the performance of the RAF's Fighter Command, Baldwin's decision would serve his country well.

Just before noon on Saturday, March 7, 1936, Adolf Hitler stood at a podium in the Reichstag examining his speech notes. Modestly dressed in a simple gray field jacket that covered his wide hips, his brown hair neatly combed, his coarse features relaxed—in repose like this, Hitler could be the minor bureaucrat his father had been. "Altogether, he looks entirely undistinguished," said a British official, who, like many British visitors to Germany in the 1930s, confused the polite, petite bourgeois figure they encountered in small gatherings with the public man. Hitler put down his notes and surveyed his audience: six hundred Reichstag delegates, almost uniformly big of body and bulging of neck. Then he began as he began many of his speeches, with a denunciation of the Treaty of Versailles. These perorations served him the way a warm-up serves an athlete. His eyes grew hypnotic; his clenched fists cut the air. His forelock became unstuck; his fleshy face tightened into an arc of anger; then the man at the podium disappeared, replaced by a wronged Germany in all its righteous wrath. Shouts of "Heil! Heil!" greeted the announcement that Germany was renouncing the Pact of Locarno and reoccupying the demilitarized Rhineland. Hitler raised his hand for silence; then he began again, this time in a lower, more resonant voice that partly obscured the grating Upper Austrian accent. "Men of the German Reichstag, in this historic hour, when in the Reich's western provinces German troops are at this minute marching into their future peacetime garrisons, we are united—" The rest of his words were drowned out by more shouts of "Heil! Heil! Heil!" This time Hitler did not resist. He stepped back from the podium, folded his arms across his chest, and allowed himself to bathe in the adulation. The next morning, when church bells rang in the little villages along the upper Rhine, German troops in field gray and French troops in horizon blue faced each other across the old Franco-German border for the first time since 1870.

A few days after the Rhineland coup Robert Boothby, a member of the December Club, a group of antiappeasement MPs, warned the House of Commons that if allowed to stand, the coup, which violated both the Pact of Locarno and the Treaty of Versailles, would undermine the postwar system of collective security in a way that all the king's horses and all the king's men could not put back together again. Churchill issued a similar warning, but he was almost the only politician of national stature to do so, and his warning, like Boothby's, was largely ignored. Paul Emery Evans, another member of the December Club, blamed Baldwin for the apathetic public reaction to the growing German threat. "The country was never told the truth, and those who endeavored to explain what was going in the world . . . were written off . . . as a small body of alarmists." Baldwin was guilty as charged, but if he committed a crime, it was telling an antiwar public what they wanted to hear. In the late 1930s, the antiappeasement movement would grow in strength, attracting other national figures besides Churchill, including Alfred Duff Cooper and Leo Amery, two former first lords of the Admiralty, as well as promising young politicians such as Harold Macmillan, a future prime minister. But young or old, most of the men who formed themselves into antiappeasement groups such as the Vigilantes, the December Club, and the Watching Committee, had been shaped by Harrow dawns and Cambridge nights. When they spoke of war, they spoke of it in the heroic language of "Vitaï Lampada," that ode to public school valor.

> The Gatling's jammed and the colonel dead
> . . . England is far and honor a name
> But the voice of a school boy rallies the ranks
> Play up, play up and play the game

To the housewife in London and the postman in Leeds, as to Stanley Baldwin and to a large part of the Labour Party, war was not a schoolboy poem, it was the first day of the Somme battle—almost sixty thousand men killed or wounded between sunrise and sunset; it was the soliloquy in Act Five of *Henry IV*: "What is honor? . . . a word. Who hath it? He that died on Wednesday. Therefore I'll none of it." A few weeks after the Rhineland coup Hugh Dalton, a senior Labour politician, spoke not just for his party but for most of Britain when he told Parliament that "public opinion . . . and certainly the Labour Party would not support the taking of military sanctions or even economic sanctions against Germany at this time." In France, public reaction to the Rhineland coup was more a shrug than a shout. Joked the satirical weekly *Le Canard enchaine*, "The Germans have invaded—Germany!" In Belgium, also a party to the Pact of Locarno, the response was close to naked fear. Except for a small sliver of the country around Ypres, Belgium had spent most of the Great War under German occupation. The Belgian government immediately revoked the alliance with France and declared that, henceforth, Belgium would adopt Swiss-style neutrality. Eventually, the Rhineland dispute found its way to the council of the League of Nations, which declared Germany in violation of both the Pact of Locarno and the Treaty of Versailles; but since the council lacked the means to enforce its judgment, the German troops remained on the old 1870 Franco-German border.

In "Omens of 1936," published in the *Fortnightly Review* in January of that year, historian Denis Brogan predicted that 1936 would be the year that faith in Never Again began to falter. And events would prove Brogan more right than wrong. In addition to the Rhineland coup, 1936 was the year civil war broke out in Spain, Hitler and Mussolini formed the Rome-Berlin Axis, Germany and Japan signed the Anti-Comintern Pact, and the European press began to report regular sightings of the death ship. Not coincidentally, 1936 was also the year when the diplomatic visit became a staple of the cinema newsreel. Typically, the newsreel would open with a panning shot of dignitaries standing on a railway platform, the politicians in top hats and frocks, the soldiers in gold-braided comic opera uniforms. A whistle is heard, heads turn, and a mighty engine appears, black as the African night, its swept-back nose creating the impression of great speed even as the train crawls into the station at ten miles per hour. Pulling to a halt in front of the platform, the pistons emit a snake-like hiss, and the waiting dignitaries disappear into a vapor of white steam. After the cloud dissipates, a flower girl appears and presents the visiting diplomat with a bouquet; pleasantries are exchanged on the platform; then the diplomat vanishes into the backseat of a big five-liter Horsch limousine with gull wing fenders or into a black Renault sedan with silver chevrons on the grille.

If the newsreel is set in the Balkans, the diplomat is French and he is there to shore up the troubled Little Entente, the alliance France has formed with Czechoslovakia, Romania, and the Kingdom of the Serbs, Croats, and Slovenes (Yugoslavia). If the newsreel is set in Spain, the diplomat could be a German—or an Italian, visiting Generalissimo Francisco Franco, leader of rebel Nationalist forces—or a Russian, visiting members of the Republican government in Madrid. If the newsreel is set in Berlin, the diplomat is Japanese, and he is in the German capital to witness the signing of the Anti-Comintern Pact between Japan and Germany. And if the newsreel is set in Rome, the diplomat could be German, or, even more likely, British, in which case he is in Italy to do the bidding of the new prime minister, Neville Chamberlain.

The House of Chamberlain, founded by the prime minister's father, Joe, lord mayor of Birmingham, and long presided over by older half brother Austen, a foreign secretary, had a history of producing able, ambitious, thrusting personalities. And Joe Chamberlain's youngest son would more than live up to that standard. When his turn to lead the family came, Neville would not only raise the roof, he also would put a new wing on the House of Chamberlain. As minister of health, Chamberlain was dynamic and innovative, and as chancellor of the Exchequer (Treasury secretary) he was very nearly great; under his guidance, Britain emerged from the Depression several years earlier than the United States. In every office he occupied, including prime minister, Neville Chamberlain delighted civil servants who admired his competency, his organized, orderly mind, and his ability to firm up the flaccid machinery of government. Among political colleagues, he was less popular. Cross the prime minister, they knew, and he would throw you to his minions in the press for a public savaging. Remarkably, this dynamic figure is completely absent from the newsreels and newspapers of the time, which gave us an image that continues to resonate to this day—Chamberlain as the undertaker on holiday: umbrella in hand, homburg on head, face pale, back slightly bent, eyes anxiously scanning the sky for signs of rain.

A photo of Chamberlain taken shortly after he became prime minister is truer to the real man. Here, the eyes are penetrating and intelligent, the sharp arc of the nose gives the face a hawk-like handsomeness, and the smile is inviting, with a hint of the warmth that always eluded the photographers but delighted intimates. The bold, almost aggressive way the prime minister addresses the camera catches another often overlooked trait. Like the Great Pyramid of Giza and the Hanging Gardens of Babylon, Neville Chamberlain's ego was a wonder of the world. In his weekly letters to his spinster sisters, Hilda and Ida, the vanity is so guileless it is almost charming. "This year has seen a record for social invitations," the prime minister notes in a weekly letter to Ida. "The Queen . . . remarked on the confidence everyone had in me," he tells Hilda in another letter. In public dealings, however, the vanity became hubris, not in the ancient Greek sense of someone who takes pleasure in shaming and humiliating, but in the sense of the book of Proverbs, "a pride that blinds." Chamberlain's view of himself as more than a match for any opponent allowed him to be played time and again by Mussolini, who thought him an old fool "not made of the same stuff as Francis Drake and the other magnificent adventurers who created the Empire," and by Hitler, who referred to the prime minister as "that silly old man with . . . the umbrella." Still, any fair assessment of Chamberlain's relations with the dictators is incomplete unless it also takes into account the decline of British power.

In 1937, when Chamberlain took office, Britain, a small island state, was sinking under the enormous military and economic burdens of a global empire, and the domestic burdens of the Depression and pacifism, and it was increasingly menaced by technological change. The advent of airpower had called into question the strategic advantages hitherto provided by the English Channel and the Royal Navy; and the fragile, spotty economic recovery from the 1929 crash had limited British rearmament. Aircraft production was rising, though not fast enough to build and equip an air force capable of fighting a European enemy; and the plan to create an expeditionary force capable of fighting a war on the Continent had fallen victim to budget cuts (including by Chamberlain) and to Never Again. The British public, said one senior politician, would be "strongly suspicious of any preparations made in peacetime with a view to large-scale military commitments on the Continent." In addition the dominions, which had contributed so much to the British war effort in 1914–18, were either growing isolationist—Canada and South Africa—or becoming burdens themselves. Australia and New Zealand looked to Britain for protection against Japan. Finally, there was the empire: the work of three centuries, the source of Britain's global power, and, now with the "hot winds of nationalism" blowing from Cairo and Calcutta, increasingly a deadweight, militarily and economically. By the mid-1930s it had become almost impossible to imagine any eventuality under which Britain could fight a major European war and emerge with the empire still intact.

In December 1937, the Chiefs of Staff addressed the consequences of British weakness in a forceful memorandum: "We cannot foresee the time when our defense forces will be strong enough to safeguard our trade, territory, and vital interests against Germany, Italy, and Japan at the same time. [We cannot] exaggerate [the importance] from the point of view of imperial defense of any political or international action which could be taken to reduce the number of our potential enemies."

Chamberlain was already thinking along similar lines: "Prepare for the worst, hope for the best"—his foreign policy—rested on two pillars: continued rearmament to deter Germany, Italy, and Japan, and appeasement to assuage their grievances. Supporters of the prime minister hailed the policy as a masterstroke. One or two of the potential enemies might be won over by appeasement, and, should the strategy fail, the year or two consumed in negotiating grievances would buy Britain time to build up its defenses, especially its air defenses, which Chamberlain, like Baldwin and Churchill, viewed as the key to victory in a modern war. The policy also had the important advantage of being in tune with public feeling.

What grievances should be appeased? In the case of Japan, no legitimate grievances suggested themselves, but Japan posed a threat to Australia and New Zealand, so Chamberlain swallowed hard and ignored Japanese infringements on British concessions in China. Italy, which was behaving menacingly in Spain and North Africa, felt aggrieved that the Mediterranean was a British, not an Italian, sea. Chamberlain swallowed hard and turned a blind eye to Italian attacks on British ships delivering goods to civil war Spain. However, lingering British guilt about the Treaty of Versailles gave German grievances a special standing in Chamberlain's eyes. Hitler was a beast, of course—a vicious anti-Semite and mad, to boot. Nonetheless, mad or not, Germany had been roughly handled at Versailles: stripped of its army, its Rhine borders, and several historic German regions. By the late 1930s, some of the injustices had been corrected, though Danzig, a historically German city, was still in Polish hands and the Sudetenland, another historic German region, was still in Czech hands. Austria was not a lost territory, but it was shrunken almost to insignificance by Versailles, and many Germans felt its rightful place was inside a Greater Reich.

In November 1937, Lord Edward Halifax, a member of the

Chamberlain cabinet and one of the prime minister's most trusted advisers, met with Hitler. This was Halifax's second visit to the "new" Germany. After the first one, he returned to London sounding like a botanist who had discovered a bizarrely florid but probably benign new species of plant life during his travels. Halifax "told me he . . . was much amused by the visit," a friend said. "He thinks the regime absolutely fantastic, perhaps too fantastic to be taken seriously." In late 1937 Halifax still thought the Hitler regime fantastic, but he was becoming aware of its dangers, and, like millions of his countrymen, he did not want Britain dragged into a war on the far side of Europe over issues that did not affect its security and that, in British eyes, had a measure of legitimacy. During his second visit, Halifax told Hitler that, provided peaceful means were employed, Britain would be prepared to accept "possible alterations in the European order, which might be destined to come about with the passage of time. Amongst these questions were Danzig, Austria, and Czechoslovakia."

Hitler assured Halifax that Germany wished to have good relations with all its neighbors. Four months later, the Wehrmacht marched into Vienna and Austria became a part of the Reich. Two months after the Anschluss—May 1938—rumors began to circulate that ten German divisions had been moved to the Reich border opposite the Sudetenland. "Those d——d Germans have spoiled another weekend for me," Chamberlain complained to his sister Hilda on May 22. Britain issued a mild warning; Germany denied that it had troops on the Sudetenland border; then, in an inspired piece of diplomacy, it was decided to blame the crisis on the Czechs, the only party to the dispute incapable of starting a world war on its own.

June and July of 1938 passed calmly, but it was not the normal calm of summer. In the Rhineland, construction crews worked double and triple shifts under arc lights to complete the West

Wall, a new defensive system that the Allied powers called the Siegfried Line. In Paris Georges Bonnet, the French foreign minister, scrutinized the French-Czechoslovakian treaty for loopholes. In Moscow Stalin, who also had a treaty with the Czechs, watched carefully to see who would emerge victorious from the Sudeten confrontation, Germany or Britain and France. In Washington the Roosevelt administration prepared an appeal for moderation. And in London the Chiefs of Staff issued a new warning: In the event of an Anglo-German war over Czechoslovakia, "it is more than probable that both Italy and Japan would seize the opportunity to further their own ends and that in consequence the problem we have to envisage is not that of a limited European war but of world war." In July, when Chamberlain spoke at Birmingham's centenary celebration, the Chiefs' warning was still on his mind. "The government of which I am at present the head intends to hold on its course, which is set for the appeasement of the world."

The Essex village of Tolleshunt D'Arcy took note of the speech, though to one Tolleshunt resident, Margery Allingham, Czechoslovakia remained a faraway country with an all but unspellable name until the end of July, when Margery and a group of friends gathered in her yard one afternoon to plan the annual village cricket party. It was a lovely Saturday, the air heavy with the smell of freshly cut grass, and overhead, a few fat cumulus clouds drifting idly eastward toward the sea—just the kind of day that always made Margery feel smug about abandoning a glamorous London publishing career for life in an obscure Essex village whose sole distinction was its possession of one of the two surviving Maypoles in England. The state of the village cricket field dominated most of the afternoon's discussion, but toward evening one guest brought up the Czech crisis, and Margery, who was thirty-four, found herself thinking back to her childhood in the Great War. She remembered a recurring dream she had had then: "a soldier galloping up on a great grey horse to kiss [a] tearful nurse goodbye . . . then death . . . and not ordinary dying either . . . but death final, empty and away somewhere." She remembered other things about that time: "the women and old people all in black . . . standing about in the village street reading the enormous casualty lists . . . ; [and] the village boy on a bike with not one telegraph spelling tragedy but sometimes two or even three." Then an astonishing thought occurred to Margery: war, which had savaged the generation before hers, now seemed about to savage the generation after hers. The thought was so staggering, she found it "hardly to be borne."

By early September 1938, reminders of 1914 were everywhere. Poland and Hungary, eager to participate in the dismemberment of Czechoslovakia, were massing troops along the Czech border; in Prague the Czech government proclaimed martial law; in Nuremberg, Hitler pledged unshakable support for those "tortured creatures," the Sudeten Germans; and in Britain the Royal Navy was put on partial alert. Passing the Cenotaph in Whitehall that Munich summer, Alec Douglas-Home, a Chamberlain aide and future prime minister, noticed that several fresh bouquets had been placed at its base.

"Well, it has been a pretty awful week," Chamberlain wrote his sister Ida on September 11. Four days later, the prime minister was flying down the Thames on his way to visit Hitler. Approaching Bavaria, the British Airways' Lockheed Electra swooped under a heavy storm and set down smoothly at the Munich airport. The cabin door was flung open and, to the tattoo of drums and the snap of swastika flags flapping in a sharp wind, Neville Chamberlain stepped into Hitlerland.

A few hours later, the prime minister was standing in Hitler's enormous Berchtesgaden office, admiring the Wagnerian view;

across the valley, a range of high mountains was half shrouded in a late-afternoon mist. He turned and examined the office. There was a huge globe next to the desk and an oak conference table at the far end of the office. "I have often heard of this room, but it is much larger than I expected," Chamberlain said, hoping to ease the tension with a little small talk.

"It is you who have big rooms in England," Hitler replied. Then, having exhausted his store of small talk, he demanded the return of the Sudetenland.

"I'd rather be beat than dishonored," Alexander Cadogan, permanent secretary at the Foreign Office, said upon hearing that Chamberlain had acquiesced to Hitler's demand. In the days following the prime minister's return to London, there was much talk of national honor in certain quarters of Whitehall, Westminster, and the press. But what was national honor to "he that died on Wednesday"? To Chamberlain, such talk only led to more Sommes and Passchendaeles. The Sudeten crisis had to be viewed through the lens of national interest. Was it worth going to war for a small country on the other side of Europe? The prime minister did not believe it was, and it quickly became apparent that most of the British public agreed with him, as did the dominions: Australia, New Zealand, South Africa, and especially Canada. "I approve wholeheartedly of the course [Chamberlain] has adopted," said Mackenzie King, the Canadian prime minister. After several weeks of intense pressure from the British and the French, who also favored a peaceful resolution of the crisis, the Czechs agreed to cede to Germany the regions of the country that were more than 50 percent ethnically German. On September 22, Chamberlain returned to Germany, expecting to sign an agreement. Instead, Hitler handed him a new set of demands: incorporation of the Sudetenland into the Reich and the annexation of several strategic regions beyond the German-speaking parts of Czechoslovakia.

"Hitler has given Chamberlain the double cross . . . [And] it looks like war," William Shirer, the CBS correspondent in Berlin, wrote on the twenty-third. By the end of the week, Shirer's premonition seemed about to come true. The British fleet and the RAF were on full alert, searchlights scanned the London sky, every significant building in the imperial capital was cordoned off with sandbags, territorials (reservists) were digging trenches in Hyde Park and St. James Park, and the government was requisitioning cellars and basements as air raid shelters. Shocked Londoners felt as if they had stepped through the looking glass into *Things to Come.* This "is like a nightmare in a film," Rob Bernays, a junior government minister, wrote. "We are like people waiting for Judgment." At a dinner party, Bernays made a joke to lighten the somber mood and was immediately cut off by another guest, who snapped, "Damn you! [Don't] you realize we may be dead next week?"

Meanwhile, in Downing Street, Chamberlain was facing a cabinet revolt. After explaining at some length his indignant reaction to Hitler's new terms, he recommended that the terms be accepted. This was too much, even for Lord Halifax, the foreign secretary and Chamberlain's closest ally in the cabinet. "Personally, I believe Hitler has cast a spell over Neville," he told a colleague. Other cabinet members felt that Chamberlain had been undone by his vanity. And, unquestionably, Chamberlain's desire to be hailed as a peacemaker did cloud his judgment, though other factors also went into his thinking. On September 20, two days before Chamberlain returned to Germany, a memo by General Hastings Ismay of the Imperial General Staff had counseled prudence: If "war with Germany has to come," Ismay wrote, "it would be better to fight her in, say, 6 to 12 months than to accept the present challenge."

In late September, the Czech crisis resolved itself at the Munich

Conference, which was convened at Mussolini's suggestion and was the source of some of the most evocative images of the prewar years: There is a famous photo of Chamberlain, looking more the coroner than the undertaker as he poses reluctantly for photographers in front of the two-engine Lockheed Electra that will fly him to Germany. There is one of Édouard Daladier, the French premier, at the Munich airport, looking physically massive but with vacant eyes that suggest that the premier's nickname, the Bull of Vaucluse, may overstate the case; and there is one of Hitler standing at the conference table, his expression a compound of all his favorite words: "unshakable," "invincible," "triumphant," "decisive"; and there is one of Mussolini, arms crossed, head tilted at an odd angle to hide the mole on his bald skull. And the most famous photo of all: Chamberlain, on his return from Munich, standing in front of a bank of microphones, promising "peace in our time" under a gray autumn sky. Lost among the lesser footnotes of the Munich Conference are two appeals from President Roosevelt, one urging Hitler to attend the conference, the other an appeal for a peaceful resolution of the Sudeten crisis.

Such was the residual strength of Never Again, not just in Britain but globally, that the morning after promising "peace in our time," Chamberlain awoke to find himself a world hero. In Munich, Germans, some with tears in their eyes, flocked to the hotel where the prime minister had stayed, like pilgrims to a shrine. In France a subscription was raised to build the prime minister a country house and a trout stream. In Britain streets were named after Chamberlain. Dinners were held in his honor; crowds followed him to Buckingham Palace, where he appeared on the balcony with the king, and on fishing holidays in the Highlands crowds followed him through Scottish railway stations. Babies were named after him, there were Chamberlain dolls, and Chamberlain bouquets with the inscription "We Are Proud of

You." In Brussels a medal was struck in his honor; from Holland came tulips by the thousands; and from the people of New York and the people of South Africa, grateful thanks for the prime minister's work on behalf of peace.

"All this will be over in early October," Chamberlain told Halifax not long after his return from Munich. He was right about the fleeting nature of fame, wrong about how quickly it could flee.

A new Gallup poll taken less than a month after Munich indicated that public support for an antiappeasement government had risen sharply. Another new poll found that 71 percent of the respondents favored keeping the German colonies awarded to Britain at Versailles, even at the risk of war. The sudden stiffening of public resolve owed less to an upsurge in patriotism than to post-Munich disillusionment. Chamberlain had gotten a piece of paper at Munich, and Hitler had gotten the Sudetenland. Emotionally exhausted by two and a half years of lurching from crisis to crisis, people began to rethink their position on war. The pacifism of the interwar years had been driven by the conviction that European civilization had come very close to self-immolation on the battlefields of the Great War. All the peace ballots, debates, and pacifist marches of the thirties were energized by the belief that such a thing must never be allowed to happen again. Munich became the midwife to a new perception among the French and British elites: Terrible as war was, it might be the only way to prevent Hitler and his regime from plunging Europe into a "new dark age." Munich also gave birth to a new perception among ordinary people, but it was more prosaic. "Living with Hitler," said one man, "was like living in a neighborhood with a wild animal on the loose."

In March 1939, when Germany occupied the non-German

parts of Czechoslovakia, public opinion hardened further. Lingering guilt about the Treaty of Versailles had restrained Britain's reaction to Hitler's earlier occupations. Austria, the Rhineland, and the Sudetenland were historic German lands. In Hitler's place, Bismarck—or almost any German statesman—would have made it his goal to reconstitute the historic Germany dismembered at Versailles. There was no explanation for the occupation of the ethnic Czech rump except pure, naked aggression. In late March, when the Chamberlain government extended a guarantee to Poland, there was broad public support for the decision.

In late August, after Hitler and Stalin signed a nonaggression pact, and a German attack on Poland became all but certain, the *News Chronicle*, one of the big London dailies, decided to test the strength of Never Again. The poll the paper commissioned found that only 11 percent of the British public still remained resolutely pacifist—that is, willing to embrace peace even on German terms. Yet anyone with a feel for public opinion knew the requiems for Never Again were premature. There remained a significant, if hard to quantify, substratum of antiwar feeling in Britain. "It was a vague body almost nebulous . . . and fortunately [had] no leader," recalled Alfred Duff Cooper, who was on the opposite side of the war debate, having resigned from the Chamberlain cabinet to protest the prime minister's appeasement. The substratum, said Duff Cooper, "was composed of disparate entities. The left wing of the Labour Party . . . whose detestation of war was so intense that they doubted anything was worth fighting for, . . . the right wing of Conservatism, . . . [whose members] believed that Communism was the greater danger and felt that Hitler had rendered his country a service by suppressing the Communists and might render Europe one by protecting it from the red peril.

"There existed also an attitude even less definite and harder to define, originating probably in the fact that the public mind was ill prepared for war. People had been told recently by ministers, and some sections of the press never ceased to tell them, that there was no longer any danger of war, so that when it [became imminent] they could hardly believe it . . . and clung obstinately to the hope that the whole thing could somehow be patched up."

Duff Cooper's list omits one other important center of antiwar feeling: the small but influential section of the British establishment who had grave reservations about risking the British economy and empire in a second conflict with Germany. Members of the group included former prime minister David Lloyd George and Montagu Norman, governor of the Bank of England, and several peers of the realm, among them Lord Londonderry and the Duke of Westminster. Though not members of the group, two powerful press barons, Lord Rothermere, publisher of the *Daily Mail* and the *Daily Mirror*, and Lord Beaverbrook, publisher of the *Daily Express* and the *London Evening Standard*, also feared that the British Empire would not survive another total war.

Should war come, the government would have to take these various strains of opinion into account in making decisions about war aims, defense spending, rationing, and a host of other related issues. And should the war go badly for Britain, the government would have to be prepared for the eventuality that all or some of these strands of opinion would coalesce and demand a negotiated peace settlement to save the country from another four years of "death and death and death."

CHAPTER TWO

AGAIN

In August 1914, war had come all at once, in a frightening rush on a glorious August day from a faraway land. One minute the country was at the seashore; the next, everyone was waving miniature Union Jacks, singing "Rule Britannia," and young men were marching off to France. In the summer of 1939, war approached like the "slow ticking of a clock in a dentist's office," recalled one woman. Occasionally an event would shatter the summer calm. The Hitler-Stalin pact, announced on August 23, produced a terrific shock, but a week later everyone had gone back to complaining about the weather. July and early August of 1939 were frightful—heavy rain almost every day. Then, abruptly, just after the signing of the pact, the sun reappeared, and, as if to make amends for its absence, produced two weeks of brilliant, warm, sunny weather. People hiked the Lake County, walked the beaches of Blackpool, Bath, and Brighton, took day trips to Calais, and organized cake sales and cricket matches, secure in the knowledge that Britain's astrologers and spiritualists unanimously agreed: there would be no war in 1939. Polling in late August showed that only one person in five expected a war, and one in three felt that "anything" would be better than one. When war finally did come on Friday morning, September 1, it came as quietly as a church lady. "There was no bravura, no sudden quickening of the blood, no secret anticipation," Margery Allingham remembered. "We seemed to go to war as a duty, a people elderly in soul, going in stolidly to kill or be killed."

The morning that the wireless announced the German invasion of Poland, the smell of bonfires, which drifts across rural England in late summer, hung in the air in Margery's village. She went out to the garden, sat down in the old wicker chair she had been meaning to get rid of for ages, and finally removed her gas mask from its pouch. Margery had no idea what an elephant fetus looked like, but running her hands across the large plastic eyes and long, trunk-like rubber nozzle, she imagined it must look something like a government gas mask. Elsewhere in Britain that morning, millions of people were already being swept up in the gravitational pull of war. The first news of the German attack had come at about 4:00 a.m. Greenwich Mean Time; by 8:00 a.m. preparations were under way to transport hundreds of thousands of mothers and children, tens of thousands of hospital patients, and enormous quantities of food to safe zones in rural Britain. Parks bristled with antiaircraft batteries, fields with antiparatrooper defenses; barrage balloons floated above London, Birmingham, and Manchester; in the London zoo, the snakes were put down. Later in the morning, veterinarian clinics across the country would be inundated by pet owners eager to euthanize the family dog or cat before the air raids began. At 1:00 p.m. television screens in the Greater London region went black just as a Greta Garbo–like cartoon character was saying: "Ay tank, Ay, go home." The war had shut down the world's first television service.

In Downing Street, Neville Chamberlain opened the morning cabinet with a requiem for "peace in our time." We "meet under the gravest possible conditions," the prime minister told his colleagues. "The events against which we have fought so long and so earnestly have come upon us. But our consciences [are] clear. There should be no possible question now where our duty lay."

After Chamberlain finished, Lord Halifax, the foreign secretary, rose to brief the cabinet on his early morning talk with the German chargé d'affaires, Dr. Theo Kordt. Uncoiled to his full six feet, four inches, the foreign secretary was an imposing figure. The enormous bald head rose above the face like a cathedral dome in miniature, and the voice, cultivated and effortlessly authoritative, suggested what the British Empire might sound like if it could speak. Halifax said Kordt had made the invasion sound more like a schoolyard fight than an invasion. Last night, the Poles had begun shooting across the border, and German troops had responded in kind.

The cabinet continued marching resolutely toward war until the conversation turned to what kind of note Britain should send Germany. The predicate for implementing the Polish guarantee was a German attack, and the early reports of air attacks on Warsaw and other Polish cities had the indefinite character of rumor. "At present," said one minister, we have "no very definite information as to what hostile action had taken place in Poland." Another believed that there might be "some further peace effort on Herr Hitler's part." A third warned that implementing the Polish guarantee would give Hitler a false sense of security, though how or why it would, the minister failed to explain. Chamberlain was also wobbling. "The big thing was a European settlement," he told Joseph Kennedy, the US ambassador. "It could be done, if only I could get the chance." In cases of aggression, the prescribed formula was to send the aggressor nation an ultimatum with a deadline. The note Halifax sent Germany on the night of September 1 was only a warning, and the warning did not include a deadline. In France, Poland's other guarantor, there were also signs of indecision; just before midnight the French news agency Haves reported that France had given a positive response to an Italian proposal for a conference to settle "the Polish question and all of Europe's other difficulties." The Duce was apparently eager to reprise the peacemaker role he had played in Munich.

The next morning, September 2, a good part of London was on a train to somewhere else. The statue of Eros in Piccadilly Circus was gone—taken to a hiding place in Scotland. The paintings in the museums were gone—taken to Wales for safekeeping. The children were gone—scattered to thousands of villages, hamlets, and towns. The zoo animals were gone—on the morning train to Edinburgh. And the light was gone—a victim of the blackout that went into effect the previous evening. At 5:00 a.m., when the first filaments of sunlight crept over the silver barrage balloons above St. James Park, early-rising Londoners sighed in relief. Toward evening on September 2, Vera Brittain, whose Great War memoir *Testament to Youth* was a foundational text of the pacifist movement, stood on a rise in rural Hampshire, watching the parade of London refugees pass by. "The road [was] alive with a restless ribbon of traffic—lorries filled with troops; 'relief' buses crammed with passengers; small cars packed with children, their parents, perambulators, and cots; vans from furniture repositories loaded with household goods." How different this war was from the one she had served in as a nurse, Brittain thought. In 1914–18, "the front was a limited area, and the lives lost were chiefly those of young men between eighteen and forty. Today, the suffering and suspense are universal. . . . There is no emotional barrier between men and women, parents and children, the old and the young; the battle is shared by all ages and both sexes."

Lord Halifax began September 2 at the Buckingham Palace Gardens, with his number two at the Foreign Office, Alexander Cadogan. Striding through the fields of freshly bloomed autumn crocuses, the two men made an odd pair. The six-foot, four-inch

Hailfax, long-legged and physically awkward, resembled a large, ungainly water bird. The petite Cadogan, huffing and puffing behind him, looked like a gnome chasing his master. For both men, the garden visit would be the high point of a day otherwise crowded with sorrows. At 5:00 a.m., when the British ambassador in Warsaw made his first call of the day, the Luftwaffe had already carried out twenty air strikes against Poland. When the ambassador called again a few hours later, he simply said that the Germans had achieved "very pronounced air superiority." In the interim there had been so many air strikes it was impossible to keep an accurate count. What the Germans called "Hitler weather"—sunny, dry days—had also proved a great boon to the Panzer columns traversing the dried-up rivers, marshes, and watercourses on the Polish plain. Before the invasion, the Poles had estimated that they could hold for three months; now three weeks sounded like an optimistic prediction.

The reports from Paris were also worrying. The French appeared to be chasing the Italian mediation offer with unseemly haste. Paris had set only one precondition for talks: an armistice, with German troops halting in place. London was demanding a German withdrawal to the Polish border. Just before noon, Halifax instructed Sir Eric Phipps, the British ambassador in Paris, to infuse some "courage and determination into M. [Georges] Bonnet," the French foreign minister. This was easier said than done. Bonnet, the leader of the antiwar faction in the government of Édouard Daladier, combined the slipperiness of an eel with the "cunning of a fox on alert." In its brief life, the Italian offer would die numerous deaths, and each time Bonnet would find a way to resuscitate it—sometimes with guile and cunning, other times with outright lies. When Count Ciano, the Italian foreign minister, called Halifax at 2:30 p.m. on September 2, he said he had just spoken to Bonnet, who had assured him "that if Hitler would suspend hostilities and agree in principle to a conference ... Great Britain and France would participate." Halifax told Ciano that he had been misinformed.

Two hours later, Bonnet called the Foreign Office. Hitler had agreed to study the Italian proposal under French terms—the German Army halts in place. Halifax said the French terms were unacceptable; Britain would not agree to mediation unless Germany withdrew from Poland. That would be desirable, certainly, Bonnet said, but why should a German withdrawal be an essential precondition? The important thing was to convince the French and British publics that their governments had made every effort to save the peace. Halifax promised to present Bonnet's views to the cabinet.

As the hot, sultry September afternoon moved toward evening, consternation and alarm grew in the House of Commons. Thirty-six hours had passed since the German attack on Poland, and Britain and France continued to quibble over terms and deadlines. When the prime minister's 3:00 p.m. speech was postponed to 6:00 p.m. without explanation, the bar in the Commons smoking room began to fill with rumors, each growing more lurid as the consumption of alcohol increased. It was said that Bonnet had told the Polish ambassador to France, "You don't expect us to have a massacre of women and children in Paris." It was said that Premier Daladier had gone "wobbly." It was said that the French wanted to give Germany a full week to reply to an Allied ultimatum; and as the September light faded from the late-summer sky and the alcohol continued to flow in the smoking room, it was proposed, only half in jest, that "Britain declare war on France."

When Churchill arrived in the smoking room late on the afternoon of the second, he was already ripping mad at the French. Earlier in the day he had warned Charles Corbin, the French ambassador in London, that if the Daladier government "ratted" on Poland, he, Winston Churchill, lifelong friend of France, would wash his hands of the French. When Corbin blamed France's slowness in mobilizing on technical difficulties—time was needed to get the army into position and evacuate the civilian population—Churchill shouted, "Technical difficulties! I suppose you would call it a technical difficulty for a Pole if a German bomb dropped on his head."

Edward Spears, a prominent antiappeasement MP, believed Downing Street was within Churchill's grasp that afternoon. "His name was on many lips, [and] the more the Cabinet vacillated, the more eyes turned to him." Churchill was less sure about the size and intensity of the "Winston" boomlet. No British politician had been more insightful about the German threat. As long before as 1932, he had warned that "all those bands of sturdy Teutonic youths marching through the streets and roads of Germany with the light of desire in their eyes . . . are not looking for status." "They are looking for weapons, and, believe me, when they have the weapons, they will then ask for the return of lost territories and colonies."

At his best, said a friend, Churchill could say the "fine true thing with a force that was like an organ filling a church." But in 1939 what most people remembered about Churchill was how often he had played the organ off-key. The egotism, the waywardness, the ambition, the publicity-seeking, the bellicosity: all were legendary. "Mr. Churchill constantly prefers the large, simple conclusions of the battlefield," noted a reviewer of Churchill's biography of his ancestor the duke of Marlborough. There were also the disloyalties: jumping from one political party to another, then back again. And there were the policy mistakes: some—like Gallipoli, opposition to Indian reform, and the decision to return Britain to the gold standard—epic. "Winston was often right," said his friend F. E. Smith. "But when he was wrong: well, my God."

Churchill's greatness was peculiar in character in that it only became "fine and true" in a particular set of circumstances, and on the afternoon of September 2, the man who would later be called the "most remarkable human being to ever inhabit Downing Street" sensed that those circumstances had yet to form. In the name of national unity, Churchill would put away his ambitions for the time being and accept the cabinet post that Chamberlain had secretly offered him the day before, first lord of the Admiralty.

A little before 6:00 p.m., when the Speaker of the House announced that Chamberlain's speech would be postponed for a second time, from 6:00 p.m. until 7:30, Henry Channon, the Conservative MP for Southend-on-Sea, Essex, was crossing the House floor on his way to his office. Passing a mirror near the smoking room, Channon paused, examined himself, and was pleased at the face staring back at him. "Quite handsome!" he congratulated himself. Politics by its nature attracts egotists, but the egotism of Henry Channon, husband of Honor Guinness, the brewing heiress and member of the most glamorous social circles in London, was singular. In post–World War One Paris, the Chicago-born Channon had been a Truman Capote–like figure: a young man of fawn-like beauty, ambiguous sexuality, and the social ambitions of a Hapsburg duchess. Jean Cocteau once told Channon that his eyes "looked like they had been set by Cartier," and Proust called his essays on Parisian life charming. In 1925, tiring of Parisian decadence, Channon had moved to London and reinvented himself as an English gentleman. Now he was parliamentary secretary to Rab Butler, the undersecretary of state for foreign affairs, and had transferred his affections from Jean Cocteau to Neville Chamberlain.

Shortly after Channon reached his office, Butler called. The cabinet had just risen and the meeting had been "stormy." Over the past twenty-four hours, the mood in the cabinet had stiffened considerably. At the afternoon cabinet on the second, the air minister, Kingsley Wood, heretofore prone to appeasement, expressed dismay about the previous evening's warning note to Germany and cautioned that further postponements in issuing an ultimatum would have a bad "moral effect." Leslie Hore-Belisha, the war minister, said that Britain should demand a complete German withdrawal from Poland that night, and John Simon, the chancellor of the Exchequer, dismissed the Italian proposal as worthless. Even if Hitler agreed to attend a conference, said Simon, he would never make any meaningful concessions. A few hours later, the prime minister would get an even rougher handling in the House of Commons.

Channon blamed the House's reaction on the long interval between the afternoon cabinet, which ended at about 5:00 p.m., and Chamberlain's arrival in the Commons at 7:30. In the interim, "the nervous House, chafing under delay and genuinely distressed . . . [had continued] to quench their thirst in the Smoking Room and when they returned to hear the PM . . . many of them were full of Dutch Courage . . . and ready to fight . . . the whole world."

Channon was right. Aroused by the gravity of the hour, the House wanted to hear "Come the three corners of the world in arms, and we shall shock them." Instead, members got an irresolute old man sickened by the thought of sending another generation of young men to war. Speeches are rarely memorable for the things left unsaid, but this one was. Chamberlain made no mention of a British ultimatum or of the British ambassador in Berlin requesting his passport; he made no mention of British honor or of Polish valor, of "sunlit uplands" and "better days to come." There was just the tired, uninflected voice of a disappointed politician explaining the current state of negotiations. As the prime minister sat down, row after row of hard faces glared at him from the backbenches.

Arthur Greenwood, an unprepossessing North Country man, rose to speak for the Labour Party. A former teacher, Greenwood had a reputation as a drinker, and he possessed no outstanding talents other than the ability to be in the right place at the right time. That talent had won him the assistant leadership position in the Labour Party; it had put him, and not the party leader, Clement Attlee, who was recovering from prostate surgery, in the House on this historic evening; and it had put Leo Amery, a vocal Chamberlain critic, in the Conservative backbenches. Having spent most of the afternoon in the smoking room bar, Greenwood began unsteadily, "I am speaking under very difficult circumstances."

"Speak for England, Arthur!" Amery shouted.

Greenwood steadied himself, the drink left his voice, and, as Amery requested, the former schoolteacher spoke for England in the simple, unaffected language of a North Country man. "I wonder how long we are prepared to vacillate at a time when Britain and all that Britain stands for and human civilization is in peril." As Greenwood finished to thunderous applause, Channon sat on the Tory benches, disconsolate at the House's reaction: "All the old Munich rage all over again. . . . All those who want to die abuse Caesar." The chief Conservative whip, the imposing David Margesson, fearing a backbench revolt against Chamberlain, signaled the Speaker to gavel the session to a close.

As the crowd thinned out, Channon pushed his way through the departing MPs to the chief whip. Margesson was the kind of Englishman Channon would like to have been. He had an admirable war record, an impeccable bloodline, implacable self-assurance, and he possessed the kind of elegant masculine physical glamour now only seen in movies of the 1930s. Can't anything be done to help the prime minister? Channon asked. Margesson shrugged. "It must be war, Chip, old boy; there is no other way out." Later in the evening, the chief whip gave the prime minister the same advice, though in rougher language.

The civil defense authorities had warned that, should war come, it would begin with a German air strike on London. On the night of September 2, Londoners received a foretaste of what that would be like. The day had been hot and sultry, and, as darkness descended, the dense, humid air congealed into huge black pillars of cloud that billowed upward into the evening sky. At about nine, lightning crackled over the Thames. For a moment, Parliament flashed a brilliant gold, then vanished back into darkness; the wind picked up, the barrage balloons tossed and turned and strained at their cables, and then great torrents of rain began to pelt down on southeastern England, flooding byways, clogging traffic, and sending hundreds of tons of garbage flooding through the blacked-out streets of the imperial capital.

It rained on the Royal Navy ships leaving port to take up blockade positions along the German coast; on the army lorries slipping through the liquid darkness toward embarkation points; on the antiaircraft crews shivering under tarps in Hyde Park; on "the Kennel Farm and Aviary," which offered "evacuation facilities for pets"; and on the ticket offices of P&O (Pacific & Orient shipping line), where uncertain patriots could book a "cruise 1,000 miles up the Amazon" for only £75. It rained on the darkened streets where no child's voice had been heard for days; on the empty museums; on the memorials to the "glorious dead"; and on the surplus women, deep into their forties and dreaming of Leslie Howard now.

In Downing Street, where an emergency late-evening cabinet was in session, a shaken Chamberlain announced that "the strength of feeling in the House of Commons" had convinced him that an immediate display of resolve was needed to steady the country. Therefore, Sir Neville Henderson, the British ambassador in Berlin, had been instructed to present an ultimatum to Joachim von Ribbentrop, the German foreign minister, the next day at 9:00 a.m.; the ultimatum would expire at 11:00 a.m. If Bonnet "could not accept our time for delivery and expiry, the French Ambassador [can deliver the French ultimatum] at a later hour."

At 11:15 a.m. the following day, the prime minister addressed the nation. "I am speaking to you from the Cabinet Room at Number Ten Downing Street," he said. "This morning the British Ambassador in Berlin handed the German government a final note, stating that unless they were prepared to withdraw all their troops from Poland, a state of war would exist between us. I have to tell you now that no such undertaking had been received and that consequently this country is at war with Germany." No one who heard Chamberlain's broadcast that morning could have had any doubt about the depth of his disappointment. As the prime minister reached the penultimate passage of his speech—"consequently this country is at war with Germany"— sorrow and despair sang through the melancholic old voice. But then he ruined the effect with a concluding sentence that bubbled over with self-pity and solipsism: "You can imagine what a bitter blow it is to me that my entire long struggle to win the peace has failed."

At 11:27 air raid sirens wailed, and Londoners huddled together in cellars, tube stations, and shelters, awaiting the arrival of the bomber stream and the thud of the antiaircraft guns. A little after noon, the "all clear" sounded, and thousands of dazed men and women climbed back into the brilliant September sunlight, blessing their good fortune. An off-course plane had triggered the alert.

At 5:00 p.m. the French ultimatum went into effect.

"Thus we tumbled into Armageddon without heart, without songs, without an ally except France (and she lukewarm), without aircraft, without tanks, without guns, without rifles, without even a reserve of raw commodities and feeding stuffs," wrote Bob Boothby. A week later, when Italy and Japan announced their neutrality, the gravest threat to British security, a world war, receded. For now only Germany would have to be confronted, and, while it would be poked and prodded, it would not be poked and prodded hard enough to incite the holocaust of total war for a second time. Under Chamberlain, Britain would fight a limited war for limited ends and with limited means.

While the pace of rearmament would be quickened, for the time being the prime minister planned to emphasize two other components of his war plan. The first was propaganda. During the autumn of 1939, thousands of copies of dozens of different propaganda pamphlets were dropped on Germany, including *Hitler and the Working Man*, the best, though not the only, example of why the academics and literary figures the Ministry of Information employed to write propaganda were too genteel for the job. *Hitler and the Working Man* began by describing national socialism as "an honorable experiment" and noted that its early leaders had had many "fine ideals." The second component of the Chamberlain war plan was economic blockade. Chamberlain believed—and it was a belief shared by the British intelligence services and many senior civil servants—that the huge cost of rearmament had overstretched the German economy, leaving Hitler incapable of fighting anything but the kind of short, sharp war he was fighting in Poland. Historians would later dismiss the belief in German economic weakness as a myth, but new research has shown that Chamberlain was at least half right. Until the summer of 1940, when the wealth of Western Europe fell under Hitler's control, the German war machine was under intense economic pressure. In 1939, Britain was spending only 12 percent of its national income on defense, while Germany was already spending 23 percent and its economy was operating at 125 percent of capacity, while the British economy had yet to fully mobilize.

Chamberlain's miscalculation was in thinking that Germany's financial weakness would make it even more vulnerable to a British blockade than it had been in the Great War. Blockades, which are intended to deny the enemy resources, only work if they are airtight. And, as Lloyd George, Britain's prime minister in the Great War, lost no opportunity to point out, this time, unlike last time, the British blockade had a gaping hole. The German-Soviet pact had given Hitler access to Russian oil, to copper—to enough raw materials to sustain a ten-year war. Indeed, when it came to his successor's faults as a war leader, Lloyd George did not know where to begin or end. The previous March, Chamberlain had blithely handed Poland a security guarantee unenforceable without Russian help; then, when an opportunity arose to strike an alliance with Stalin, he had let it slip away. And because Chamberlain refused to put British industry on a full wartime footing, Britain would not have ten divisions in France until the spring of 1940, and had only 1,270 first-line aircraft and a few hundred tanks, many outdated models. Against this force, Germany could field up to 157 divisions—10 of them armored—nearly 4,000 modern warplanes, and 3,000 modern tanks. It was true that 90 to 94 of France's 117 divisions also faced Germany, but the French army's 3,254 tanks and 1,562 aircraft were in the hands of soldiers and airmen preparing a 1939 army with 1918 training and strategies.

No one who lived through the Great War was surprised that Lloyd George had emerged as Chamberlain's principal critic. The personal vendetta between the two men began in August 1917, when then prime minister Lloyd George dismissed Chamberlain as director of National Service, the organization that oversaw conscription. It was Chamberlain's first—and, until the collapse of his appeasement policy, almost only—public failure, and Lloyd George was not inclined to let him forget it. In his *War Memoirs*, he described Chamberlain as "not one of my most successful selections." Eighteen years later Chamberlain got his revenge. In 1935, when Stanley Baldwin proposed appointing Lloyd George to the cabinet, Chamberlain, who was then chancellor of the Exchequer, said he would not sit at the same table with that man.

In the autumn of 1939, Lloyd George was seventy-seven, and had a large, intact ego and a controversial past. On Mussolini and Franco, on the Munich settlement—on many of the great issues of the 1930s—he had been on the right side of history; but there had been one egregious lapse. On several occasions, Lloyd George had praised Hitler, not because he admired national socialism, but because he believed the Führer, like himself, was a historic leader. In the late 1930s, not many British politicians could have called Adolf Hitler the "George Washington of Germany" and lived to tell the tale, but Lloyd George was admired for his Great War leadership, and, like Churchill, he was one of those larger-than-life, fabulously gifted figures whom the public grants a latitude they deny mere mortal politicians. As "artful as a cartload of monkeys" is how one aide described Lloyd George; "a mind like a scorpion," said another. One of nature's slyer jokes was to fashion Lloyd George into an almost perfect physical facsimile of the Wizard of Oz: a great white mane of hair, perfectly matched by a great white mustache and, in between, twinkling blue eyes full of mischief.

The dispute between the former and current prime ministers would dominate most of September and October 1939, and while it began as an argument over the conduct of the war, it quickly turned into a debate about a negotiated peace settlement with Germany; and as it did, the broad middle of the British public, those who had gone to war "stolidly to kill or be killed," would make their voices heard. The day Britain declared war, Lloyd George pledged to support the Chamberlain government, though he could not bring himself to mention the prime minister by name. "I am one of the tens of millions in this country who will back any government that is in power, in fighting through this struggle," he had told the House. However, after the quick German victory in Poland, Lloyd George began to fear Britain was overmatched. On September 27 he told the All Party Group, a collection of Liberal, Conservative, and Labour MPs, that if Britain's chances of prevailing in a war with Germany were less than 50 percent, the government should seek a settlement. Privately, Lloyd George was blunter. "If [the government] rejects the chance of making peace," he told a friend, "it will not be long before Britain will realize that they [sic] have committed the most calamitous mistake perpetuated by British statesmanship since the days of Lord North." (Frederick Lord North was the British statesman who lost the American colonies.)

On October 3, the day Poland fell, Lloyd George made the case for a negotiated settlement in a House of Commons speech. Armageddon might be taking its time in coming, he said, but no one should fool themselves, Armageddon was coming. For MPs who had already met Armageddon once before—at Passchendaele, on the Somme, or on Vimy Ridge—that was a sobering thought. The "flood waters are still holding," Lloyd George said. Let us hope "that as in the time of the deluge, the dove of peace will appear with an olive branch in its beak." A faint ripple of assent went through the Conservative backbenches. But that was not what most people remembered about the speech. What they remembered later was the shock at hearing a prominent public figure utter the words "negotiated settlement" in the seat of government. Duff Cooper was furious. "What sort of terms would Germany offer?" he shouted from the Tory benches. "And who would be fool enough to believe in their sincerity?" The Labour MP David Grenfell was also aggrieved. After declaring himself an admirer of Lloyd George, Grenfell ripped the old Welshman apart. "If it had been anybody else," Chamberlain wrote his sisters a few days later, "I should have felt sorry for him, but I can't credit LlG with a spark of real humanity or generosity."

Outside of a handful of aristocrats with ancient titles—Londonderry, Tavistock, Bessborough—and odd opinions, almost no British public figure of significance praised the Lloyd George speech. The public response was more enthusiastic. "Thousands and thousands have written him about peace," A. J. Sylvester, Lloyd George's chief aide, noted a few days after the House speech. Mail also flooded into Downing Street. In one three-day period in early October, Chamberlain received 2,450 letters, and 1,860 of them demanded an end to the war "in one form or other." The sandal-wearing pacifists, the Oxbridge leftists, and the food faddists who drove George Orwell to distraction accounted for some of the mail, but most of the letters were from people in the broad middle of British public opinion. Members of this group were prepared to fight, but first they wanted all reasonable peace proposals explored.

Hitler's speech on October 6 kept the peace debate alive and enhanced Lloyd George's public standing. When the German leader said, "I believe even today that there can be . . . real peace in Europe and throughout the world, if Germany and England come to an understanding," he seemed to be speaking directly to Lloyd George—and with Lloyd George, flattery went a long way. Watching him work a large crowd a few days after Hitler's speech, Sylvester was reminded of an old "peacock with his tail in full show." One moment "he was playing up to blue-blooded Tories... talking about our superb air force and the greatest navy in the world. Next, he was playing up the peace mongers, by advocating a conference and peace. He carried everybody off their feet and there was not even a single heckle or question. He had them so, he could make them laugh or cry at his will and pleasure." Though no government official would admit it, the public conversation about a negotiated settlement also had an influence on official thinking. Like Lloyd George, the leaders of the dominions—Canada, Australia, South Africa, and New Zealand—complained that Chamberlain's response to Hitler's peace proposal on October 12 had gone "too far in the direction of slamming the door on further discussions." It would be an exaggeration to say that the views of the king; Halifax; Sam Hoare, the home secretary; and Leslie Hore-Belisha, the secretary of war, mirrored Lloyd George's, though not a large exaggeration. In private conversations in September and October 1939, all four men would warn that a German war of any length could result in "the complete economic, financial, and social collapse" of Britain.

Despite all the mutual antipathy, Chamberlain and Lloyd George actually agreed about the desirability of ending the war at the negotiating table. Where they differed was on how to make Hitler honor a peace agreement. The Munich settlement had lasted less than a year. What would prevent a new peace agreement from collapsing just as quickly? Lloyd George's answer was guarantors. Hitler would not dare violate a settlement guaranteed by Russia, Italy, and the United States. Chamberlain believed guarantors were insufficient. Germany also had to learn, once and for all, that aggression does not pay, and his war plan had been crafted to achieve that end. With a minimum of bloodshed, Britain—and France—would make the price of aggression intolerable for Germany. Stalemate on the Western Front would drain its military strength, blockade would break its economy, and propaganda leaflets such as *Hitler and the Working Man* would undermine the morale of its people. Publicly, Chamberlain was predicting a three-year war; privately he expected starvation, public discontent, and raw material shortages to force Hitler—or hopefully, a new German leader—to the negotiating table much sooner. In early November 1939, he told Joe Kennedy, the US ambassador, "I don't believe [the war] will go beyond spring."

In the autumn of 1939, Americans could be forgiven for thinking that Chamberlain did nothing without first consulting Kennedy. "You and Hitler are running neck and neck to see who has his picture more often in the New York papers," a friend wrote the ambassador from America. "It is 'Kennedy goes to Downing Street,' 'Kennedy sees Halifax,' 'Kennedy has his shoes shined' . . . the implication in the New York newspapers is that Chamberlain does not dare to go to the lavatory without you." Even more than making money, Joe Kennedy's special gift was self-promotion. In 1939, there was scarcely a literate American unfamiliar with at least one part of his biography, whether it be his years in Hollywood; his Wall Street career; his chairmanship of the Securities and Exchange Commission; his large, photogenic family; or his 1938 appointment as American ambassador to Britain. Even readers unfamiliar with the details of his life recognized Kennedy's big, toothy Irish grin from a dozen magazine covers. Two weeks after the German invasion of Poland, *Time* hailed the ambassador as the war's "indispensable man." "With 9,000 Americans to shepherd in England, with tangible U.S. business interest under his command, with British bigwigs to see, Franklin Roosevelt to keep informed, Joe Kennedy has a bigger job."

Time had it backward. Kennedy's "bigger job" was essentially that of a concierge. In the early weeks of the war, while the White House and State Department debated the US response to the European crisis, Kennedy was booking passage for Americans anxious to flee Britain. In early October, when a British colleague mentioned that Roosevelt and Churchill had initiated a private correspondence, the ambassador, who had not been informed of the correspondence, had to hide his surprise. In Washington, Kennedy's stock began to fall in 1938 when he suggested that the democracies and the dictatorships should "bend their energies toward . . . solving common problems and attempt to establish good relations" in a Trafalgar Day speech. In Downing Street and in certain precincts of Whitehall, however, he remained a welcome presence. In August 1939 he encouraged Rab Butler, the undersecretary of state for foreign affairs, who needed little encouragement, to offer Hitler a proposal "he could hang his hat on," and in early September he urged Chamberlain to "put in some war regulation that would make the British public think twice about going to war."

After the Soviet Union occupied eastern Poland on September 17, Kennedy's appeasement turned into defeatism. From the autumn of 1939 through the summer of 1940, he sent Washington a stream of cables questioning British resolve. "They [the British] have no intention of fighting," he wrote in one. King George VI, who had been made aware of the cables, complained publicly about Kennedy's defeatism, and the Foreign Office found the ambassador's attitude worrisome enough to open an investigation. Was Kennedy a defeatist because of his association with the pro-German aviator Charles Lindbergh? Because he was politically ambitious and "did not want to be tarred with the pro-British brush"? Or because he was an Irish American and thus "predisposed to tweak the lion's tail"? Oddly, the Foreign Office overlooked the most obvious explanation: Kennedy was an American.

By mid-September 1939, it was becoming difficult to traverse a road or a byway in America without encountering a "Keep the US out of War" sign. A month later, a Gallup poll reported that, by a 95 to 5 percent margin, Americans favored neutrality. Even Abraham Lincoln did not poll that high. "The country is literally drunk with pacifism," a French journalist wrote from New York. The reasons for the antiwar feeling were many, starting with the nearly universal American belief that, in the Great War, Britain and France had outplayed the United States. For its 116,708 dead, the US had gotten roughly $10 billion in still unpaid European debt and precious little else. Beyond that, every American had his or her own personal reasons for supporting isolationism: German and Irish Americans because of a historic enmity toward Britain; midwestern isolationists from the conviction that the only country an American should defend was his own; businessmen because a world war would disrupt the international economy; and the parents of draft-age sons, such as Ambassador Kennedy, for fear that American boys would be dragged back into the European abattoir.

In the late 1930s, Congress responded to isolationist sentiment by passing the Neutrality Acts, which forbade the sale of US arms and other war materials to belligerent countries. Under pressure from President Roosevelt in early November 1939, the acts were amended to allow belligerents to purchase war materials in the United States. The cash-and-carry provision, abrogated in 1937, was also reinstated. This allowed other nations to make purchases in the United States, provided they paid immediately and shipped their purchases on non-American ships. The change was expected to benefit the Allies, as Germany had virtually no foreign currency reserves; beyond the amendment, though, Roosevelt was unprepared to go. "Consistent in his inconsistencies, cold and distant behind the . . . warm personality, listening always to some private voice whose tones we can recognize but never overhear and whose advice we can imagine but never verify," Roosevelt's thinking was opaque, even to his closest advisers. Still, by the autumn of 1939, his views on several war-related issues seemed clear enough. He recognized that Nazi Germany posed a unique historical threat; he hoped events would educate Americans about the Nazi peril; but, as he was contemplating a run for an unprecedented third term in 1940, he was unprepared to get too far ahead of public opinion.

In the case of the Americans, Chamberlain told a colleague, it was "best not to expect anything but words."

One morning toward the end of October 1939, a middle-aged man, burly of build and with a sharp-featured, lively face, stood in a bunker ten feet below the Maginot Line, breathing in the close air and peering through a periscope. The man's suit, discreetly well tailored, and his speech, flavored with the sparkling vowels of the English upper classes, suggested an official of some sort—a touring diplomat perhaps, or an undersecretary of some obscure but interesting government department secreted away in a Whitehall basement. However, anyone with an eye for such things could tell from the visitor's bearing and the informed questions he asked that he had a military background. Edward Louis Spears, KBE, retired colonel, and currently Member of Parliament for Carlisle, knew this part of northern France well. During the Great War, Spears had visited the region several times. Except for the birds that had come back grudgingly in the late 1920s and the soldiers who arrived in the 1930s to man the Maginot Line, not much had changed since Spears's last visit in 1918. The line of raised earth that ran across the abandoned field in front of the French positions marked the remains of a trench line; the rusty objects in the field, the unexploded shells that the wet season threw up in this part of France; and the broken tree line behind the field, the aiming point of some long-ago artillery barrage.

Spears was chairman of the Anglo-French Committee, a parliamentary group created to promote Allied solidarity. Unlike the United States, France was viewed as essential to British national security, and the front-line tours and talks with French colleagues allowed committee members to assess French morale and military readiness. Spears owed his chairmanship to his unique background. Born in France of English parents in 1886, he had spent part of his childhood in the country and had headed the British military mission in Paris in the final years of the Great War. As a professional soldier, he also had an understanding of the ways in which the British and French military did and did not complement each other.

Britain had a large navy and a growing air force, but its army, decimated by budgetary cuts during the interwar years, still existed largely on paper. Presently, there were only four regular army divisions in France, all short of artillery, tanks, radios, and ammunition. Six more regular divisions would join them, upon completion of their training in Britain. But beyond those ten divisions, there was nothing available except a wilderness of conscripts and part-time reservists who would take a year or more to train up to a professional standard, and several dozen battalions of the Indian Army, who were needed in India. On a recent visit to the French High Command outside Paris, Anthony Eden, the secretary of state for the dominions, had flushed with embarrassment upon examining the High Command's map of the Western Front. Amid the forest of tricolor flags, Eden counted only two Union Jacks. The War Office planned to create a fifty-five-division army at some unspecified date in the future, but until money could be found to arm the divisions and soldiers found to man them, the main British weapon on the Western Front would be the French Army.

The best army in the world, people said of the French Army after the Great War, and twenty years later that trope had been repeated so often, French military superiority was taken for granted. "The most perfectly trained and faithful mobile force in Europe," Churchill had said recently, and the Bastille Day parade the previous July seemed to give proof to the first lord's words. Under a fleshy pink summer sky, down the Champs-Élysées marched Algerian, Moroccan, and Senegalese colonial regiments without end; "cannons of all calibers . . . tanks of all sizes. . . . [While] squadrons at high and low altitude [flew] over Paris from the Arc de Triomphe to the Obelisk." The army gave "an impression of order, discipline, irresistible force," said one spectator. A generation later, the producers of the classic BBC series *The World at War* would use footage from the 1939 parade to send up the myth of French invincibility. As grainy images of the marchers flickered across the screen, the narrator, the actor Laurence Olivier, noted that the French army of 1939 relied on trains and horses for transportation. A long, stagey pause followed; then Olivier added, "especially horses."* He was right, but he had the benefit of hindsight. In 1939, the French public and the British politicians and generals believed what Churchill believed: the French Army was incomparable.

---

*In fairness, the German army also relied heavily on horse power.

And nothing symbolized that incomparability more than the Maginot Line. Embodying all the defensive lessons of 1914–18, the line, a series of large forts or *ouvrages*, was hailed as a military masterstroke, the kind of achievement only the French Army was able to execute: an impenetrable defense system capable of chewing up an invading German army at minimum cost in French lives. The line also had its critics, among them Colonel Charles de Gaulle, a leading proponent of armored warfare, who warned that in the next war, France would not be fighting the German army of 1914. But de Gaulle's warnings were ignored. A champion of the offense, the prickly colonel was viewed as out of step with the French public, who remembered the offensive battles of 1914, when as many as twenty-seven thousand men had been killed in a single day. Never Again.

When anyone asked how France, with barely half Germany's population (39 million versus 80 million) and only a third of its steel production (6.6 million tons versus 19 million tons) could hope to prevail in a new conflict, the answer was always the same: the Maginot Line. In the interwar years, belief in the Maginot Line became the principal article of faith in the French catechism of war. Whenever its effectiveness was questioned, defenders would set upon the heretics with a fury. They would point to the twelve to sixteen miles of artillery, antiair, and machine-gun emplacements that made up each strongpoint in the system, and ask how the Boche could hope to penetrate such a killing field. And the defenders were right: the Germans could not, not if they made a 1914-style infantry attack. But a mobile army led by tank columns could maneuver through gaps in the line left by poor planning and budgetary constraints. From Switzerland in the south to Luxembourg in the north, the French border bristled with defenses, except along the Belgian border, the German invasion route in 1914.

There were also skeptics who questioned the commitment of the French political class to the war. The parties of the right viewed communism, not Nazism, as the main threat; the French Communists viewed capitalism as the greater evil; and, between the two extremes—in the broad middle of French politics—there was equivocation and division about the war. Some prominent members of the center-right and center-left parties, such as Georges Mandel, the minister of the colonies, and Paul Reynaud, the minister of finance, supported the war without reservation. Others, such as Georges Bonnet—who, though no longer foreign minister, remained an influential figure—and Pierre Laval, a prominent French senator, regarded the new contest with Germany as tantamount to national suicide; and Laval and his followers in particular were working energetically behind the scenes to reach an accommodation with Hitler.

Finally, there were the French people.

On the early November day Spears arrived in the capital for talks with senior French politicians, the boulevards and cafés were crowded, and every radio in every sidewalk café seemed to be blaring out Maurice Chevalier's new hit, "Paris Reste Paris." But this Paris of barrage balloons, sandbag emplacements, and *flics* (French slang for policeman) with tommy guns did not feel like the Paris that Spears knew. There was no energy or gaiety in the crowds, no silhouette of the Eiffel Tower illuminating the night sky, no noisy American tourists, and almost no young or middle-aged men, except at the railway stations, where conscripts as old as forty-five and fifty were boarding trains for the front. The Champs-Élysées was bedecked in tricolor flags, and periodically a voice on the radio would announce, "We shall prevail because we are stronger," but not many people found the voice convincing. There was more than a grain of truth in the observation that on September 3 France had gone "to war looking over her shoulder, her eyes seeking peace." Hitler's October 6 speech had produced such a clamor to end the war that for a time William Bullitt, the American ambassador, feared the Daladier government would be unable to resist it. "In this city of bronze memorials and dreadful rolls to the dead," wrote Janet Flanner, the *New Yorker*'s Paris correspondent, there are "millions . . . [who] continue to think [war] could be avoided even after it has been officially declared."

The day after his arrival, Spears told Jean Giraudoux, the minister of information, that he was surprised at how much anti-British sentiment he had encountered in Paris. It is the fault "of German propaganda," Giraudoux said, which was not exactly a falsehood, but not exactly the truth either. Comparing the French and British war efforts in October 1939, the average French man or woman could be forgiven for thinking there was still truth in that old Great War jibe "The British intend to fight the war with French soldiers." France was fully mobilized; its people were working extended wartime hours, paying wartime taxes that undercut their standard of living—and every able-bodied male fifty or younger was being mobilized. By contrast, Britain had yet to institute rationing, had raised taxes only two shillings in the twenty-shilling pound, had confined conscription to men in their twenties, and had not yet put its industry on a full wartime footing. In the second month of the war, the British unemployment rate still stood at near depression levels: 1.4 million men. Toward the end of the conversation, Giraudoux did permit himself one mild criticism: he told Spears that anti-British feeling in the capital might subside if fewer British soldiers were seen on leave in Paris and more at the front.

A few days later, while visiting Georges Mandel, an old acquaintance from the Great War, Spears asked how committed Édouard Daladier, the French premier, was to the war. Spears had heard rumors that the Bull of Vaucluse possessed "the horns of a snail." Mandel chuckled at the question, then made one of his rare forays into humor: "No truer quip had been evolved in the Chamber [of Deputies]."

Not long after Spears returned to London, the Chamberlain government canceled the annual Armistice Day celebration at the cenotaph in Whitehall. The announcement set off a debate in the offices of a London pacifist group. "If we win this war," said a member of the group, "shall we have another Armistice Day and a new monument to the Glorious Dead? Or shall we again contrive to end the war at the eleventh hour of the eleventh day of the eleventh month, so as to save inventing another ceremony?"

Neither, replied a colleague. "Ever seen the French monument to the dead of 1870 [the Franco-Prussian War] in the churchyard at Camiers? After the last war, they economized by adding a brief inscription commemorating the heroes of 1914–18. We shan't have any money when we've won this war—so we shall probably just have to do the same."

CHAPTER THREE

EUROPE IN WINTER

In January 1940, the war was entering its fifth month and the only fighting to be found in Europe was closer to the Arctic Circle than to France. The previous September, when the war began, Josef Stalin looked west and saw peril everywhere. Germany—despite the Soviet-Nazi Nonaggression Pact—represented the gravest danger, but a conflict with anti-Communist France and Britain was not beyond the realm of possibility. Consequently, Stalin concluded that the western flank of the Soviet Union needed bracing. Under pressure from Moscow, the Baltic states—Latvia, Estonia, and Lithuania—agreed to grant the USSR military bases. Next, Stalin turned his attention north. In early October, the Finns were presented with a list of territorial demands, including the annexation of a large portion of the Karelian Isthmus, the thinly populated strip of high-forest, steep-hill, and marshy swamp that forms a land bridge between Finland and Leningrad (St. Petersburg). The Soviet demands were rejected; Stalin abrogated Moscow's mutual assistance pact with Helsinki and assembled a twenty-one-division army along the Finnish border. Early on the morning of November 30, the preternatural quiet of the Karelian Isthmus was shattered by artillery fire. In between shell bursts, the clank of tanks could be heard approaching through the high forest from the east. Farther to the north, a second Soviet force stormed the arctic port of Petsamo. So confident were the

Soviets of a walkover that the invasion forces brought along brass brands to celebrate their victory.

A month later the Red Army was bogged down in a bloody war of attrition on the Karelian Isthmus; the military reputation of the Soviet Union was in tatters; and Britain, France, and the United States were in the grip of Finnish "mania." Like Spain before it, gallant little Finland had become an international symbol of democratic resolve. Here, at last, thought wakeful-minded Europeans and Americans weary of the ludicrous "phony war," was "a real war, a man's war." Across Western Europe and America, balls and galas were held for Finnish relief and sweaters knitted for Finnish soldiers. At art galleries in New York, London, and Paris, the fashionable gathered under stark black-and-white photos of the Winter War to sip wine and lament the unhappy state of the Western democracy. "The fortified front of Karelia evokes, simultaneously, the Maginot Line and a season of winter sports," wrote a Frenchman who likened the Finnish war to "a highly seductive glossy magazine for skiing amateurs." In Allied chancelleries, maps of Finland were taken out and examined; eager fingers measured the distance between Finland and the iron ore fields of neutral Sweden, which fed the Nazi war machine; and eager minds imagined shifting the war's center of gravity from France, with its lovely countryside and crowded cities, to the north, where the vast, empty wastes were perfect for a war of maneuver and the only civilians put in harm's way would be the reindeer and the Finns.

Meanwhile, along the Western Front, barely a shot had been fired in anger. Well into the autumn of 1939, power plants in the German Saar were still providing French border towns with electricity, and when the French city of Strasbourg was evacuated, it was

German Army searchlights that illuminated the way for the evacuees. "They are not wicked," an indignant French soldier replied when a visiting British journalist asked him why he did not shoot the German soldier bathing in a river fifty meters away. In the winter of 1939–40, visitors could be forgiven for thinking that the primary function of the Western Front was to provide photo ops for the celebrated and glamorous. The Duke of Windsor was photographed visiting Fort Hochwald; the journalist Dorothy Thomas, shooting a French .75; and there was almost no place on the Western Front where Clare Boothe, playwright, journalist, scriptwriter paramour of Bernard Baruch and Joe Kennedy and soon to become Mrs. Clare Boothe Luce, had not been photographed. The air of unreality that hung over the war that winter undermined military discipline and raised questions about the combat readiness of the Allied armies. French soldiers strolled around in bedroom slippers—cigarettes dangling from their lips, jackets unbuttoned, hands thrust in pockets. The British Expeditionary Force had a crisper, more disciplined air, but its troops were not trained up to the standard of the best German units; and the BEF's commander, Lord John Gort, an amiable Anglo-Irishman, was more interested in the aspects of war that fascinated readers of *Boy's Own*, such as how to mount a trench raid, than in the broader strategic questions that are the proper province of an army commander. Asked about the Maginot Line's weaknesses, Gort exclaimed, "Oh, I haven't had time to think about that!" "Queer kind of war," William Shirer of CBS news wrote after a tour of the Western Front.

It seemed like a queer kind of war to civilians, too. The British public had expected the war to begin as the Great War had, with a series of epic encounter battles on the plains of Belgium and northern France. Instead, there was a brief French foray into the Saar, then nothing. The autumn of 1939 brought all the annoyances of war—price rises, blackouts, unheated flats, evacuations, censorship, conscription, long queues—without any of the dramatic events that make civilians feel their sacrifices have purpose and meaning. "It's a war of nerves," said a man in a Blackpool pub. "War of nerves, my arse," said his companion. "It's boring me bloody stiff." "The British people [are] prepared to accept great sacrifices," observed Sam Hoare, the home secretary. "But not minor irritations."

In folk memory, Britain went to war to the voice of Vera Lynn, singing

> They'll be bluebirds over
> The white cliffs of Dover . . .

In reality, Britain went to war to the voice of the nanny state admonishing the citizenry, in pamphlets and posters: "Don't spit, it's a bad habit"; "Make your family gargle before they go to the shelter"; "Keep your feet dry"; "Keep Calm and Carry On"; "Try not to lie on your back—you are less likely to snore"; "Make your home safe now!"; "Don't dig a deep trench unless you know how to make one properly." Even British officialdom's attempts at inspiration, such as the poster "Your Courage, Your Cheerfulness, Your Resolution, Will Bring Us Victory" just sounded like Nanny in a patriotic mood. That poster also set people to wondering who this "us" was and for whom this "us" was going to win the war. Many working-class Britons suspected they were "us" and that they were being called on to win the war for their social betters.

In time, a sense of duty and confiscatory tax rates would make the wealthy more like the rest of us; but in the winter of 1939–40, that time was still some way off. At the Dorchester, top-hatted doormen still greeted guests; at the Savoy, strawberries and cream were still available, at the Connaught, grouse, oysters, and partridge. And at the dinner parties of Lord Kemsley, the owner of the *Times* of London, guests were still attended by a "galaxy of footmen," the food was still "vast and excellent, and the wine flowed like water." In the East End, one of the poorest neighborhoods in London, a wealthy couple and their chauffeur descended upon a grocery store, snatched four twenty-eight-pound bags of sugar from the shelves, and carried them to the cash register. The store owner refused to sell the sugar. "I don't think that sort of thing is right," he said. "They don't give the poor a chance."

By January 1940, the absence of a real war was making many of the nanny state's rules almost impossible to enforce. Hardly anyone carried a gas mask anymore, the blackout was honored more often in the breach, and tens of thousands of parents were reclaiming their evacuated children. Alarmed by this latter development, the Ministry of Health rushed out a cautionary poster, which depicted Hitler whispering into the ear of a British mother: "Take them back, take them back." "Don't do it, Mother," a banner line at the bottom of the poster warned. The logic behind the poster was obscure. First, *Hitler and the Working Man*; now Hitler, the champion of maternal love? By January, most of the eight hundred thousand children evacuated in September were home; but with the schools still closed, the children had nothing to occupy them. Eventually the government would cobble together a home school network, but food, gasoline, and heating fuel shortages were left unaddressed, as were the dangers of the blackout, which caused four thousand civilian injuries in its first several months of operation and produced headlines such as "He Stepped from Train, Fell 80 Feet." The harsh winter of 1939–40, the worst in decades, further soured the public mood. In Blackpool the snowdrifts were fifteen feet high; in Sheffield, four feet high; in London, where the Thames froze over, "snow lay deep and hard as iron beneath 25 degrees of frost"; and on January 21, the coldest day ever recorded in England, ice storms snapped tree branches and brought down telephone wires. "As the harsh days slowly [pass]," Vera Brittain wrote one day that winter, "my author friend writes me from the country that she is working with numb fingers in a room where in spite of the fire, there is ice inside the windows. 'It is bitterly cold here,' she reports. 'So cold my brains seem frozen in my head.'" The fifteen-day blackout on weather news meant that technically the snow and freezing temperatures remained a state secret for two weeks, but in a concession to reality, official-dom allowed plows to clear the roads in the meanwhile.

In January 1940, Giuseppe Bastianini, the Italian ambassador in London, told Rome that there was "constant talk [here] of how the war could be liquidated. If severe military reverses were sustained, the social situation in this country might become serious." Bastianini was overstating the fragility of British morale, but the government intrusions into everyday life, the shortages, the cold, and the confusion about what Britain was fighting were eroding support for the war. As a reward for their sacrifices, the British public wanted to be inspired, wanted to hear Nelson at Trafalgar: "England expects that every man will do his duty." Instead they got

> An elderly statesman with gout
> When asked what the war was about
> Replied with a sigh
> My colleagues and I
> Are doing our best to find out.

In October 1939, when the British Institute of Public Opinion asked, "Would you approve or disapprove if the British government were to discuss peace proposals with Germany now?," only 17 percent of the public had approved. In early 1940, when the institute asked the question again, 29 percent, nearly a third of the public, favored immediate discussions.

"People call me defeatist," Lloyd George told a journalist at the turn of the year. But "tell me how we can win! Can we win in the air? Can we win at sea, when the effect of our blockade is wiped out by . . . Russia? How can we win on land? When do you think we can get through the Siegfried Line [Germany's version of the Maginot Line]? Not until the trumpet blows, my friend."

On the Continent, the winter of 1939–40 was also severe. By early January, weeks of heavy snow had transformed northwestern Europe into an icy white plain where sky, earth, and river blended seamlessly into one another. In this almost featureless landscape villages, market towns, and tree lines became navigational aids for aircraft, tank crews, and lorry drivers. On the rare warm days when fog formed over the snow, the villages and towns would also disappear, and navigation often broke down completely. January 10, 1940, was such a day. That morning, the Essen–Cologne road was so fogged over that Major Erich Hoenmanns, a Luftwaffe pilot, turned his plane west and began searching for the Rhine, which also ran up to Cologne, where his wife was awaiting him. At some point Hoenmanns realized the river beneath him was not the Rhine, it was the Meuse; he was flying west toward the Allied lines, not north toward Cologne. Panicked, he began fumbling with the controls of the Messerschmitt BF-108 Taifun. The engine stalled, and a moment later the ground was coming up at Hoenmanns at several hundred miles an hour. A pair of trees sheared off the Taifun's wings, and the plane landed in a snowy Belgian field with a hard thump. In the next few moments, danger and absurdity would intersect in a way that only happens in war. Hoenmanns was standing in the snow, worrying what would happen if he was interned and the Luftwaffe mistakenly sent his mistress's belongings to his wife, when his passenger, Major Helmuth Reinberger, announced that he was carrying one of the greatest secrets of the war—the plan for the long-rumored German offensive in the West.

By the time the plan arrived at the Belgian High Command that evening, it had survived two attempts by Reinberger to burn it, but, even scorched, it still had an important story to tell. The German offensive in the West would begin with a variation of the Schlieffen Plan, which had shaped the encounter battles of the Great War—a thrust through Belgium and into northern France. Four days later, the phone rang in the flat of Alexander Cadogan, Halifax's number two at the Foreign Office. Cadogan looked at the clock: it was 3:45 a.m. When he picked up the receiver, the voice on the other end said, "Telegram from Brussels. Belgians expect invasion of Belgium, Holland, and Luxembourg today." Cadogan was unable to fall back to sleep.

In its brief four and a half months of existence, the plan the Belgians retrieved from Hoenmanns's plane had unnerved almost everyone who had come into contact with it, starting with the German High Command, who were first introduced to the plan on September 27, the day Warsaw fell. The setting was the new German Chancellery, whose austere lines and monumental size spoke of the Roman and Greek influences on its architect, Albert Speer; and its 480-foot-long Grand Hall, 17-foot-high bronze doors, and statues of nude Aryan athletes spoke of the Wagnerian influence on its principal occupant, Adolf Hitler. The old Chancellery next door had been preserved, but only for its metaphorical value. Entombed in decades of Berlin grime, it stood as a symbol of defeat and humiliation, of Versailles and French occupation, of breadlines and runaway inflation, while its glittering successor proclaimed *"ein Volk, ein Reich, ein Führer."*

The first car to arrive at the Chancellery that morning held Hermann Göring. The reichsmarschall, who was colossal in everything—girth, ego, ambition, even bad taste—was wearing a gold-trimmed white uniform and a cap whose chinstraps disappeared into the folds of his neck fat. The other lead cars held General Walther von Brauchitsch, commander in chief of the German Army, and his naval opposite number, Grossadmiral Erich Raeder; von Brauchitsch was dressed in standard army field gray, Raeder in navy blue. The cars in the rear held a bevy of aides and advisers, their shoulders adorned with gold braids, their chests spangled with medals. For a moment the Chancellery courtyard echoed with the sound of car doors slamming shut; then the assemblage gathered itself up and marched down the marble corridors to Hitler's office, which *Life* magazine had recently called the largest office in the world. Inside, the Führer awaited his guests in a simple gray uniform, under a mural illustrating the capital virtues—Wisdom, Prudence, Fortitude, and Justice.

During the meeting, Hitler introduced his guests to what was still the germ of an idea with a lecture on "general time." Every day of quiet in the West gives Britain and France another day to mobilize their industries, to build up their armies, to cut further into Germany's superiority in the air and on the ground. Therefore, said Hitler, Germany must strike in the West this year—1939. General George Thomas, director of the War Economy Department, was appalled. German steel production was currently running tens of thousands of tons below target each month, and there were serious shortages of gunpowder, vehicles, ammunition, and spare parts. Many of Hitler's other guests agreed with Thomas; the plan was recklessly audacious. The armored and motorized divisions returning from Poland would take months to refit; airpower could not be brought fully to bear in autumn, due to the uncertainty of the weather; and the army was not ready to face a professional, well-equipped Western army. In Poland, some machine-gun units had refused to fire for fear of giving away their positions, and some platoons and companies had refused to attack unless goaded by an officer. These deficiencies would have to be corrected before the Wehrmacht could undertake a major campaign. In the collective opinion of the Supreme Command, Germany would be incapable of launching a decisive offensive in the West until the spring of 1942. Strike now, warned one general, and the cost will be four hundred thousand dead.

At a second meeting, on October 10, Hitler reframed his offensive plan for the generals. It was no longer just a clever strategic move designed to catch the Allies off guard. The offensive was now fundamental to Germany's survival in a struggle with a Britain and France bent on its obliteration. Evoking "general time" again, Hitler warned that unless Germany struck soon, the Allies would press neutral Belgium and Holland into the war and, from bases in the Low Countries, Britain and France could mount an annihilating air campaign on the industrial Ruhr, the engine of the German war machine. Over the next six weeks, what had begun as a relatively modest offensive plan—an enveloping movement through Belgium and southern Holland—grew steadily more ambitious. Responding to the Luftwaffe's demand for airfields on the Channel coast, the plan was expanded to include the occupation of all of Holland. The role of German forces in the Ardennes region was expanded as well. Instead of supporting the main thrust through the Low Countries with a limited penetration into eastern France, the Ardennes force would sweep westward across France and capture the Channel coast. Chamberlain's rejection of Hitler's peace offer on October 12 may also have had an effect on German planning. Five days later, on October 17, Hitler told the army's commander in chief,

General von Brauchitsch, and his chief of staff, Colonel General Franz Halder, that "the British will only be ready to talk after a beating. We must get at them as quickly as possible. No use holding back." A week later the offensive had a name, Case Yellow, and a starting date, November 12, but still not much support from senior German commanders.

In early November, General Halder compressed the army's objections to Case Yellow into three points. One, "At the moment, we cannot launch an offensive with a distant object." Two, "*None* of the higher headquarters think that the offensive . . . has any prospect of success." And three, "On the whole, the assessment of the enemy is the same as that of the Army High Command." (The Allies were also aware of the German Army's shortcomings.)

On November 5, General von Brauchitsch presented Hitler with a memo on Case Yellow that drew heavily on Halder's conclusions. As head of the army, von Brauchitsch was the logical choice to confront Hitler, but he was perhaps not the best choice. Blandly handsome and apolitical, he had demonstrated great physical courage at Verdun, but physical courage is not the same as moral courage, and Halder had reservations about his superior on that score. The meeting began well enough. Hitler was almost playfully ironic when von Brauchitsch complained about the logistical problems created by the autumn rains: he reminded the general that "it rains on the enemy, too." But an ominous silence greeted von Brauchitsch's request that the Army Supreme Command be allowed to run the war without interference, and when von Brauchitsch criticized the army's performance in Poland, Hitler erupted: The army had always opposed him. The army was cowardly. One day he would crush the army! Then, abruptly, the outburst ended and Hitler asked, "What are you planning?" in a voice that carried the insinuation of holding cells, midnight interrogations, and rubber truncheons. An hour later, when he met Halder outside the old Chancellery building, von Brauchitsch was chalk white. The two men talked for a while; then von Brauchitsch told Halder about Hitler's question "What are you planning?" That is all that is known about their conversation, but both men must have wondered what Hitler knew or suspected about their ties to the German opposition.

Contacts between the German opposition and the British government dated back to at least 1938. On the eve of the Munich crisis, word reached London that Colonel Hans Oster, a member of the Abwehr, the German intelligence service, was organizing a coup against Hitler; but, reluctant to lose a last chance to preserve peace, Chamberlain ignored the reports and flew to Germany. When he returned, promising "peace in our time," the Oster coup collapsed. In the autumn of 1939, London was more welcoming when news of a new opposition coup arrived. Oster and Colonel Helmut Groscurth, another Abwehr officer, had been in contact with Halder and von Brauchitsch, and both men had expressed an interest in implementing "fundamental changes" in the German government. On October 31, three weeks after Hitler's peace offer, Chamberlain was so confident a coup was imminent, he told a colleague the Wehrmacht was about to "take the leading part in the formation of a new government" that would return Germany "to peaceful, friendly, tranquil relations with the world." If it sounded too good to be true, it was.

Whatever remaining faith London had in the German opposition was destroyed by the Venlo incident. A few weeks after von Brauchitsch's talk with Hitler, Gestapo agents masquerading as opposition members kidnapped two British agents in the Dutch town of Venlo and dragged them across the border to Germany. Shortly thereafter, London received a note from the kidnappers:

"Negotiations for any length of time with conceited and silly people are tedious. You will understand therefore that we are giving them up. You are hereby bidden a hearty farewell by your affectionate German opposition, [signed] the Gestapo."

On November 17, General Winter finally achieved what the German High Command could not. Heavy snows postponed Case Yellow from the seventeenth to the twentieth, then to December 3, December 11, December 17, and December 27. As a precaution, the offensive was postponed yet again, after the Belgians retrieved a signed copy of the plan from Major Hoenmanns's crashed plane. Case Yellow would not become a reality until May 10, but during the late winter and early spring of 1940 rumors about a German offensive in the West would undermine the last serious attempt to reach a negotiated peace and make a war in distant Finland look ever more attractive to the British and French governments.

Throughout December and into January 1940, the Finns continued to more than hold their own in a war that ranged northward into the Arctic, southward into the Gulf of Finland, and eastward across the high forest of the Karelian Isthmus. But except for the dramatic light and the snow-covered high forests, the war possessed none of the "Nordic charm" that the British, French, and American supporters of Finland imagined. At Suomussalmi, at Ousul, and in a hundred places in between, the pattern of battle was always the same: wave after wave of half-trained Soviet troops attacked into volleys of machine-gun fire to little or no profit except for driving the occasional Finnish machine gunner mad from all the killing. Visiting the battlefield at Suomussalmi before the snows had an opportunity to tidy it up, James Aldridge, an American war correspondent, was shocked. "It was the most horrible sight I've ever seen. There were two or three thousand Russians and a few Finns, all frozen in a fighting attitude. Some [of the dead] were locked together, their bayonets within each others' bodies, some were frozen with their arms crooked, holding the hand grenades they were throwing. . . . Fear was registered in their faces. Their bodies were like statues of men throwing all of their muscles and strength into some work, but their faces recorded something between bewilderment and horror."

Finally, in the latter part of January 1940, the weight of Soviet power began to tell. The Finns were losing a thousand men a day, an unsustainable casualty rate for a nation of four million. On the morning of February 1 an artillery barrage swept across the Karelian Isthmus, the key front in the Winter War. Six days later, the Russian guns were still firing. On the seventh day, three Soviet divisions attacked. Behind the soldiers came the tanks—150—and above the tanks flew squadron after squadron of Soviet planes. Machine-gun fire crackled. Entire Soviet battalions fell dead in the snow, but half an hour later a fresh battalion would emerge from the tree line, pick up the rifles of the dead, and charge into the machine guns again. This would continue until the guns ran out of ammunition or a lucky shot from an eighteen-year-old Soviet recruit killed the machine gunner. Facing defeat, the Finns turned to Britain and France for assistance—and the British, eager to seize the Swedish iron ore fields adjacent to Finland, and the French, eager to relocate the German offensive from France to Scandinavia, promised Helsinki twenty-five thousand troops and then fifty thousand troops. Strategically, the decision made little sense at the time, and in the long light of history, it makes even less.

Writing about the February 5 meeting, where the Allied Supreme Council decided to send troops to Finland, J. R. M. Butler, author of the official British history of the Second World War, could barely hide his exasperation. "An air of unreality pervaded the proceedings . . . as shown in the readiness to lock up troops in Finland that were so urgently needed elsewhere, in the underestimation of the administrative difficulties of such a campaign, in the slight regard paid to the danger of Soviet hostility, in the miscalculation of German efficiency and resources and . . . in the wishful thinking which discounted the determination of the neutral governments [Sweden and Norway] to maintain their neutrality."

In the midst of the Finnish crisis, Washington made a surprise announcement: At the end of February Sumner Welles, a prominent State Department official, would visit Rome, Berlin, Paris, and London "for the purpose of advising the President and the Secretary of State as to the present conditions in Europe." This bland announcement in the February 10, 1940, edition of the *New York Times* failed to do justice to the brief given to Welles, a well-born, discreetly ambitious New Yorker. Welles's assignment was to assess the prospect of ending the war peacefully before serious fighting in Scandinavia or France made a negotiated settlement impossible. Welles also carried several subsidiary briefs, including instructions to counter Hitler's influence on Mussolini. The Duce had kept Italy out of the war the previous September, but he had ten battleships, two aircraft carriers, and more than seventy divisions, and whenever he came within Hitler's orbit, his desire to use them increased noticeably.

In Congress, where isolationist feeling was intense, the Welles mission aroused deep suspicion. Senator Hiram Johnson of California reminded his Senate colleagues that on the eve of the Great War Woodrow Wilson had sent Colonel Edward House to Europe on a similar mission, and three years later American boys were dying on French fields. The president is trying to "entangle us in Europe's quarrels," Johnson warned. Similar accusations were made by Representative Roy Woodruff of Michigan, Senator Robert Reynolds of North Carolina, and several other prominent senators and congressmen.

London was also unenthusiastic about the Welles mission. The phony war was making it harder and harder to impose curfews, rationing, and evacuations on a public less and less enthusiastic about a war whose purpose remained obscure. Polling in February showed that a stubborn quarter of the British public continued to favor a negotiated settlement with Germany in one form or another. In a letter to Roosevelt, Prime Minister Chamberlain cautioned that an Allied public excited by Welles's "sensational intervention" might force London and Paris into a patched-up peace settlement "that apparently righted the wrongs done in recent months," but "sooner or later . . . [would] result in a renewed attack on the rights and liberties of the weaker European States." A few weeks later Chamberlain again cautioned the president about the Welles mission, this time evoking Finland. "We fear that . . . if the Governments of [neutral] Sweden and Norway get the idea that some peace suggestions are likely to be set afoot, they will refuse to grant [the Anglo-French Expeditionary Force] the passage we want in order to save Finland." This was a half-truth at best. To London, the most attractive aspect of saving Finland was that British troops would pass the Swedish iron ore fields on their way north.

Reaction to the Welles mission in Berlin and Paris was also unenthusiastic, but Rome, Rome was different.

Two weeks after the *New York Times* announcement, Welles was sitting in Mussolini's office on the Piazza Venezia. For a man who embodied grandiosity in its most florid form, the Duce's office was surprisingly restrained. High-ceilinged and long, the room sought its effects in the play of light on empty space and in clean, unadorned lines. There were no furnishings except Mussolini's desk, which sat at the far end of the office and the three chairs in front of it, and no light except for the natural light flooding through the windows, and that from a single lamp on the Duce's desk. The aged figure who rose to greet Welles was also a surprise. In person, Mussolini looked "fifteen years older than his actual age of 58 . . . moved with an elephantine motion . . . and was very heavy for his height." For most of the nearly two-hour interview, the Duce sat sphinx-like behind the desk, the small lamp illuminating the folds of skin on his fleshy face, his eyes shut except when a question particularly interested him. When Welles asked if he thought a negotiated peace settlement was still possible, the eyes popped open.

"Yes!" Mussolini replied, "emphatically." None of "the people now at war desired to fight. The situation . . . in that regard [is] utterly different from that which existed in 1914"; but if a "real war breaks out, with its attendant slaughters and devastations, there will be no possibility, for a long time to come, of any peace negotiation." Welles left the meeting feeling that one part of Mussolini was genuinely interested in brokering a peace settlement, but that part was at war with the Roman emperor, who was fond of proclaiming, "I was born never to leave the Italians in peace." Welles had heard the rumors about a German offensive in the West, and believed its outcome would determine which of the two Mussolinis prevailed. If "Germany obtains some rapid apparent victory, such as the occupation of Holland and Belgium," Welles cabled Washington, "I fear very much that Mussolini would then bring Italy in on the German side."

Four days later Welles stood in a cold Berlin wind, examining two monumental black nudes in the Court of Honor, the entrance to Hitler's Chancellery. The statues were the sole expression of humanity in the court, and they failed to express it convincingly enough to relieve the acute sense of oppression that Welles felt standing in a rectangle of "high blank walls" open only to the sky. It was March 2, and Welles was in Berlin to confer with Hitler, who proved even more unlike his public image than did Mussolini.

Charlie Chaplin's comic Hitler in *The Great Dictator* had made such a deep impression on the Western public, it was almost impossible for a non-German to imagine the Führer doing anything except goose-stepping, tugging at his mustache, or throwing a temper tantrum. The Hitler who greeted Welles under the mural of the cardinal virtues bore little resemblance to the Chaplin creation. In person, Hitler was taller and more physically prepossessing than he appeared in newsreels; he also spoke a surprisingly "beautiful German" in a "low, well modulated voice" and was dignified in manner and temperate in his observations. Indeed, European peace had no better friend than Adolf Hitler until Welles asked about the prospect of negotiating an end to the war. "I can see no hope for the establishment of any lasting peace until the will of England and France is itself destroyed," Hitler replied. "There is no way by which the will to destroy Germany can be itself destroyed, except through a German victory. I believe that German might is such as to ensure the triumph of Germany, but if not, we will all go down together." How much of this Hitler really believed, Welles was unsure, but he was sure that the average German believed it. The Treaty of Versailles and a decade of Nazi propaganda had convinced the German people that the Western powers were committed not just to Germany's defeat but also to its annihilation. The outburst over, Hitler assumed the statesman's mantle again, and the meeting concluded on a cordial note. "I appreciate your sincerity and that of your government," he told Welles. As Welles was boarding the Paris train a few hours later, Hitler was issuing a secret directive for Fall Weserubung: the occupation of Norway and Denmark.

"There is only one way to deal with a mad dog," Georges Clemenceau, France's Great War leader, once observed. "Either kill him or chain him with a steel chain that cannot be broken." During his visit to Paris, Welles heard several versions of the Clemenceau doctrine from his successors. Albert Lebrun, the French president, said that after three German wars in seventy years, "it was a vital need of France to ensure herself that at least one generation of Frenchmen can be born to live a normal span of life." Jules Jenneney, president of the French Senate, put that thought more fiercely: Germany, he said, had to be "taught such a lesson as to make it impossible for the German people ever again to bring about a European conflagration." The only major French politician who spoke of a negotiated settlement was Édouard Daladier, the premier, who told Welles he believed an agreement with Germany was still possible, but, just before leaving Paris, Welles heard that France was assembling a fleet at Brest to carry the fifty-thousand-man Allied Expeditionary Force to Finland. Had Welles spoken to the former foreign minister Georges Bonnet, or to Pierre Laval, a prominent French senator, he would have left Paris with a different impression of French resolve.

In London, Chamberlain and Lord Halifax spoke of punishing Germany for its aggression, but in the company of intimates, the foreign secretary took a slightly different view. One day, when his undersecretary, Rab Butler, said the war was a mistake, Halifax thought for a moment and then replied, "I agree." However, below Chamberlain, Halifax, and a few other cabinet ministers, everyone else Welles met in London was in full war paint. Admiral Dudley Pound, the first sea lord, talked of burning Berlin to the ground, dividing Germany into small principalities, and imposing a fifty-year occupation. Oliver Stanley, the secretary of war, and Churchill, the first lord of the Admiralty, favored a hundred-year occupation. The German people should have no illusions "as to where the mastery in Europe lay."

Of all the personalities that Welles met on his trip, none made as deep an impression as Churchill.

Mr. Churchill was sitting in front of the fire smoking a 24 inch cigar and drinking a whiskey and soda. It was quite evident that he had consumed a good many whiskeys before I arrived. As soon as the preliminary courtesies had been concluded, Mr. Churchill commenced an address which lasted exactly one hour and fifty minutes, during which I was never given an opportunity to say a word. It constituted a cascade of oratory, brilliant and always effective and always interlarded with considerable wit. It would have impressed me more had I not already read his book . . . [of] which his address to me constituted a rehash.

By March 16, when Welles returned to Rome for a second visit with Mussolini, rumors of war were everywhere. From Norway to Spain, people sensed a real shooting war was coming, maybe in Scandinavia, maybe in France, maybe somewhere else, but it was coming, and with spring, the traditional campaign season almost upon Europe, it was coming very soon. "The minute hand is pointing at one minute before midnight," Mussolini said, then told Welles about his recent conversation with Joachim von Ribbentrop, the German foreign minister. According to von Ribbentrop Germany "would consider no solution other than a military victory." Hitler expected to conquer France within three or four months and for Great Britain to crumble shortly thereafter. The prospect of war seemed to energize Mussolini. Welles noticed that "the nervous oppression" that the Duce had evidenced at their first meeting was gone. Mussolini's eyes closed less frequently, his fleshy face was more animated, and his manner more relaxed and casual. Two days later, at a conference on the Brenner Pass, the Duce pledged to Hitler that Italy would march with Germany.

Welles returned to Washington convinced that the principal obstacle to peace was not the statuses of Poland, Austria, and Czechoslovakia. As serious and difficult as those issues were, the principal obstacle was insecurity. Each side was preparing for total war because each side believed its enemies were bent on its annihilation. Hitler was responsible for fomenting the atmosphere of distrust, but the Treaty of Versailles and the subsequent humiliations imposed on Germany had given him a lot to work with. In Welles's view, the only solution to what was essentially an existential crisis was a security guarantee imposed by an outside force strong enough to enforce the guarantee. In his final report, he suggested that the force might take the form of an American-led coalition of neutral states. But even supposing an isolationist Congress would agree to sanction such a measure, by the time Welles filed his report it was spring, and spring was the campaign season in Europe.

CHAPTER FOUR

SEARCHING FOR SOMETHING SPECTACULAR

To her admirers, the Comtesse Hélène de Portes was a great beauty. It was true that the comtesse had a large nose and a chin that was not all a chin should be, and in certain quarters of Paris her taste in hats was regarded as almost tragic. "Perfectly silly," Edward Spears said, of "the ridiculous saucer shaped contraptions" the comtesse favored. To admirers, however, these minor flaws were more than offset by a head of wonderfully thick, dark, curly hair, sparkling eyes, "very good feet and ankles," and a figure so perfect it constituted a French national treasure. "She had a way of walking," wrote Elie Bois, a columnist for *Le Petite Parisian*, "that disclosed the suppleness of her limbs and the agility of [a] whole body maintained by physical exercise." Clare Boothe, who was spending the spring in Paris, thought Bois was being ridiculous. Describing Hélène de Portes as the "du Barry of France" is like "describing Mrs. Eleanor Roosevelt as the Cleopatra of the New Deal," she said.

The journalist René Benjamin once described the Marquise de Crussol, the comtesse's great rival, as "a pretty little gilded goat," but Benjamin's was a minority opinion. Small, with "peculiar fea-

possessed none of the comtesse's
additional burden of a humili-
qui estee Cure Sole"—the sardine
eference to the advertising slogan
g business. The rivalry between two
emmes du monde had many sources,
rival salons, but at bottom it was a
wer. The marquise's lover, Édouard
Daladier, was the premier of France, and the comtesse's lover,
Paul Reynaud, the minister of finance, wanted to be the premier of
France. Of the two women, the comtesse was the more aggressive
and controlling. A persistent and intrusive presence at the Ministry of Finance, where a special telephone line had been installed
for her use, on at least one occasion the comtesse had been seen
presiding over a meeting of ministry officials in Reynaud's office.
There was much speculation about why Reynaud put up with it.
The most widely accepted explanation was height; he was barely
five feet tall and the comtesse "made him feel tall and grand and
powerful." If Reynaud had been three inches taller, the history of
the world might have been changed," said one Parisian.

For years, the comtesse had been relentless in her efforts to
advance Reynaud's career, and for years those efforts had floun-
dered on the same two objections. A national leader required a
political base, and Reynaud, a lawyer and a financial technocrat,
lacked a base. The second objection was linked to the first—and
perhaps also to Reynaud's height—he threw off a fume of superiority that was politically toxic. In group photos, Reynaud always
seems to stand a foot or so in front of everyone else: his smile full of
self-pleasure; his slightly slanted eyes giving his small, handsome
face an exotic oriental cast; and his perfectly cut suit suggesting
that he was a man who paid more attention to his appearance
than a man should. There were two schools of thought about

the origins of Reynaud's nickname. One held that he was called "Mickey Mouse" because of his diminutive stature, the other that the nickname was a backhanded tribute to Reynaud's tremendous energy. The French, who liked their politicians with a little dirt under their fingernails, found it easy to imagine the earthy Daladier as a resident of the "real France," that mystical national homeland where men spent their days in a field, back to the sky, face to the black earth; Reynaud, they found impossible to imagine anywhere except where he in fact lived, in one of Paris's most exclusive districts. Reynaud had much to offer France: intelligence, competency, and determination to wage the war aggressively. Still, it is likely that he would have ended up marooned on the shoals of history had not a political crisis at the end of the Finnish war done what all the Comtesse de Portes's efforts had failed to do.

In no nation had the "great and glorious" cause of Finland aroused more passion than in France. On February 10, 1940, when Daladier announced that the Allies would send fifty thousand men and a hundred aircraft to Finland, the Chamber of Deputies erupted in applause. Here, at last, was the France the deputies had been waiting for, the France the French people had been waiting for: the France of Verdun, of the Marne, the France who defended the weak and helpless and embodied liberal democracy. Daladier's popularity soared after the announcement, but then, in early March, Finland surrendered, the Allied Expeditionary Force disbanded, and the languorous rhythms of the *drôle de guerre* reasserted themselves. The press returned to printing photos of Allied generals pinning medals on one another, while, along the Western Front, Allied and German troops resumed "pranking" one another. In one famous incident, a German unit posted a sign near the French line: "Soldiers of the Northern Army, beware of the English. They are destroying your properties, eating your food, sleeping with your wives, raping your daughters." The next day the French troops responded: "Who gives a damn? We're from the South."

In Paris, the femmes du monde, bored with war work for a nonexistent war, resumed their long champagne lunches, and shopkeepers ignored the boring blackout regulations. "What does the word 'war' really mean?" the writer Simone de Beauvior wondered. The previous September, "when all the papers printed it boldly across their headlines, it meant horror, something undefined but very real. Now, it lacks all substance and identity." As the old malaise reasserted itself, Daladier's political fortunes fell.

Entering the French Chamber of Deputies on March 19, the premier looked like a man who had been invited to his own funeral. The vote of confidence that afternoon went overwhelmingly against him. "The Bull of Vaucluse has received something more than darts this time," wrote Elie Bois. "The toreador ha[s] planted the sword firmly between his ribs." On March 21, Paul Reynaud assumed the premiership, promising to reinvigorate the war effort with a spectacular new plan.

By late March, Prime Minister Chamberlain was also feeling the need to do something spectacular, and for the same reason. Boredom and disaffection were undermining civilian discipline and morale. To many Britons, the war was beginning to feel unreal, as if it was something Whitehall, Westminster, and Downing Street had concocted for their own personal amusement. "Keep out," declared a cartoon in the *Picture Post*. "This is a private war. The War Office, the Admiralty, the Air Ministry and the Ministry of Information are engaged in a war against the Nazis. They are in no account to be disturbed. Nothing is to be photographed. No one is to come near."

In early March Mass Observation, a social research and public opinion organization, warned the government that "for the mass of people," the war "seems increasingly pointless. A new restlessness is setting in . . . a desire for something to happen."

In a March 25 memo to Chamberlain, Reynaud proposed something spectacular, a three-point plan to energize the Allied war effort. Point one was to provoke Germany into battle by seizing control of the Norwegian territorial waters; point two was using the German counterstroke as cover for landing troops in Norway and Sweden; and point three was the seizure of the Swedish iron ore fields. This was the most modest of the premier's proposals. Reynaud also wanted to bomb the Russian oil fields at Baku and to send submarines into the Black Sea to stop the flow of Soviet oil to Germany. About Stalin's likely response to such a provocative action, the memo had little to say; and about the risk of fighting a two-front war—against the Soviet Union, which had 3.4 million men under arms, and against Germany, which had 2.5 million, the memo had even less to say. Reynaud did acknowledge that "the absence of a state of war between the Allies and Russia will perhaps be seen as a legal obstacle to this enterprise [the Black Sea oil blockade]," but said, "the French Government . . . for their part, consider that we should not hesitate to set [the obstacle] aside."

Chamberlain went "through the ceiling" when he read the memo. The British rearmament program, far behind the German program at the start of the war, had benefited from the relative peace of the past seven months, but in March 1940, the program was still a year from completion. How many British planes and tanks would get built if the Luftwaffe was over Coventry and Sheffield every night? How would the small British army survive if Stalin moved one hundred of his divisions west? The Chiefs of Staff considered the Reynaud memo of interest only as an example of the excitable French temperament. "The lack of spectacular military events tends to create pressure to undertake projects that offer little prospect of decisive successes and are calculated to impair our resources and to postpone ultimate victory. This tendency should be resisted."

Two days later, Chamberlain was still fulminating about the Reynaud memo. At a meeting on March 27 he described himself as "horrified"; the memo conveyed "the impression of a man who was rattled and who wished to make a splash to justify his position. That Reynaud should mention submarines going into the Black Sea without mentioning Turkey [which sat on the Black Sea and had a vital interest in anything that happened there] seemed fantastic." The prime minister's idea of "spectacular" did not include national suicide. He wanted an action large enough to impress the Germans and engage a bored, disaffected British public, but not so large as to provoke a powerful German response.

Behind these differences lay a fundamental difference about what the Allies were fighting for. France's war aims possessed the virtue of consistency, the imprimatur of history, and the clarity of a propaganda poster. The Reynaud government, like the Daladier government, subscribed to the Clemenceau Doctrine: "There is only one way to deal with a mad dog. Either kill him or chain him with a steel chain." In practice, this translated into two demands: the defeat of the German Army in the field and the dismemberment of the German state so that future generations of Frenchmen could live in the peace and security denied their fathers and grandfathers. The third French demand was also a testament to the power of memory and loss. Three German wars in three successive generations had convinced the French that there was a systemic wickedness in the German character that extended to the German people; a postwar settlement would have to take this character deformity into account in meting out punishment to a defeated Germany. If the Clemenceau Doctrine shaped France's war aims, the Treaty of Versailles shaped Britain's. On September 3, 1939, Chamberlain went to war with the two core convictions: Germany must be taught that aggression does not pay and that it would be self-defeating to impose another Carthaginian peace on it. Look what Versailles had wrought: torchlight parades, goose steps, Poland and Czechoslovakia, concentration camps, pogroms, Hitler, Göring, Goebbels. The desire for revenge had twisted an entire generation of young Germans.

Consequently, well into the spring of 1940, Britain's war aims were kept vague and ill defined. Was Britain fighting the Nazi regime or the German people? The government was looking into that question. Was Britain fighting for a "just [peace] for all nations, including Germany," or to liberate Poland and Czecho-slovakia? The government was looking into that as well. Was Britain fighting to end Hitlerism or just to depose Adolf Hitler? Another matter requiring careful study. What was Britain fighting for, then? To this question, the Chamberlain government did have a clear answer. Britain's ultimate war aim was to induce a "change of heart" in Germany, which Britain would do by showing it, once and for all, that aggression does not pay. A German withdrawal from Poland and Czechoslovakia would provide evidence of this "change of heart," but in and of itself it was insufficient. A with-drawal was a mechanical act; a change of heart, a spiritual one. The Chamberlain government was never able to clearly define what constituted an authentic change of heart. Still, the prime minister was confident if Germany had one, he would recognize it. Did Britain seek the military defeat of Germany? The Chamber-lain government also had a clear answer to this question: only as a last resort. Until about March 1940, the prime minister remained confident that blockade and propaganda would produce victory, either by inducing a collapse of the German economy or by triggering a revolt of the German masses—or, perhaps, both.

During a meeting of the Allied Supreme War Council in December 1939, then premier Daladier made it clear to Chamberlain that vague British talk of punishing aggression was insufficient. It was "essential . . . to make it impossible for Germany to disturb the peace once more." That was French for dismembering the German state. A few days later General Henry Pownall, a BEF staff officer, told Chamberlain that General Alphonse Georges, the deputy commander of the French Army, had warned that "if the British again stood in the way of what the French considered a fair solution, they would never forgive us." In a January 1940 speech, the prime minister attempted to appease his French critics by blaming the German people as well as their leaders for the war. Chamberlain was careful to qualify the accusation, though. "To put it about that the Allies desire the annihilation [of Germany] is a fantastic and malicious invention. . . . On the other hand, [the] German people must realize that the responsibility for the prolongation of this war and of the suffering it might bring in the coming years is theirs, as well as the tyrants who stand over them." To keep the French sweet, on occasion other cabinet ministers would make similarly bellicose pronouncements. In a November 1939 speech, Lord Halifax talked of "secur[ing] the defeat of Germany," and in a February 1940 interview, Oliver Stanley, the secretary of state for war, told the *Daily Telegraph*, "I have only one war aim, to win the war." By early March, with the British public confused about Britain's war aims and the French government alarmed by them, Chamberlain was feeling the need to take bold action. Hence he decided to revisit an idea he had discussed with Daladier the previous December: Britain and France would pledge not to sign a separate peace agreement with Germany; such a pact would ease French suspicions about British resolve and provide an umbrella under which French and British differences over war aims could be hidden. Within weeks, the no-separate-peace pledge was placed on the agenda of the March 28 Allied Supreme Council meeting in London. But before addressing the pledge, Chamberlain intended to put Reynaud in his place.

On the evening of the twenty-seventh, the new French premier arrived in London amid a swirl of rumor and innuendo so dense it constituted its own weather system. It was said of Reynaud that he was overly dependent on his mistress, the Comtesse Hélène de Portes, that he had "the proclivities of a pocket Napoleon," that he had a "small man's arrogance," that he was a "lightweight" and "high-strung," and that he was less representative of the real France than his predecessor, the earthy Daladier.

The next morning, at the opening meeting of the Allied Supreme Council, Chamberlain set to work on the premier. One of the other guests, General Edmund Ironside, the chief of the Imperial General Staff, marveled at the prime minister's skill. Chamberlain opened the meeting "with a ninety minute monologue on the general situation . . . [that] took all the thunder out of Reynaud and left him gasping with no electric power," Ironside noted. "All the 'projects' that Reynaud had to bring forward, Chamberlain took away. It was masterly and very well done. Little Reynaud sat there with his head nodding in a sort of 'tik,' understanding it all, for he speaks English very well." By the end of the meeting, Reynaud looked "for the entire world like a little marmoset."

Reynaud, who knew a thing or two about political infighting himself, transcended the humiliation. He had brought along one good card—the fragile state of French public opinion—and, a gifted orator, he played the card with flair and drama. He told the Supreme Council that the French people were angry at being dragged into the war by the reckless British guarantee to Poland, angry at the pretense that eight underequipped British divisions in France (each with twelve thousand to fifteen thousand men) represented an *effort du sange* (effort of the blood); and he warned that his countrymen and -women were becoming increasingly susceptible to German claims that France was fighting Britain's war for it. The speech tapped into a deep vein of British guilt. Seven months into the Great War, Britain had established twenty-nine divisions in France, all fully equipped.

Chamberlain, whose eagerness to do something "spectacular" had not previously included setting a date for doing it, now agreed to a schedule. On April 1, the Allies would issue a warning to the Norwegian and Swedish governments, and on the fifth the Allies would commence Operation Wilfred, the mining of Norwegian waters. Wilfred was one of the three most important measures approved by the Allied Supreme Council on the twenty-eighth. The second was Royal Marine, the mining of German waters, which would commence a day earlier than Wilfred, with the mining of the Rhine, and conclude on the fifteenth, with the mining of the German canals. On April Fools' Day, the plan for Wilfred was expanded to include a British ground force, bearing orders to land in Norway if the Germans landed first or if "there is clear evidence they intend to do so." The third measure was the no-separate-peace pledge, which was widely hailed by the French and British press the next day, but which would be remembered by posterity for its tragic ending.

March had also been a busy month in Germany. Late in the month, British intelligence reported that the Germans were "concentrating aircraft and shipping for operations [against] . . .

Norwegian aerodromes and ports." On the twenty-eighth, the day the Allied Supreme Council met, there was another warning about a German operation against Norway. Two days later, in a radio address to the British public, Churchill said, "It seems rather hard, when spring is caressing the land . . . that all our thoughts must be turned and bent upon sterner war." Then he warned his listeners to prepare themselves for an "intensification of the struggle."

The first days of April brought more ill tidings. From the intelligence services came reports of a large troop concentration in Rostock, the German port closest to Norway; and from France came a request from Daladier, now minister of defense in the Reynaud government, for a three-month delay in the implementation of Royal Marine. The mining operation would provoke retaliatory German bombing raids, and Daladier wanted more time to prepare France's air defense and to evacuate men and war industries from threatened areas. Was Daladier telling the truth? In part, yes, but there were also rumors that the request was an act of spite. One rumor had it that Daladier was jealous of Reynaud's success in London; another, that he was "a peasant" and that the French peasant was famously vindictive. But the most persistent rumor linked Daladier's request to the feud between the Marquise de Crussol and the Comtesse de Portes, and there may have been something to that. When Daladier refused to dine with him and Reynaud during an early April visit to Paris, an abashed Churchill declared, "what will centuries to come say if we lose this war through lack of understanding?" Spears knew what Paris would say: "All Paris recognized that unless a bomb eliminated both the ministers' dulcineas [mistresses]," the Reynaud-Daladier feud would continue. For those inclined to enjoy such a spectacle, Spears's friend Georges Mandel had a warning. If Daladier brought down the Reynaud government out of spite or for some other reason, Édouard Herriot, president of the French Chamber of Deputies, and Pierre Laval, an influential French senator, would come to power on a peace platform.

In early April, with the British war budget (for 1940) still 40 percent below the German, and the British unemployment rate—another metric of war readiness—still at nearly a million, Chamberlain was facing a political crisis of his own. The Vigilantes, the All Party Group, the Watching Committee, and other opposition groups were intensifying their calls for a change of government. Linked only by a shared fear of Chamberlain's complacency and incompetence, sixty-five-year-old Leo Amery, a Liberal imperialist whose loyalties were to an England that died at the Battle of the Somme in 1916, had little in common with Hugh Dalton, a Labour MP whose gaze was fixed on the welfare-state Britain of 1945, or with Clem Davies, a Unilever executive and political moderate, other than the desire to remove Chamberlain from office.

Davies, founder of the All Party Action Group, and Lord Salisbury, founder of the Watching Committee, were slower in embracing this ambition than many of the prime minister's other critics. Both men had founded their groups with the intention of providing advice and counsel to Chamberlain and his cabinet. Only when the prime minister showed little interest in accepting advice did Davies's and Salisbury's desire to assist the prime minister become the desire to unseat him. In this journey from friend to enemy, the events surrounding the reshuffle of the Chamberlain cabinet on April 3 played an important role.

Despite mounting criticism from the opposition groups, at the beginning of April Chamberlain still looked politically invulnerable. In the March Gallup poll he had a 57 percent favorability rating—a high number but, as events were about to show, an empty one. By the beginning of the eighth month of war, a large segment of the British public had developed significant reservations about the prime minister's leadership. But, as yet, the doubts and reservations had not found a catalyzing event. The cabinet reshuffle would provide it. For months, the press and Parliament had been urging Chamberlain to bring new faces into the cabinet and to lighten the departmental duties of the cabinet ministers so they could devote more time to oversight of the war. There had also been calls to bring Labour and Liberal MPs to the cabinet so the government would have a national rather than a narrowly partisan character. Little of this advice was evident in the cabinet reshuffle of April 3. Chamberlain's inner cabinet went into the reshuffle with nine ministers, all Tories and all burdened with heavy departmental responsibilities that interfered with their war work; and the inner cabinet emerged from the reshuffle with eight ministers, all Tories and all burdened with heavy departmental responsibilities besides their war work. The absence of Labour and Liberal ministers was not Chamberlain's fault—no member of either party would serve under him—but the cautious, unimaginative character of the cabinet changes were. More to the point, they were also reminders of everything that people disliked about the prime minister. Whatever one thought of Hitler, in newsreels he looked dynamic, vigorous, youthful, in command; Chamberlain looked like an old man with an umbrella and a funny Adam's apple that bobbed up and down above his wing-tip collar when he spoke.

Except for Churchill, who became head of the Military Coordination Committee as well as first lord of the Admiralty, the prime minister's new cabinet looked like his old cabinet. The only tangible difference was that almost everyone now occupied a different office. On April 4 the *Times* usually a reliable champion of Chamberlain, described the cabinet changes as depressing and unimaginative. "So toughly has the game been played that in no fewer than three separate cases ministers have simply exchanged offices." The *Manchester Guardian*, less friendly to the prime minister, likened the cabinet reshuffle to "a sort of musical chairs of the old stuff"; another opposition paper called the changes "proof that it is almost impossible for the PM to part with his best and oldest friends." Unfazed by the criticism, Chamberlain defended his war leadership that same day in a rousing lunchtime speech to a Conservative Party conclave at Westminster Hall, a brooding medieval structure whose history of regicide might have given pause to a politician less confident than Chamberlain on a day when half the papers in the country were calling for his head. The prime minister began:

> When the war broke out, German preparations were far ahead of our own and it was natural then to expect that the enemy would take advantage of his natural superiority. . . . Is it not a very extraordinary thing that no such attempt was made. Whatever may be the reason . . . one thing is certain: [Hitler] *missed the bus.*

A few days later, Chamberlain wrote to his sister Hilda, "My speech to the Party . . . was very warmly received and the informality and jauntiness" of "'[Hitler] missed the bus' seems to have given peculiar satisfaction." Not to everyone. Before Chamberlain spoke, Dick Law, a Conservative MP and member of the Vigilantes, gave a "biting little speech" opposing a resolution endorsing the prime minister's war leadership. Law finished, expecting to be torn "limb from limb." Instead, dozens of the party faithful—men and women who had stood by Chamberlain through Munich and Poland; who had defended him against charges of smugness, lethargy, cronyism, and complacency—leaped to their feet, applauding. "Why, this resolution is going to fail!" exclaimed a Chamberlain loyalist. On an appeal to party loyalty, an amended version of the motion did eventually pass; nonetheless, the incident placed a new thought in the public mind: perhaps it was not Hitler but Chamberlain who had "missed the bus."

Until 1904 Scapa Flow, a thinly inhabited Scottish waterworld of low horizons, cold islands, and deep drafts, dwelled in the eternity of geological time. Then the Royal Navy arrived, military time replaced geological time, and the British Home Fleet replaced the local fishing fleet. Piers, workhouses, minefields, artillery emplacements, brothels, and pubs arose; a war came and went; and a generation of young naval officers returned to Scapa Flow, proud of their service at Jutland, the climactic Anglo-German sea battle of the Great War, and certain that nothing like it would ever be seen again. Through the 1920s and 1930s, the prospect that airpower would render sea power obsolete darkened the days of the senior naval officers at Scapa Flow, and that darkness persisted down to the afternoon of April 7, 1940, when news arrived that large elements of the German fleet had put to sea.

Despite the recent intelligence reports, the German action came as a surprise. On April 3, Churchill, who as first lord of the Admiralty was privy to the latest naval intelligence, had told the cabinet that he "personally doubted whether the Germans would land a force in Scandinavia." Two days later Chamberlain also dismissed rumors of a German action in Norway. Berlin would issue furious protests when the Royal Navy began the mining of Norwegian waters, he said, but the German government would "take no retaliatory action."

Forty-eight hours later, a Coastal Command pilot sighted a German task force of eight destroyers and a cruiser heading northward in a heavy sea. A few hours later there was another sighting— three German destroyers also heading north. Then, at one thirty on the afternoon of the seventh, came a third sighting. An RAF pilot counted fourteen destroyers, three cruisers, and one other vessel, possibly a transport; this force was also sailing north. At eight thirty that evening the Home Fleet, which had been on alert since early afternoon, raised anchor and sailed out into the April night. The Second Cruiser Squadron, at Rosyth (another Scottish port), set sail an hour and a half later, leaving behind several battalions of angry British soldiers. The squadron had been preparing to ferry the troops to Norway when news arrived that the German Navy was at sea. Roused from their bunks, the troops had been ordered off the cruisers without explanation, without new orders, and without their equipment. At about the same time, the naval units accompanying British troop ships across the North Sea to Norway peeled away from the convoys and disappeared into the darkness.

The German naval movements were a feint designed to draw the Home Fleet away from the Norwegian coast by the prospect of a historic sea battle along the lines of Jutland. As the British Home Fleet took up battle positions on the night of April 7–8, German warships and merchantmen, holds crowded with troops and engines of war, were taking up attack positions along the unguarded Norwegian coast. "Up the other side of the channel steering came merchant ship after merchant ship. . . . Great tempting tankers, heavy laden ships . . . the German invasion of Norway going north." So wrote a British submarine captain who was under orders not to attack northbound merchantmen. In the Far North, one German battle group bore down on Narvik, the port through which Swedish iron ore was shipped to Germany; farther south, another force approached Trondheim, a central Norwegian town with a good port and a historic past as the capital of medieval Norway. Below Trondheim, where the weather was treacherous, a third German battle group pitched and rolled in the sea off Stavanger, the site of a strategically important air base. Other German units steamed eastward toward Oslo in force-11 gale winds that reconfigured the sea into canyons of whistling black water.

The Admiralty's first indication that the German fleet was

not where it imagined it was came the following morning, April 8, when the *Glowworm*, a British ship attached to the mine-laying operation, encountered the *Bernard von Arnim*, a German destroyer, off the Norwegian coast. During the running gun battle that ensued, the German ship lost its equilibrium in the pitching sea; its bow heaved, its forecastle (upper deck) snapped off, its hold flooded, and two deckhands were swept away. The *Glowworm*, smaller and more nimble in the heavy seas, was closing in on the destroyer when the *Hipper*, a large German cruiser, emerged from a snow squall and blew off the *Glowworm*'s bridge. The British ship fired several torpedoes and made smoke to cover its retreat. Just before the *Hipper*'s guns caught it emerging from the far side of the smoke screen, the *Glowworm* made a final transmission to the Admiralty—"Germans at sea"—and then turned into the wind, rammed the *Hipper*, and blew up. A moment later, the morning sea held more sorrows than the hills of Jerusalem.

In London that morning General Hasting Ismay, secretary to the Imperial Defense Committee, awoke to the sound of a ringing telephone. The duty officer at the War Office was on the line; his words were so garbled that at first Ismay thought his caller had forgotten to put his dentures in. Ismay instructed the officer to do so and then to repeat the message. The caller steadied himself and reported that, overnight, the Germans had seized the main Norwegian ports and Denmark. Hanging up, Ismay realized that until this moment he had never fully grasped "the devastating and demoralizing effect of surprise."

The next morning, April 9, the intelligence services reported that, overnight, the Germans had occupied three important Norwegian population centers—Oslo, Bergen, and Trondheim—and were about to occupy Stavanger and Narvik. A cable from Ronald Campbell, the British ambassador in Paris, further deepened the gloom in Downing Street and Whitehall. The cable concerned Daladier and Reynaud, who were scheduled to visit London later in the day. Campbell warned that due to "acute differences . . . on private and personal matters . . . [Daladier] was now determined to embarrass Reynaud in every possible way." Spears, always au courant with Parisian gossip, identified the source of the discord thusly: "The Marquise backs the one and the Comtesse backing the other [and both women] having a grand old time, all claws and no holds barred."

Campbell's warning proved to be a false alarm. When the Allied Supreme Council convened at four on the afternoon of the ninth, Reynaud and Daladier, conscious of the gravity of the hour, were models of professionalism and seriousness. The French offered an alpine division to assist in the reconquest of the occupied Norwegian ports and agreed that Narvik, the bright, shiny object in British military thinking since the start of the war, should be a priority target. There was also a long discussion about the significance of the German action. Was Norway a one-off or the beginning of the long-anticipated German offensive in the West? On the streets of Brussels, Amsterdam, London, and Paris, that question was also a topic of lively and nervous debate on this early spring afternoon. "Will it be Holland and Belgium [next] or the Maginot Line, or a great air attack on this country—or altogether?" wondered the young Downing Street aide John Colville. The council concluded that the threat of a general offensive was grave enough to press neutral Belgium for permission to set up Allied defensive positions along its border.

"These will be fateful days, these next few," General Ironside wrote in his diary that night.

The politicians, though slower than soldiers to grasp the dimensions of the German success, had awakened to it by the next morning, April 10. "The Germans have seized the [Norwegian] ports . . . and to dislodge them [would] be a difficult operation," Chamberlain said at the morning cabinet meeting. The announcement would have greatly surprised readers of the *Daily Mail* and the *Daily Express*. The morning papers were reporting that Trondheim, Oslo, and Bergen had already been recaptured. "England's waking up" and "We've started on them now," people told one another on the bus to work; miniature Union Jacks appeared in shop windows; "Rule Britannia" echoed through lunchtime pubs. On the eleventh, when Churchill rose from his seat to brief the House of Commons on Norway, there was a noticeable tingle of expectation in the chamber. Ah, thought Harold Nicolson, an MP at the Ministry of Information, "tales of victory and triumph" from a master orator. What a pleasant prospect!

That happy thought did not survive Churchill's first few sentences. As the first lord told a scandalous tale of British setbacks and defeats transformed into victories by unverified rumors emanating from New York and Stockholm and from an irresponsible tabloid press, Nicolson could feel "a cold wave of disappointment" pass through the House. As news of Churchill's speech spread across the country, the first reaction was confusion. How could that be? people wondered. The government said we've already recaptured Oslo, Bergen, and Trondheim! Then people became angry, and then depressed. In a scathing report on the handling of the news from Norway by the government and press, Mass Observation noted that the early erroneous good news about Oslo, Bergen, and Trondheim had the effect of intensifying the negative impact of Churchill's bad news.

> Many people expected that we should immediately smash Hitler out; wipe his troops and air force and navy off the face of Northern Europe. The First Lord of the Admiralty encouraged this view. And two days after the invasion the press and BBC

proclaimed magnificent victories and rumor ran wild.... When the rumor was exploded all the uncertainty came up again ... insidious, magnified.

What came out of all this? ... A growing belief that Hitler is infinitely cunning, infinitely clever, and immensely strong. A suspicion that he is some sort of ultra-human devil born to curse our days.

In the weeks to come, Norway would become the graveyard of several political careers and the making of several others. It would prove, once again, that Churchill was born under a lucky star, and it would expose glaring weaknesses in the British military's command structure, most notably in the area of interservice cooperation. General Mackesy, who had been appointed ground commander of the Narvik expedition, and Lord Cork, the naval commander, left Britain on separate ships from separate ports after receiving separate briefings. General Mackesy received his from General Ironside; Lord Cork, his from the first sea lord, Dudley Pound, and a second briefing from Churchill, in the backseat of the first lord's car just as Cork was about to depart for Norway. Then, amid Admiralty complaints that it had no information about the ground plan for Narvik, War Office complaints that it had no information about the naval plan for Narvik, and Mackesy's and Cork's complaints about each other, the war cabinet would decide that Narvik was not that important after all. The Norwegian government wanted first priority given to Trondheim, and Chamberlain and Lord Halifax were inclined to agree with the Norwegians. Churchill half agreed.

At 1:00 a.m. on April 12, General Ironside heard a knock on the door. When he opened it, Churchill was standing in the doorway. Behind the first lord were the first sea lord, Dudley Pound; the first sea lord's deputy, Admiral Phillips; and the air chief marshal, Cyril Newall. Ironside, who was six feet four, stood in the half light of the doorway, examining his guests, the tallest of whom was a half head shorter than he. "Tiny" Ironside was not a man easily intimidated. He had faced down the Boers in the Boer War, the Germans in the Great War, the Red Army in revolutionary Russia, and innumerable War Office officials. Still, Ironside knew from experience that late-night visits generally brought trouble, and late-night visits involving Churchill generally brought serious trouble. "Tiny," the first lord said, "I want several of the battalions earmarked for the assault on Narvik diverted south to stake a claim on Trondheim." Ironside, who as chief of the Imperial General Staff had to approve the request, said no. "A convoy packed in one place is not suitable for landing in another." After an often heated argument, Churchill went home frustrated, and Ironside, who was acquainted with the first lord's determination, went to bed uneasy. "I shall not get much sleep tonight," he wrote in his diary.

On the fourteenth, Churchill again made a late-night visit to the general. "Tiny," he said, "we are going to the wrong place. We should go for Trondheim." In the past seventy-two hours, the Royal Navy had scored a series of spectacular victories in the waters around Narvik; and with the town now seemingly on the edge of recapture, Churchill believed that British forces could be safely diverted to the Trondheim operation. "The Navy will make a direct attack on [Trondheim]," he said. "I want a small force of good troops, well led, to follow up the naval attack. I also want landings north and south of Trondheim . . . to cooperate with the assault when it comes off." Ironside again pointed out that diverting troops to Trondheim would cause insurmountable logistical difficulties; Churchill again insisted that Trondheim was the priority now. The argument went back and forth for several minutes; finally, a resigned Ironside asked Churchill if he was acting in his capacity as first lord of the Admiralty or as the chairman of the Military Coordination Committee. Churchill said in his capacity as chairman of the MCC, which had authority over all three fighting services. Absolved of responsibility for an order he believed foolhardy, Ironside agreed to release the troops.

Almost immediately, the British Chiefs of Staff began to have second thoughts about Trondheim. To reach the town, the invasion fleet would have to force a heavily defended fifty-five-mile fjord. The more the chiefs studied the operation, the more the word "Gallipoli" came to mind. That was the last time the Royal Navy attempted to force a heavily defended, enclosed body of water, and the effort had cost three battleships. The chiefs were also worried about Narvik again. While British troops sat offshore, waiting for the snow to melt on the landing beaches, the Germans had reinforced the town. On April 16 an attack on Narvik looked a good deal more formidable than it had on the fourteenth.

On April 17 the naval assault on Trondheim was scheduled for the twenty-second; on the eighteenth it was rescheduled for the twenty-fourth; and on the nineteenth it was canceled for good, in favor of a land operation. A British force moving south from the fishing village of Namsos, and a second force moving north from the town of Åndalsnes, would attack Trondheim from the landward side. For experienced troops, traversing a hundred-plus miles of snow-covered road in subzero temperatures against heavy opposition on the ground and in the air would be a remarkable feat of arms. For the inexperienced troops of the 146th and 148th Brigades, it would require something akin to a miracle. The 146th and 148th were territorial units made up of citizen soldiers, much like American National Guardsmen. Ten months earlier, most of the men had been ironmongers, farmhands, factory workers, insurance clerks, teachers, and bus drivers. Young men, they knew the names of all the popular bandleaders of the day, but the British army had not yet had time to teach them how to be proper soldiers and did not have enough machine guns and motors to arm them properly.

In France, public reaction to Norway went through three stages. In mid-April, when Clare Boothe arrived in Paris, almost none of her French friends had a good word to say about the Anglais. The British were the senior partners in the Norwegian campaign, but the Parisians Boothe spoke to complained that they were not acting that way. "Where [was British] intelligence when the Germans were planning [the invasion]? Where was the [Royal] Navy? Where was the British Expeditionary Force?" Then, one morning, French radio announced the British assault on Trondheim, and Union Jacks sprouted up across the capital like some wild new jungle growth. They hung from balconies, windows, storefronts, and flagpoles. In the streets, French soldiers who had previously refused to salute British officers started saluting them smartly. "At last we are real allies," a French captain said. "Not since the affair of Joan of Arc have the English and French so well understood each other."

"Oh, isn't it wonderful!" Boothe said to Colonel Horace Fuller, whom she met during a visit to the American embassy in Paris in late April.

"What? What's wonderful?" asked Fuller, who was the military attaché at the embassy.

"Norway!"

"Oh, sure," Fuller replied. "Hitler missed the bus, all right, but he caught the transport plane instead."

Then Fuller took Boothe into his office, unfolded a map of Norway on his desk, and explained "what it meant to force an enemy-held fjord in ships, how much tonnage and how many men it would take and how many guns. Norway . . . was the kind of country which if you got there first and with the most, you could not be got out in a day or a year or perhaps ever," Fuller said. "And Hitler got there first."

The cancellation of the Trondheim operation initiated the third stage of French feeling about Norway, a French officer who served in the campaign summed up the change in a coy little parable about the Zulus. The British, he said, had planned Norway as if it were "an expedition against the Zulus, but unhappily, we and the British [turned out to be] the Zulus, armed with bows and arrows against the onslaught of modern scientific war."

In *The Gathering Storm*, the first volume of his war memoirs, Churchill was frank about his good fortune in escaping political ruin after Norway. "Considering the prominent part I played in these events . . . it was a marvel that I survived and maintained my position in public esteem." In the unedited version of that sentence, Churchill was franker. "It was a marvel—I really do not know how—I survived and maintained my position in public esteem while all the blame was thrown on poor Mr. Chamberlain." In a note on the galleys of *The Gathering Storm*, Clementine Churchill told her husband why he survived: "Had it not been for your years of exile & repeated warnings re: the German peril, Norway might well have ruined you." Chamberlain had no such history to shield him from criticism.

By early May, a majority of the British public agreed with the young lieutenant, who told a reporter on the road to Trondheim, "I'll tell you what's wrong. It's that bloody Chamberlain." Chamberlain's favorability rating, which had stood in the high fifties in March, was now in the thirties, and in the press and in the House of Commons there was much noisy speculation about whether he would still be prime minister at the end of May.

Chamberlain himself was confident that he would be. "I don't think my enemies will get me this time," he told his sister Hilda in a May 4 letter.

CHAPTER FIVE

CHAMBERLAIN MISSES THE BUS

Early on the Sunday morning of May 5, 1940, a large crowd of middle-aged men could be seen gathering around the fountain in Finsbury Square, an acre and a half of treeless London lawn enclosed in a cheerless rectangle of commercial buildings just south of the Wesley Chapel burial grounds. Except for the bowling green and easy access to the numbers 21 and 43 buses, the fountain—fifteen feet high, constructed of gray and white stone, and built in the shape of a church steeple—was the square's only notable feature. Erected by two Victorian worthies, Thomas and William Smith, to honor the memory of their mother, Martha, the fountain was for many years the sole province of the neighborhood birds; but after the Great War the birds were forced to share it with the Old Contemptibles, who, on the morning of their annual march to St. Paul's Cathedral, would gather around the fountain to drink, smoke, and tell old war stories.

The first British troops to arrive in France in 1914, the Old Contemptibles owed their name to Kaiser Wilhelm, who dismissed them as that "contemptible little army," and their special place in the heart of the British nation to the honor of being the first British troops to the fight in 1914. During the 1920s and 1930s, the Contemptibles' parade became a highlight of London's spring season.

Every May, through slumps and booms, coronations and abdications, international crises and international peace conferences—through pacifist protests and Mosleyite marches (Oswald Mosley was leader of the British Union of Fascists)—the old soldiers would gather in Finsbury Square and march down to St. Paul's Cathedral: the Scots Guards band in front, piping out the old tunes of glory, and the crowds singing along. Now, nearly thirty years on, the lean bodies and hard faces of war had given way to fleshy, middle-aged jowls and expanding waistlines, which made the old warriors as unrecognizable as the nation of their young manhood: the old Edwardian Britain, supreme in all things.

At 9:00 a.m. the trumpets of the Life Guards blared; the marchers snuffed out their cigarettes, slipped their whiskey casks into a coat pocket, and fell into line; on the far side of the square, a *Manchester Guardian* reporter took out his pen and described the scene forming before him. "In caps, bowlers and silk hats, tweeds and morning coats, the men were still regimental in their way of marching and it was hard to believe that these were the same men who were at Mons and the first Ypres twenty six years ago. All wore at least three medals and some six or seven." By the time the reporter closed his notebook, the old soldiers had vanished into the crowd below the square and the Scots Guards band was beating out "It's a Long Way to Tipperary" for all they were worth.

Normally, the parade would receive a big write-up in the following day's papers, but May 6 was an unusually busy news day. The two-day parliamentary debate on the Norwegian campaign would begin the next day, and the *Times*, the *Manchester Guardian*, the *Daily Telegraph*, and the other major papers were full of speculation about the fate of Chamberlain, Churchill, and other members of the government. The other big news story of the day was the return of the 146th and 148th Territorials, who had made the "death march" to Trondheim. Readers looking for tales of valor and self-sacrifice could find them in the soldiers' accounts, as could readers looking for explanations of why Norway had gone so wrong. "All the boys felt that if only we had some fighters to deal with their bombers, we could have smashed the Germans," an infantry captain told a *Guardian* reporter. A sergeant who fought in central Norway told a similar tale to the *Daily Mail*'s man. "There was never a break in the [bombing] attacks. . . . If we had had tanks and fighter air craft we could have done really good work." In interview after interview, the soldiers spoke of inferior British airpower, inferior British tactics, inferior British organization, leadership, and equipment, or of no equipment at all.

During a visit to Downing Street the previous Wednesday, May 1, Major Millis Jefferis, newly returned from Norway, told Chamberlain that another factor had also contributed to the poor British performance. Being bombed was a new experience, and some units had not stood up well to it. At the sound of an airplane, the troops would flee into the woods or into a cellar. The first day of May also brought a stream of other worrying news to Downing Street: from Turkey came a warning that the Germans planned to follow up their victory in Norway with a massive air strike on Britain, followed by a landing; from the Admiralty came a report that German planes had begun mining the Thames and the Tyne River; and from Yugoslavia came news of an imminent German attack on Holland. The first of May also brought Churchill to Downing Street; he arrived at about six in the evening, dripping wet and in a foul mood. "If I were the First of May," he said, gazing out at the pelting rain, "I should be ashamed of myself." Jock Colville, who was aware of Churchill's four changes of mind over Trondheim, bristled at the remark: "Personally, I think he [Churchill] ought to be ashamed of himself." The intelligence reports that arrived on Chamberlain's desk the following day, May 2, included one particularly intriguing item: during a discussion of Anglo-Italian relations with an English acquaintance, Signor Giuseppe Bastianini, the Italian ambassador to Britain, had suddenly burst into tears. The ambassador's behavior remained a puzzle for two days. Then, on May 4, a report from Myron Taylor, the American envoy to the Vatican, suggested a possible explanation. According to Taylor, Mussolini planned to enter the war on Hitler's side as soon as he was confident that Germany would win.

On the fourth, the Chiefs of Staff submitted a new report to the war cabinet. *Review of the Strategical Situation on the Assumption That Germany Has Decided to Seek a Decision in 1940* examined the three options open to Hitler if he made an attempt to win the war that year. Of the three, the chiefs rated as most likely the one the Turkish report mentioned: "a major offensive against Great Britain," starting with an air campaign and culminating in an invasion aimed at knocking Britain out of the war. Less likely—though not to be discounted, said the chiefs—was the second option: Germany seeks military and economic hegemony in Scandinavia and in parts of the Balkans, severs Britain's sea routes, then calls for a peace conference in which the German conquests allow Hitler to dictate the terms. The chiefs rated a German offense in France, the third option, as least likely. Attacking the Allies at their strongest point would produce unacceptable losses. Chamberlain scanned the report, but not very attentively. By early May he was engaged in two wars: one against Germany, the other against his critics in Parliament.

It is impossible to say when Chamberlain's fall became inevitable. Opposition to appeasement had been growing in fits and starts since Churchill's 1932 warning about a rearming Germany—and opposition to Chamberlain personally, at least since the Munich conference in 1938. Yet if one had to choose a moment when the prime minister's fall became inevitable, it would probably be his talk with Lord Salisbury the day after the Norway invasion. Salisbury was a member of one of the most influential and storied families in England. For four hundred years the Cecils had tumbled down through English history like the notes of a particularly sparkling tune. There had been Cecil prime ministers, Cecil secretaries of state, Cecil lord privy seals, and Cecil ambassadors and proconsuls. Salisbury, the current leader of the family, was seventy-eight and had a commanding presence that owed something to breeding, something to the old-fashioned Victorian frocks he favored, something to personal rectitude, and something to a stare of displeasure that carried such moral weight that even brave hearts withered under it.

Salisbury was also the leader of the Watching Committee, which he founded, not to unseat Chamberlain but to help him and his ministers execute the war more effectively. A few bomb throwers had managed to slip by Salisbury's watchful gaze and become members of the committee, but in the main its members were like him: thoughtful public men of steady temperament who believed that differences between the government and its critics could be resolved if the prime minister adopted three measures, which Salisbury laid out for Chamberlain during his visit to Downing Street the day after the Norway invasion. None of the measures was particularly novel. For months, critics had been urging Chamberlain to bomb Germany, to create a smaller, more nimble war cabinet, and to bring more new faces into the government. And for months Chamberlain had resisted the advice. Perhaps because he was tired of hearing it, after Salisbury finished, the prime minister forgot who he was talking to and snapped: "If people did not like the present administration of the government, they could change it."

On April 29, during a talk with Lord Halifax at the Foreign Office, Salisbury again pressed for a more vigorous pursuit of the war. From Argentina to Sweden, Germany was viewed as always swift and daring, Britain as always too late with too little. "A formidable air offensive against German military targets . . . would have a profound and . . . favorable effect on neutrals, including the United States," Salisbury said. Lord Halifax, who also had grown weary of unsolicited advice from uninformed notables, thanked Salisbury and his companions, Leo Amery, Edward Spears, and Harold Nicolson, for their concern, and assured his guests that the government was aware of the dangers facing the country. "Lord Halifax, we are not satisfied," Salisbury said with the sharpness of a man unaccustomed to being patronized. Then he rose from his chair and walked out of the foreign secretary's office, taking with him his colleagues and whatever remaining hopes he had of working with the Chamberlain government.

"Oh! The excitement, the thrills, the ill concealed . . . nervousness, the self interest . . . when there is a crisis on." So wrote Henry Channon of the intoxicating blend of political intrigue, deception, backbiting, phone taps, and war that was London in the first week of May 1940. Sensing that Norway had made Chamberlain politically vulnerable, on May 2, the day the government announced the Trondheim failure, Clement Davies and Leo Amery, two of the most influential opposition leaders, decided to mount a challenge to the government. Every May before adjournment for the Whitsunday holiday (the Feast of Pentecost), Parliament held an adjournment debate, an unstructured session during which MPs could introduce almost any subject for discussion and debate. Amery and Davies arranged to have the Norwegian campaign put on this year's debate schedule. Next, Davies asked Clement Attlee and Arthur Greenwood, the leader and deputy leader of the Labour Party, to request a confidence motion—a vote of confidence—at the end of the debate.

The Labour men refused. Without the support of Conservative MPs, the motion would fail, and Attlee and Greenwood found it impossible to imagine any set of circumstances under which rank-and-file Conservative MPs—those business-friendly go-getters from the suburbs and upright Tory knights of the shire—would vote a Conservative prime minister out of office.

Meanwhile, the prime minister's supporters, sensing a challenge to his leadership, began to plot a defense. In late April, Alec Douglas-Home, a senior Chamberlain aide, collared Henry Channon in the House and "pumped" him for information: "Did I think Winston should be deflated? . . . Ought he leave the Admiralty?" Douglas-Home's interrogation was one of the first indications that Chamberlain's allies planned to mount a whispering campaign against the first lord, who was widely viewed as the prime minister's most probable challenger. Harold Nicolson, a Churchill supporter, also noticed that "the Tapers and Tadpoles [Chamberlain's operatives] were putting it around that the whole Norwegian episode is due to Winston." Out in the Conservative Party heartland, the home counties, where people spoke of England rather than Britain, the anti-Churchill campaign grew vehement. "W. C. they regard with complete mistrust," Nancy Dugdale wrote her soldier husband, Tommy, in Palestine. "They hate his boasting broadcasts. W. C. is really the counterpart of Göring in England, full of the desire for blood—blitzkrieg and bloated with ego and over feeding, the same treachery running through his veins, punctuated by heroics and hot air. I can't tell you how depressed I feel about it."

As the Whitsun debate approached, Churchill's supporters mounted a whispering campaign of their own. "Winston is being lauded by both the Socialist [Labour] and Liberal opposition and being tempted to lead a revolt against the PM" the ever-watchful Henry Channon noted in his diary. "Tonight, [he] sat joking in the smoking room surrounded by A. V. Alexander [a Labour Party official] and Archie Sinclair [leader of the Liberal Party], the new Shadow Cabinet. A Westminster war added to the German one." Chamberlain was also suspicious of Churchill's intentions. Winston "is too apt to look the other way while his friends exalt him," he complained to his sisters in a letter. In the debate over Churchill's loyalties, the final word is usually given to John Colville, who had heard from a trusted source that "Winston was being loyal to the P.M. but his satellites (e.g., Duff Cooper, Amery etc.) were doing all in their power to create mischief and ill feeling." Perhaps, but at the very least, it is likely that Churchill was aware of his friends' politicking. In early May, a time when Chamberlain was still expected to survive the Whitsun debate, Churchill felt confident enough about his own political future to ask Lloyd George if he would accept a post in a Churchill government. Unsurprisingly, the former prime minister refused to give him a straight answer.

The March Gallup poll had indicated that fully a quarter of the British public favored "a discussion of peace proposals with Germany now," and, as Lloyd George was the only politician of national standing who represented that point of view, he was also spoken of as a possible successor to Chamberlain. "People call me a defeatist," Lloyd George told Cecil King, editor of the *Sunday Pictorial*, a 1940s version of *People* magazine. "But what I say to them is this: Tell me, how can we win? Can we win in the air? Can we win at sea, when the effect of our naval blockade is wiped out by Germany's connections with Russia? . . . Hitler cannot win any more than we can. . . . The Germans cannot get through the Maginot Line. . . . The war will drag wearily on."

Other well-informed Britons agreed. In March, when a reporter asked Basil Liddell Hart, Britain's leading military analyst, what the government should do, he replied, "Come to the best possible terms as soon as possible. . . . We have no chance of avoiding defeat." Lord Rothermere, owner of the *Daily Mail* and the *Sunday Pictorial*, also favored a quick end to the war and was willing to say so in public. "When the moment comes, I intend to campaign for your recall as PM," Rothermere told Lloyd George in late April. Lord Beaverbrook, another propeace press magnet, also promised to support the former prime minister in his papers. By early May, a majority of the Watching Committee believed that Lloyd George would succeed Chamberlain. And Nancy Astor, an influential Virginia-born MP, considered the old Welshman's return to Downing Street probable enough to arrange a sit-down to see if Lloyd George still had the "root of the matter" in him.

A sharp-tongued, fading Southern beauty, Lady Astor had a titled, wealthy husband—Waldorf Astor; a history as an appeaser for which she had repented; and a history as an anti-Semite, for which she had half repented. For her saucy Scarlett O'Hara–like manner, Lady Astor had repented not at all. "You're the kind of woman my mother warned me about," one alarmed young man had said when she offered to give him a personal tour of Parliament. Lady Astor also had many influential friends, and on May 7, the first day of the Whitsun debate, she invited several of them to a luncheon at 4 St. James Place to vet Lloyd George. The guest of honor arrived a few minutes late—and, as always, perfectly turned out. His mane of snow-white hair was combed into a Prince Valiant bob; his suit and tie were impeccably matched. Lady Astor, who was famously blunt, asked her guest point-blank if he wanted to return to Downing Street—and Lloyd George, who was famously evasive, provided his vetters with an hour of incisive, witty, amusing, and occasionally nasty word portraits of Chamberlain, Churchill, Reynaud, Clemenceau, and Lord Liverpool. The interview "brought all his evasive techniques into play," said one exasperated vetter, Tom Jones, a prominent civil servant and educator. Jones left the luncheon feeling that the guest of honor desired high office but "preferred to await his country's summons a little longer and . . . he expected to receive it as the peril grew." Jones was not far off the mark. Lloyd George had already decided what conditions he would and would not accept if he were offered Downing Street again; in the latter category was a mandate for victory. "I could not produce a decisive victory as I did last time," he told his aide, A. J. Sylvester. "We have made so many mistakes that we are not in nearly so good a position."

The Whitsun debate was one of the most anticipated events of the spring. By 9:00 a.m. on May 7, six hours before the start of the debate, Parliament Square was already half full, and each arriving bus and car seemed to deposit a new group of spectators. Some of the early arrivals had brought along a newspaper to read; others passed the time in conversation or closed their eyes and turned their faces toward the morning sun. May had brought spectacularly good weather. Something about the slant of the light that spring, people said. Later in the month, when the news from France grew grave and the sky remained a flawless robin's-egg blue, people would feel mocked by the beauty of the days. Not then, though, after the bitter winter of 1940—the corridors of light that flooded through the tired, war-weary May streets seemed like a miracle.

The early arrivals included a sprinkling of pensioners, off-duty civil servants and policemen, a handful of surplus women (in their fifties now and close to becoming Great War artifacts), a few soldiers too fresh-faced and unmarked to have served in Norway, a few Old Contemptibles, a smattering of housewives, some stockbrokers from the City, and pro- and antiwar advocates, easily distinguishable from one another by their dress. The former appeared smart in freshly pressed Irish linens; the latter affected the disheveled, proletarian look favored by radical academics and the members of Victor Gollancz's Left Book Club.

The prime minister was scheduled to open the debate with a speech on the Norwegian campaign, and Churchill to close it the next evening with a defense of the government. But when the first group of MPs arrived in the House of Commons around noon, almost everything else about the debate remained unsettled, including who the other speakers would be and whether the debate would end with a vote of confidence. Clement Davies was still pressing Attlee and Greenwood to introduce a confidence motion, but the matter of victory or defeat would turn on how many Conservative backbenchers voted with the government, and on that point Attlee felt Chamberlain had reason to feel confident. On the morning of the Norway debate, the press was also predicting a government victory. The spirit of rebellion "does not run so deep [in the Conservative Party] that the Prime Minister will be embarrassed in the House of Commons today," said the *Daily Express*. The *Manchester Guardian* took a similar line. "When it comes to a choice between accepting the present government or finding an alternative . . . even the most critical Tories, never mind the everlasting 'Yes men,' will pause." The *Daily Mail* offered the most succinct and credible explanation of why the government would prevail: David Margesson. Nature had endowed the Conservative chief whip with the qualities of personality essential to the efficient conduct of a whip's duties: a bullying manner; an encyclopedic memory for slights, double crosses, and wrong votes; and a bottomless supply of invective. "You utterly contemptible little piece of shit," Margesson snarled at one young Tory MP who failed to vote as instructed, and the MP considered himself fortunate to have gotten off so lightly. The denial of patronage, of campaign funds, and of appointments to important parliamentary committees; insidious whispering campaigns: the chief whip had a cornucopia of political punishments, and he sprinkled them like fairy dust over the errant, the rebellious, and the careless. "Brave politicians have been known to quake before the Chief Whip," said the *Daily Mail*.

One of the few journalists to express skepticism about the government's prospects was a *Guardian* reporter whose weekend of man-on-the-street interviews had revealed an important change in public opinion. People were now personalizing Britain's military setbacks. They "talk of Chamberlain—rather than the Government. They say, 'Why did Chamberlain say this or that?' [Or] it's like Chamberlain to believe 'this or that.' Some of the phrases used by the Prime Minister have been so unfortunate . . . that they have stuck in the [public's] mind." In an editorial, the *Guardian* said, "Whatever happens today, it is unlikely that Mr. Chamberlain will remain in office much longer. He is losing ground."

The morning cabinet meeting on May 7 helped the prime minister put his political concerns into perspective. A new intelligence report indicated that the Chiefs of Staff had gotten it seriously wrong in *Review of the Strategical Situation*. The report warned of an imminent German offensive in the West, perhaps as imminent as the next day or the day after. Such warnings had become almost routine since Hoenmanns's plane crash in January, but the Dutch, who expected to be attacked first, found the new report sufficiently convincing to suspend all army, navy, and air force leaves and to cancel all outgoing and incoming calls to the Netherlands. How should Britain respond if the report were to be proved true? the ministers were asked.

Sam Hoare, the new secretary of state for air and usually a

reliable "wet" on matters of national security, took an unexpectedly aggressive stance. "If we fail to take immediate advantage of the German invasion of Holland to launch our air attack on Germany, an opportunity so favorable to us might never recur." Churchill, who spoke next, also sounded out of character. The first lord urged restraint. "It would be very dangerous and undesirable to take the initiative in opening unrestricted warfare at a time when we possessed only a quarter of the striking power of the German air force."

Kingsley Wood, the minister without portfolio, raised another objection to a British first strike. In response to a request from President Roosevelt the previous autumn, Britain had pledged not to wage an unrestricted air war unless Germany did. "We [should] scrupulously observe the rules until they have been broken by the enemy," Wood said. After some discussion, the cabinet agreed that the decision about a British response should be postponed until the matter was studied further. Then the ministers dispersed, some worrying about the next day and the day after that; some worrying about that afternoon.

Just before three, Henry Channon ran into the prime minister in the Commons. "We chatted for a moment," Channon wrote in his diary that night, "but it was he who made the conversation, as I was suddenly stilled by my affection for him." Channon's affection was the last bit of human warmth Chamberlain would experience that day.

At 3:48 p.m., the prime minister rose from his seat and approached the dispatch box, the traditional forum for ministerial speeches. Normally at such moments Chamberlain was a supremely commanding figure. But that afternoon there was a tentativeness to him. The gleam of self-satisfaction was missing from his smile, conviction from his voice. Standing at the box, surveying the raucous House, he looked like a matador who had lost his nerve; and the House, always quick to sense vulnerability in a minister, pounced. Jeers and sneers rippled through the backbenches; the Speaker gaveled the session to order and Chamberlain began.

He "spoke haltingly and . . . fumbled his words and seemed tired and embarrassed," said Channon, who was sitting almost directly behind the prime minister. A tribute to the "magnificent gallantry" of the troops brought a brief burst of "Hear! Hear!"s, but by the time Chamberlain reached the third paragraph of his speech the House had had enough of him. His observation that "our withdrawal from Norway created a profound shock both in this House and in this country" produced angry shouts of "And abroad!" and "And all over the world!" Chamberlain navigated through the next few sentences without incident; then he made a fatal error: he retreated into self-pity. "Ministers, of course, must be expected to be blamed for everything."

"Missed the bus! Missed the bus! Missed the bus!" the House chanted.

Chamberlain tried to talk through the taunts, which only made the taunters shout louder. The Speaker banged his gavel again: "Honorable Members are anxious to hear the prime minister." No one believed that.

"Missed the bus! Missed the bus! Missed the bus!"

"I will not allow it!" The Speaker banged his gavel a third time.

By the time Chamberlain reached the tenth paragraph of his speech, the Egyptian ambassador had fallen asleep, Henry Channon was close to tears, and the opposition MPs had concluded that the only lessons the prime minister had learned from Norway were lessons he should have learned in 1935. Mocking cheers greeted Chamberlain's observations on the devastating effect of airpower and on the mobility of the "vast and well-equipped

German armies." It took a while for the prime minister to realize that he was being mocked. When one MP shouted, "What about production?" he replied earnestly, "Yes, production in materiel, planes, guns, everything." Only when another MP shouted, "We said that five years ago!" did Chamberlain finally get the joke.

Realizing the damage he had done himself, a younger Chamberlain might have ended with a promise to make major changes in the war cabinet. But, now seventy-one, the prime minister's political instincts had so atrophied that he had no idea his stubbornness on the cabinet issue had become a metaphor for everything that was wrong with his leadership. The day after the debate, the *Manchester Guardian* would note that it was a sign of how out of touch Chamberlain had become that he had failed to foresee that his one concession to demands for the cabinet change—the appointment of Churchill as a kind of ersatz minister of defense—would backfire and produce a lot of noisy speculation about how the prime minister was trying to subvert a popular rival by burdening him with an impossible job. "The earlier Chamberlain would have done it much more adroitly," the *Guardian* noted.

Clement Attlee spoke next, but this was not the Clement Attlee of history, the architect of the British welfare state. *That* Attlee was still a war and half a decade away. The Attlee of the Whitsun debate was a journeyman politician with a clerk's mustache, a constituency in Stepney, and an unruly prostate that was threatening his leadership of the Labour Party. Behind Attlee's back there were growing complaints about his frequent absences for convalescence. A prosaic speaker, Attlee had nothing particularly memorable to say, but his care in balancing criticism of Churchill with praise was the first indication that the House was going to try to salvage Churchill from the wreckage of Norway.

No speaker threaded this particular needle with more skill than Sir Roger Keyes, a retired admiral and the MP for North

Portsmouth. "I have great admiration and affection for my right honorable friend, the first lord of the Admiralty," Keyes said after delivering a withering critique of the Trondheim operation, without mentioning Churchill by name. However, threading the needle was not what made Keyes's speech memorable. It was who he was, a war hero; and how he was dressed, in the uniform of an admiral of the fleet. Years later, people who had been in the House that night would still remember the uniform and the simple dignity of slight, jug-eared Keyes, who for a moment seemed to step outside himself and become a symbol of what Britain stood for in the world and what it was the House's duty to see that it continued to stand for.

Keyes concluded his speech, to tumultuous applause, at seven thirty, and the House began to empty out for dinner. By eight, everyone was gone except Leo Amery (who was scheduled to speak next), a few sleepy diehards, and the Speaker of the House, an ally of the chief whip, David Margesson. The Speaker had scheduled Amery's speech for the dinner hour to ensure that if he made trouble, no one but a few half-deaf octogenarians would know about it. As the Speaker waited for the House to empty out a little more, Amery contemplated the moral ambiguities of his position that evening; they were almost Shakespearean in dimension. Joe Chamberlain had given Amery his start in Birmingham politics, and that night Amery planned to publically humiliate Joe's son Neville to help Winston Churchill, a lifelong rival and sometime enemy.

The Churchill-Amery relationship was a saga in itself. It began on a summer's day a half century earlier, when a young Winston Churchill pushed a young Leo Amery into the swimming pool at Harrow. The rivalry that arose from that "rosebud" moment persisted through five decades, during which Amery and Churchill's mutual antagonism always proved stronger than the things they shared: a devotion to King, Country, and Empire, and similar talents and interests. Gifted intellectually and ambitious politically, both men had served terms as first lord of the Admiralty and colonial secretary, and in the 1930s both had been banished to the political wilderness for opposing appeasement. Waiting for the Speaker's signal, Amery could be forgiven for thinking that in a fairer world, this would be his moment, not Churchill's.

At eight ten, the signal came; Amery rose from his seat and surveyed the House. There were barely a dozen members present, and in a chamber built for more than six hundred MPs, the twelve looked like six. Amery felt his nerve slipping. He planned to speak some hard but necessary truths about the prime minister that night, but he had to be careful. Without a chorus of supporters to give his speech a national cast, some of the things he planned to say could sound low and mean and very personal. Amery was debating whether to give a shorter, softer version of his speech when Clement Davies came up behind him and "murmured in [his] ear that [he] must at all costs state the whole case against the government." Then Davies went off to the House smoking room and the House library to fetch an audience for Amery. Meanwhile, the guests in the Strangers' Gallery (where visitors sit) began to fix their attention on the short, squat man standing in the Tory backbenches, reviewing his notes. He appeared to be in his midsixties and bore a slight resemblance to Churchill, but he was shorter and squatter than the first lord; he looked more like a beetle than a bulldog.

Amery began, as previous speakers had, with a critique of the Norwegian campaign, but then he took the debate in a new direction. Norway, he told the House, was only a symptom. The problem was Chamberlain.

> The Right hon. Gentleman, the Prime Minister [says we have] . . . been catching up on Germany's preparations. Believe

me, that is far from the truth. While we may catch up on her presently . . . there is no doubt that during these eight months, due to Germany's flying start and our slowness off the mark, the gap between German force and ours had widened enormously as far as troops . . . equipment, tanks, and all the paraphernalia of land war are concerned. It has widened in the air even, if we reckon in things which may accrue to us. . . .

We cannot go on as we are. There must be change.

Clement Davies had made good on his promise. The backbenches were filling up. Reassured by the growing "murmurs of approval and open applause," Amery moved to the most provocative part of his speech.

Just as our peacetime system is unsuitable for war conditions, so too does it breed peacetime statesmen who are not too well fitted for the conduct of war. . . . Somehow we must get into government men who can match our enemies in fighting spirit, in daring, in resolution and in thirst for victory. Some 300 years ago, when this House found that its troops were being beaten again and again by the dash and daring of the Cavaliers . . . Oliver Cromwell spoke to John Hampden. . . . [He told Hampden] Your troops are most of them old and decayed serving men and tapsters and such fellows. . . . You must get men of a spirit that are as likely to go as far as *they* will go, or you will be beat still.

Amery paused. This morning he had recalled another Cromwell quote. It compressed everything he wanted to say about the prime minister into a single biting epithet, but, if used, the epithet—cruel beyond measure—would become Chamberlain's scarlet letter. It would be the first thing people thought of when they thought of Chamberlain. The epithet would follow him to

the grave and beyond the grave into the pages of ever[y]
phy written about him and into the mind of every scl[...]
who came across his name. Did Amery want to do that to Joe
Chamberlain's son? The cheers were still rising, and Amery could
feel his emotions rising with them. He looked across the House;
Lloyd George was smiling at him. Swept up in the intoxicating
"crescendo of applause," Amery made his decision.

> I have quoted certain words of Oliver Cromwell. I will quote
> certain other words. I do it with great reluctance because I am
> speaking of those who are old friends and associates of mine,
> but they are words which, I think, are applicable to the present
> situation. This is what Cromwell said to the Long Parliament
> when he thought it was no longer fit to conduct the affairs of
> the nation.
>
> You have sat too long here for any good you have been
> doing. Depart, I say, and let us have done with you. In the Name
> of God, go.

During the final hours of the debate, Cromwell's words—powerful,
contemptuous, unanswerable—resonated through the House,
making everything that came after them sound anticlimactic. At
about midnight, the debate over, the House emptied out into the
warm May night. The government had sustained a potentially
mortal blow, and the Chamberlain men knew it. In seven hours
or so, "In the Name of God, go," and "Missed the bus!" would be
bold-faced headlines in a hundred morning papers, and by the
next evening they would be the punch lines to a dozen pub jokes.
Henry Channon went to bed "most uneasy about tomorrow," and
the next morning John Colville awoke in a "nadir of gloom." A
week before, the junior whips who had descended on the depart-

ing MPs on the evening of May 7 might have extinguished a backbench revolt with an "Iron Man defense" of threats, bribes, and promises of cabinet changes. But, emboldened by Amery's speech, the dissidents now would settle for nothing less than Chamberlain's head. "The efficacy of the Government depend[s] on the character of the Prime Minister, and the [present] Prime Minister's character ha[s] not proved sufficient," Harold Nicolson wrote in his diary that night. In Downing Street, Chief Whip Margesson warned a group of government supporters that compromises, unthinkable a few days earlier, might now be necessary to save Chamberlain.

Impressed by the strength of anti-Chamberlain sentiment in the Conservative backbenches, Clement Attlee agreed to file a motion for a confidence vote. The government would win, Attlee knew; the large Conservative majority in the House ensured that. But Chamberlain needed more than a numerical majority to survive. If a significant minority of Conservative MPs defected to the opposition, the government would suffer a moral defeat and the prime minister would have to resign.

The next afternoon, the Strangers' Gallery and backbenches were abuzz with gossip when Herbert Morrison rose to speak a little after 4:00 p.m. Rumor had it that Morrison, a senior Labour politician, would introduce the confidence motion, and rumor proved correct. As Morrison was concluding—"I ask that the vote . . ."—Chamberlain suddenly sprang to his feet and approached the dispatch box. Almost for the first time since the Whitsun debate began, the House was perfectly quiet.

"I do not seek to evade criticism but I say this to my friends— and I have friends in the House." Here, Chamberlain paused and turned to the Conservative backbenches. He seemed to be expecting a show of support; none was forthcoming. The House's silence, previously respectful, now became embarrassing. "Anyhow," the prime minister resumed, "I have friends in this House . . . I accept the challenge. I welcome it indeed."

A brief burst of cheers from the Conservative backbenches produced a nod of appreciation from the prime minister, but when he returned to his seat on the front bench, the smile was gone and he looked old and tired and wounded. "Little Neville," Henry Channon thought. "[He seems] heartbroken and shriveled."

The speeches that followed retraced the pattern of the previous night. Battalion after battalion of government "yes men" rushed into the breach to defend the prime minister, and anti-Chamberlainite MPs continued to exclude Churchill from their criticism of the government. When the first lord rose to protest the exemption, Lloyd George gave the House a master class in needle threading. "The right honorable gentleman must not allow himself to be converted into an air raid shelter to prevent the splinters from hitting his colleagues."

Delivering the government's closing statement on Norway, Churchill attempted to thread the needle himself. For an hour he interspersed a factual account of the campaign with lamentations about Labour's decision to ask for a vote of confidence. He called on Conservative dissidents to end "prewar feuds," and he defended Chamberlain's right to appeal to his friends. Arguably, what Churchill left out of his speech was more significant than what he put in. He did not defend the prime minister's conduct of the war or praise his fellow ministers. Indeed, almost the only person he did praise was himself. "Let me remind the House . . . when I, with some friends, was pressing [for rearmament], it was not only the government that objected but the opposition parties."

Harold Nicolson thought the speech masterful. "Winston [sounded] absolutely loyal" while at the same time signaling that "he really has nothing to do with this confused and timid gang."

Other listeners were less impressed. John Peck, one of Churchill's Admiralty aides, thought his performance "did not ring entirely true." Violet Bonham Carter, the daughter of former prime minister Herbert Asquith and a leading figure in the Liberal Party, also detected a note of inauthenticity in the speech. In particular, Bonham Carter thought Churchill's summation sounded "forced." Dingle Foot, another Liberal politician, called the speech "the least impressive of [Churchill's] career." Like many Chamberlain supporters, Lady Alexandra Metcalfe suspected there was a reason why Churchill, usually a sublime orator, had sounded so flat. She also found his reaction to Lloyd George's air raid shelter quip revealing. "Winston [looked] like a fat baby swinging his legs on the front bench trying not to laugh" while the other ministers sat "stone faced."

After Churchill finished, shouts of "Clear the lobbies!" and "Division!" filled the air, and the ancient rhythms of parliamentary life asserted themselves. MPs rose from their seats, walked to the back of the House, and divided. Chamberlain's supporters joined the line in front of the government lobby, opponents joined the line in front of the opposition lobby. (The lobbies were long corridors.) Normally, divisions are decorous affairs, but not that night. Too much was at stake. Taunts of "Missed the bus!" and "Yes men!" "Get out! Go! In the Name of God, go!" and "Rats!" flew between the two lines.

For the Labour MPs, that night was about Chamberlain and his conduct of the war, but it was also about the hunger marches of the 1920s and the doles of the 1930s. It was about billy clubs and blood-drenched strikers and hatreds and resentments that had accumulated over seventeen years of mostly Conservative rule, the last three under Neville Chamberlain. For the dissident Tory MPs, it had the character of a family tragedy. In background, outlook, and belief, the members of the House Conservative caucus were similar. They had gone to the same schools, served in the same regiments, attended one another's weddings. They had watched one another's children be baptized, had buried one another's parents, and, except for Neville Chamberlain and his government, they had believed in the same things: in England, in Crown and Empire, in patriotism, loyalty, duty, and the Conservative Party, the party of their fathers and their fathers' fathers. If betraying one's country was the worst thing a man could do, then, for many of the dissident Tories standing in the opposition line, betraying one's party with a cabal of socialists was a very close second. It was especially so when David Margesson would be waiting to greet you at the other end of the opposition lobby, his face screwed up into an "expression of implacable resentment." Approaching the passage to the lobby, Edward Spears found himself thinking, "How many men have faced [this entrance] wondering whether they were doing the right thing, whether in four steps they had ruined their political careers?"

The outcome of the division was never in doubt. The large Conservative majority in the Commons ensured a Chamberlain victory. What mattered was the margin of victory, and here the tellers [the vote counters] had a surprise: the prime minister's customary majority, 200 to 250 votes, had shrunk to 81. The House erupted. "Go! Go!" "Resign! Resign!" "Missed the bus!" Harold Macmillan, a future prime minister, and Joshua Wedgewood, a Labour MP, stood up and sang an off-key version of "Rule Britannia." Chamberlain endured the taunts for as long as he could, then "pick[ed] his way over the protruding feet of his colleagues" and left. Watching him walk out, "following in the wake of all his dead hopes and fruitless efforts," Spears "was surprised to find himself feeling intensely sorry for him."

When Clem Davies met Joe Kennedy later that night, the prime minister's supporters were already putting it about in London clubland that Chamberlain planned to remain in office. Davies and Kennedy discussed the political situation for a while with their host, the press magnate Lord Beaverbrook. Then Kennedy said that President Roosevelt would want to be briefed on the debate, and disappeared into another room to place a transatlantic call. When Kennedy returned, he looked "haggard and shaken"—Roosevelt said Holland had been invaded, Rotterdam was in flames, and German parachute troops had seized control of all the main bridges in the Netherlands. Davies immediately placed a call to Churchill, then to Sam Hoare, the air minister. Neither man had heard anything about an invasion. Nor had the Dutch ambassador, who fainted when Davies told him the news. An hour later, the Dutch government announced that the rumor was false, and the Dutch ambassador went back to bed and slept the sleep of the saved. Joe Kennedy had a more turbulent night. The evening's events had confirmed his fears that Britain was unready to meet the real war that he was sure was imminent. "There is a very definite undercurrent of despair because of the hopelessness of the whole task for England."

The next day the press was full of speculation about Churchill succeeding Chamberlain, but, oddly, there was very little discussion or analysis of how that change would alter Britain's war aims. With Churchill in office, there would be no more talk of teaching Germany that aggression does not pay, or of inducing changes of heart and mind. Under a Churchill government, Britain's war aim would be victory, complete and unambiguous, even if that meant a return to the total war of a generation earlier.

CHAPTER SIX

THE ROGUE ELEPHANT

May 9 was another day of melting beauty and black news. The British position in Norway continued to crumble, the rumors of a German offensive in the West continued to multiply, and the leadership crisis in Westminster continued to intensify. In the May Gallup poll, Chamberlain's unfavorability rating rose to 67 percent. "That bastard Chamberlain; I can't put into words what I think about him." "Oh, Christ, he's frightfully obstinate." "He won't see any point but his own." The man-on-the-street interviews in *Political Crisis*, Mass Observation's report on the Norway debate, spoke forcefully of what the report called "genuine...mass pressure to change the Prime Minister." The morning-after coverage of the debate also spoke forcefully of the desire for change. Several major papers were administering last rites to Chamberlain on their front pages, and several others already had him dead and buried and had his political obituary on their front pages. The requiems were premature. A majority of the Conservative MPs in the House of Commons still supported the prime minister. So did the new young king, George VI, who knew something about public abuse himself.

In the spring of 1940, George VI was in the third year of his reign, just long enough to have become a favorite piñata of the chattering classes in London and Paris. "A very dull man," said the British writer Nancy Mitford. "Another snipe from the Windsor Marshes," said the MP Harold Nicolson. A "moron," declared former French premier Édouard Daladier. Daladier's remark was particularly uncharitable. It was true that George VI had placed sixty-eighth out of sixty-eight on his entrance exam for the naval college at Osborne, and sixty-first out of sixty-seven on his exam for the naval college at Dartmouth; but placed in context, the scores were not as bad as they looked. As one observer noted, the "average London club man" would not have done any better. It was also true that the king lacked personal glamour, but his older brother, Edward VIII, had possessed bucketfuls of glamour and no character—and look what that had wrought: Wallis Simpson and the yearlong abdication crisis. Devon, Dorset, Kent, Norfolk, and Suffolk were happy to have the earnest, stable, trustworthy, dull George VI and his strong-minded, porky little Scottish queen in Buckingham Palace.

The king's friendship with Chamberlain had its roots in the abdication crisis. Then chancellor of the Exchequer, Chamberlain's skillful handling of the financial side of abdication had impressed the new king, and in time respect led to trust and trust to "a bond" between the two men. Devoted to "duty and family," the king and the prime minister had much in common, says British historian Andrew Roberts. "They were both intensely private individuals. Furthermore, both wanted to regard German claims in the best possible light, feeling as they did a deep dislike for Bolshevism." Beyond that, both men were sensitive to the cry of Never Again! And, as king-emperor, George VI was particularly sensitive to warnings that a new German war could cost Britain its empire and its great power status. If 1914–18 had demonstrated anything, it was that the delicate architecture of the imperial state did not stand up well to the rigors of total war. In 1914 the German, Russian, and Austro-Hungarian empires had seemed as enduring as time; eight years later, the kaiser was a farmer in Holland, and the czar and Charles I (the ruler of Austro-Hungary) were dead. One day not long after the war began, a Foreign Office official found the king feeling "a little defeatist" after a talk with Ambassador Kennedy, who had given George VI a lecture on "the loss of prestige of the British Empire in the changed circumstances in which we live."

The relationship between Chamberlain and the king also had a political dimension. Under British law, a sovereign's political powers are severely circumscribed; but even in the twentieth century, royal prestige could make a wink, a nod, and a word from the palace go a long way; and George VI, reticent in other spheres of life, was less reticent about employing this unofficial source of power and influence. Britons who cheered the king, the queen, and Chamberlain on the palace balcony after the Munich Conference were left in no doubt about where the Crown stood on appeasement; and guests within earshot of the queen and Chamberlain at a dinner party in July 1939 were left in no doubt about the Crown's dim view of Churchill. During the Norway debate, the king pushed his unofficial powers a step further. Knowing that Chamberlain's political survival rested on convincing a reluctant Labour Party to join a national government under him, during an audience after the first day of debate, the king asked Chamberlain, "Would it help if I spoke to Attlee . . . and say that I hoped they [the Labour Party] would realize that they must pull their weight and join a national government?" The prime minister said he wanted to think on the matter, and as he was thinking on it his luck appeared to take a turn for the better.

On May 9, a sizable number of the Conservative MPs who had voted no or had abstained on the confidence motion awoke with a severe case of morning-after guilt. Heartened by the sudden shower of mea culpas raining down on the Conservative Central

Office, the Tory whips prepared a package of promises, including a pledge to form a national government and to increase Churchill's powers and offer perks, such as choice committee assignments and better constituency services. Then they invited the penitent, the mournful, and the self-seeking into the office for a talk. The third element in what became known as the prime minister's "Iron Man defense" was a whispering campaign against Churchill. Just before lunch on the ninth, Harold Nicolson heard that "the Whips are putting it about that the whole business [the confidence vote] was a snap vote cunningly engineered by Duff Cooper and Amery." For his unexpected turn of good luck on May 9 Chamberlain also owed a debt of gratitude to his opponents.

Almost to a man, the rebel Tories who voted no on the confidence motion stood under the flag of Churchill, and, almost to a man, the Labour MPs who voted no disliked Churchill as much as, and in some cases more than, they disliked Chamberlain. In many Labour homes, the name Churchill was synonymous with the name Tonypandy. In Labour Party legend, when miners in the Welsh town went on strike in 1910, Home Secretary Churchill sent the army in to break the strike; in reality, Churchill sent the army in to protect the miners from the local police. But over the years, the Tonypandy legend acquired—as legends often do—the power of truth. In Labour households, a generation of children absorbed it with their mother's milk. If Labour was going to serve under a Conservative prime minister in a national government, then Attlee, Greenwood, Hugh Dalton, and the other senior party leaders wanted that Conservative PM to be Lord Halifax. Steady of temperament and sound of judgment, the word that most naturally attached itself to the name of Edward Halifax was "blameless." Accordingly, the foreign secretary was also the first choice of the king, who was "bitterly opposed to Winston succeeding Chamberlain," and of the queen, who shared the king's feelings about Churchill.

Fearing a divisive fight over the succession question, on the morning of the ninth the leading opposition groups agreed to put aside that question for now and to focus their energies on bringing down Chamberlain.

"Don't agree and don't say anything."

It was the lunch hour on the ninth, and Anthony Eden and Churchill were sitting in a London restaurant with Kingsley Wood. Perhaps because the whips had been offering Wood's head to dissident Tories all morning, the lord privy seal was in an indiscreet mood. "Neville ha[s] decided to go and wants Halifax to succeed him, and you to endorse the choice," Wood said, then offered Churchill a piece of advice. The prime minister had called an afternoon meeting to discuss the leadership question. When he raises the succession issue, "don't agree and don't say anything." Eden was "shocked" by Wood's indiscretion. He was a Chamberlain man, and here he was, casually betraying years of loyalty and friendship over lunch in a noisy London restaurant. Still, Wood's advice was "good," so Eden "seconded it."

There were other betrayals on the afternoon of the ninth, as events forced men to choose between loyalty to country, loyalty to party, loyalty to friends, and loyalty to the truth. Clement Davies, Duff Cooper, and Bob Boothby, three of the most influential anti-appeasement MPs, began the morning pledging not to politick for individual candidates, and spent the afternoon politicking on behalf of Churchill. That day, the first lord was an easy sale. Bellicosity, tenacity, daring, certitude—qualities that had alternately annoyed, exasperated, and frightened two generations of MPs—looked different on a day when four hundred German tanks had been sighted in a wood east of the Belgian Ardennes and the German merchant fleet had switched to the frequency it had used just prior to the Norway invasion.

Later that afternoon, Lloyd George gave a remarkable speech. "When the history of [this period] comes to be written," he told an almost empty House of Commons, "it will be seen that most of this trouble has originated in the fact that the victors in the late war did not carry out solemn pledges in the Treaty [of Versailles] which they themselves gave." Many found it beyond strange that on the eve of war, Lloyd George would choose to make such an inflammatory accusation—but not his old nemesis, Neville Chamberlain. Lloyd George is "stak[ing] out a position from which ultimately he might be called on to make the peace," the prime minister told his sister Ida a few days later.

As the afternoon wore on, sentiment continued to move in Churchill's direction. Bob Boothby reported that there is "a gathering consensus of opinion in all quarters that you are the necessary and inevitable prime minister." Clem Davies said that his lobbying had left Attlee and Greenwood "unable to distinguish between the P.M. and Halifax." The euphoria in the Churchill camp was premature. Kingsley Wood's intelligence was wrong. Chamberlain opened the afternoon meeting he had called to discuss the succession question with the announcement that he would remain in office if the Labour Party agreed to serve under him. Clement Attlee, who joined the meeting at a little after six, quickly disabused the prime minister of that notion. "Our party won't have you, and I don't think the country will have you, either." Chamberlain needed a moment to digest Attlee's words. When he spoke again, he asked if Labour would serve under another Conservative leader. Attlee and Greenwood (who was also present) said they thought the party would, but that they would be unable to give a definitive answer until they spoke to their colleagues, and that would take a few days. Labour's annual party conference was scheduled to begin the following Monday, and most of the party's leaders were already in Bournemouth, the Channel resort town where the conference was to be held. After the Labour men left, Chamberlain raised the succession question. Halifax, who had had a stomachache earlier in the day, felt his gnawing discomfort coming back.

It would be an exaggeration to say that Downing Street was Halifax's for the asking on the evening of the ninth—Churchill's candidacy had developed a terrific momentum. But the foreign secretary was the establishment's choice. The king—and Chamberlain, who still led the Conservative Party—viewed Halifax as safe, and safety is what makes the establishment choice the choice of the establishment. Halifax might have known little of military affairs, but, unlike Churchill, he could be trusted not to risk the country's future on a wild adventure. Even with Churchill gaining momentum, Halifax's prudence alone might have propelled him into Downing Street on May 9, had he wanted to be prime minister. But he did not want to be prime minister—not in wartime.

The foreign secretary's objections to high office were voluminous. A wartime leader should sit in the House of Commons, the center of power in the British parliamentary system, and Halifax sat in the House of Lords. A wartime leader should have a store of military knowledge, and a few weeks earlier, when asked whether Trondheim or Narvik should be attacked, Halifax had found himself unable to provide an informed answer. There was also the matter of Churchill, and what to do about him. According to Rab Butler, a Halifax confidant, the foreign secretary recognized that Churchill possessed the talents to be an outstanding war leader, but Halifax felt Churchill needed "steadying," and was uncertain in which role he could best provide it, "as Prime Minister or as a Minister in a Churchill government?" Later Butler would say that

Halifax's decision to remain at the Foreign Office arose from his concern that "even if he did become PM, Churchill's qualities and experience meant he would end up 'running the war anyway' and Halifax would end as sort of an Honorary Prime Minister."

There are several accounts of how the leadership question was resolved on the evening of May 9. Churchill's version, which appears in *The Gathering Storm*, the first volume of his World War Two memoirs, is the most famous and dramatic.

Usually I talk a great deal, but on this occasion I was silent. . . . Mr. Chamberlain [said he] felt . . . that [there] might be an obstacle to my obtaining [Labour's] adherence at this juncture. I do not recall the actual words he used, but this was the implication. . . . His biographer, Mr. Feiling, states definitely that he preferred Lord Halifax.

As I remained silent a very long pause ensued. It certainly seemed longer than the two minutes which one observes in the commemorations of Armistice Day. Then at length Halifax spoke. He said he felt his position as a Peer out of the House of Commons, would make it very difficult for him to discharge the duties of Prime Minister in a war like this. He would be held responsible for everything but would not have the power to guide the assembly upon whose confidence the life of every Government depended. He spoke for some minutes in this sense and by the time he had finished it was clear that the duty would fall on me—had in fact fallen upon me.

William Deakin, the research assistant and fact checker on *The Gathering Storm*, believes that Churchill was "hamming [it] up" in his account of the succession. He misstates the date—the meeting occurred on May 9, not the tenth—and fails to mention that Chief Whip Margesson was present. Years later Deakin would tell Andrew Roberts, Halifax's biographer, that Churchill's account was "not to be taken seriously." Halifax's account, which was written almost immediately after the meeting—not seven years later, as Churchill's was—is regarded as the more accurate record of what transpired, not least because the account is consistent with what Halifax had been saying for days. Decisions about peace and war are the province of the House of Commons, and as a member of the House of Lords, Halifax's ability to influence the decisions the Commons made on these issues would be severely limited.

> The P.M., Winston, David Margesson and I sat down to it. The P.M. recapitulated the position and said that he had made up his mind that he must go, and that it must either be Winston or me. He would serve under either. . . . David Margesson said that unity was essential and he thought it impossible to attain under the P.M. He did not at that moment pronounce between Winston and me and my stomach ache continued.
>
> I then said that for all the reasons given, the P.M. must probably go, but that I had no doubt at all in my own mind that for me to take it would create a quite impossible position. Quite apart from Winston's qualities as compared to my own at this particular juncture, what would in fact be my position? Winston would be running Defense, and . . . I should have no access to the House of Commons. The inevitable result would be that being outside both these vital points of contact I should speedily become a more or less Honorary Prime Minister living in a kind of twilight just outside the things that really mattered. Winston with suitable expressions of regard and humility, said that he could not but feel the force of what I had said and the P.M. reluctantly, and Winston evidently with much less reluctance, finished by accepting my point of view.

Halifax's withdrawal did not automatically make Churchill prime minister. The king had yet to weigh in on the appointment, and, despite a friendly late-night talk with Attlee and Greenwood, Labour had not yet agreed to serve under Churchill. That decision would be made by the party delegates in Bournemouth, many of them crusty old veterans of the hunger marches of the 1920s and the strikes and lockouts of the 1930s. "Tonypandy!" was their battle cry, and the general strike of 1926, when Churchill did use the army against strikers, their Calvary. The Halifax threat had also not entirely receded. Overnight, several of the foreign secretary's supporters pressured him to reconsider his withdrawal, but that proved impossible. The next morning, when Rab Butler called to discuss the succession question, he was told that the foreign secretary was at the dentist's.

May 9 was also a day of political crisis in Paris, where the government of Paul Reynaud was divided over the fate of Maurice Gamelin, the commander in chief of the French Army. A General Gamelin had served France in an almost unbroken line since the time of Louis IV, though none had advanced so far or displayed such a precocious interest in military affairs as the current General Gamelin. At nine years old, Gamelin was reputed to have had the largest toy soldier collection in Paris; at twenty-one, he graduated first in his class at the French military academy St. Cyr; during the Great War, he was an aide to Marshal Ferdinand Foch, the Allied Supreme Commander; and after the war he earned distinction as a military intellectual.

Underneath this impressive dossier lay a fatalistic nature and a certain rigidity of mind, but Gamelin's expressionless face and habit of keeping to himself gave him a sphinxlike quality that allowed others to see what they wanted to see in him. Thus, to admirers such as former premier Daladier, the general's solidity of manner and body symbolized the resolve and confidence of France itself, while to detractors it symbolized a dullness of imagination and spirit. Upon assuming office the previous March, Premier Reynaud had leaned toward the latter view, but he kept an open mind until Gamelin turned out to be as surprised as he was by the German invasion of Norway. "That nerveless man, I would be a criminal if I left [him] at the head of [the] French Army."

For several weeks, Reynaud went back and forth about dismissing Gamelin, but he always ended up where he had started. Without the political support of Daladier, who was a member of his cabinet, Reynaud's government would fall, and Daladier was Gamelin's chief political patron. Meanwhile, the rumors of an imminent German offensive continued to mount, and Reynaud caught a bad spring cold. On May 8, when he called a snap cabinet meeting for the next day, he was pale and feverish and had a hacking cough. Elie Bois, that gossipiest of Parisian journalists, credits Reynaud's miraculous recovery on the ninth to the doctor who visited his apartment early that morning and "doped him to the full." The weather probably deserves some credit for the premier's recovery as well. In 1940, April in Paris could not hold a candle to May in Paris. When wartime listeners heard "The Last Time I Saw Paris" on the wireless, the Paris they thought of was the one Clare Boothe described that last May the city was free. "Chestnuts burst into leaf on lovely avenues. . . . [T]he sunlight dances off the opalescent gray buildings." Sunbathers lounge on the quays along the Seine; the Ritz [is] crowded "with lovely ladies wearing simple sun dresses or the smart uniforms of the Union des Femmes," and the great jewels in the windows of Van Cleef & Arpels and Cartier "sparkle in the sunlight."

Reynaud arrived at the afternoon cabinet meeting on the ninth with color in his cheeks and a bulky dossier against Gamelin under his arm. After dispensing with a few minor pieces of business, the premier opened the dossier and began reading. Minutes passed, then hours. When Reynaud finished, it was three o'clock and France no longer had a government and he no longer was premier. "If [Gamelin] is guilty, I am," Daladier said, then offered his resignation. Seeing no other alternative, Reynaud offered his. "As I can no longer make my point of view prevail, I am no longer Head of the government." When the meeting concluded at about 4:00 p.m., the sunbathers along the Seine were packing up, the racetrack at Auteuil was emptying out, France and Britain no longer had settled governments—and German paratroopers were making final preparations for an early morning assault on Holland and Belgium.

London learned of the German offensive at around 5:30 a.m. on May 10, about an hour after the Second Panzer Division crossed the Belgian frontier under the remains of the night sky. A few minutes later, the ablutions of the Dutch border guards were interrupted by a squadron of Heinkels passing overhead. Gazing down at the early morning countryside, one German pilot thought "How crazy . . . Children playing by the stream, a white dog jump[ing] around them barking; why is this lovely peaceful land suddenly 'enemy territory'?" In Paris, where air raid sirens had begun blaring a little before 5:00 a.m., Reynaud added a new charge to his dossier on Gamelin. Ten days earlier, the general had dismissed a warning from a Wehrmacht source about a German offensive between May 8 and May 10. In the residential quarters of the French capital, dogs, startled by the sirens, barked; lights twinkled on above the deserted streets; and faces appeared between window curtains. "Everyone like us was . . . looking upward," recalled one Parisian.

In Downing Street, the first news of the German attack arrived in fits and starts. A 6:00 a.m. report that "Holland alone" had been attacked was followed by a 7:00 a.m. report of German attacks on Luxembourg and Belgium. By the time the war cabinet convened at 8:00 a.m., the reports had become more detailed. German parachutists were fighting in the streets of The Hague; bombs were dropping on the French town of Nancy; the HMS *Kelly* had been torpedoed off the French coast. "Perhaps the darkest day in English history," Henry Channon thought as he scanned the morning headlines at a London kiosk. "Lille bombed"; "Paris raided"; "Bombs in Kent." By early afternoon on the tenth, close to a million men were moving across the northern European plain under a sublime May sky. One of them, a German sergeant, took out his journal and wrote, "The warmth and brilliance of the day is oppressive." Vera Brittain, who was attending the Bournemouth Conference, listened to the war news for a while. Then, unable to bear any more, she walked through Bournemouth, trying to lose herself in the views. "Cliffs shin[ing] luminously . . . the sweet dry scent of innumerable fir trees." For a while, the distractions worked. Then, like the German sergeant, Brittain felt a sense of oppression descend on her. "It is unbelievable that only a few miles away, across the misty sea, which looks so serene below the yellow hedge of gorse that fringes the cliffs, men are destroying one another in their thousands and the civilization of half a dozen countries is going up in smoke and flame." In Paris, André Beaufre, a young French captain, came across General Gamelin in Vincennes, the home of the French High Command. The general was striding "up and down" a corridor, "humming with a pleased and martial air." The maps in Gamelin's war room indicated that the German offensive was unfolding as he had expected: thrusts through Holland and central Belgium.

Like millions of other Britons, Randolph Churchill learned of the German offensive over breakfast. When the news crackled through on the wireless in his mess hall, Randolph immediately called his father: "What about . . . becoming prime minister today?" "Oh, I don't know about that," the elder Churchill replied. Earlier that morning, Chamberlain had announced that he intended to stay in office until "the French battle was finished." Labour MP Hugh Dalton was unhappy but unsurprised by the prime minister's decision. "The old man is an incorrigible limpet, always trying new tricks to stay on the rock." Harold Nicolson also believed, war or no war, that Chamberlain had to go. Then he heard Alec Douglas-Home, a Scottish aristocrat with Tammany Hall–caliber political skills, address a meeting of the Watching Committee. Of the Chamberlain supporters who fanned out across London on the morning of the tenth to make the case that the prime minister should stay on, none executed that brief more artfully and elegantly than Douglas-Home. Listening to the Scotsman, Nicolson found himself thinking, well, yes, there was a good deal of "sense" in Douglas-Home's argument, the dangers of the moment do require a "steady, experienced" hand like Chamberlain's. Douglas-Home's opposite number on the tenth was Brendan Bracken, a Churchill aide who possessed the temperament of a bomb thrower, an off-again, on-again relationship with rectitude, an impressive intellect, an irresistible frizz of Harpo Marx hair, bottle-thick glasses, and the knowing smile of an insider who is privy to everyone else's secrets.

Upon hearing of Chamberlain's decision to stay in office, Bracken began working the phones. A few hours later, Lord Salisbury issued a statement to the press reaffirming his support for Churchill, and the Labour Party published an official denial of the reports that the party had agreed to enter a national government under Chamberlain. In what must have been the most personally difficult moment of the day for the prime minister, Kingsley Wood, whom Chamberlain still regarded as a loyal friend, told him that the only honorable recourse was resignation. Chamberlain's lingering hopes of remaining in office were crushed at the four thirty cabinet meeting when an aide handed him a note. Chamberlain read it while General Ironside briefed the cabinet on the situation in Belgium. When the general finished, Chamberlain read the note aloud.

The Labour Party had been asked whether they would consider in principle co-operating in the government (a) under the present Prime Minister or (b) under some other Prime Minister. The Labour Party's answer ha[s] now been received. Their reply to the first question was in the negative and to second question was as follows: "The Labour Party are prepared to take their share of responsibility as a full partner in a new Government under a new Prime Minister."

Shortly thereafter, Chamberlain offered his resignation to a sympathetic and disappointed king. "[I] told him how grossly unfair I thought he had been treated and that I was terribly sorry that all this controversy had happened. We then had a talk about his successor [and] I, of course, suggested Halifax." Chamberlain told the king that Halifax wanted to stay at the Foreign Office. Below Halifax, the pickings became thin. There was Anthony Eden, the public's first choice for prime minister in a recent Mass Observation poll, but Eden's popularity owed more to his good looks than to his acumen. Senior Tory politicians considered Eden, secretary of state for the dominions, too young and untested for high office. There were also the Munichois, men such as John Simon and Sam Hoare, who had a deep knowledge of government but prewar records of appeasement. When the second tier was eliminated, only one candidate remained, Churchill, who described his accession to the premiership on May 11 as a rendezvous with destiny. "[I felt] all my past life had been but preparation for this hour and for this trial." Generations of readers have thrilled to the description, but it was precisely this kind of romanticism that made the prospect of a Churchill government so disturbing to the king and to many of the new prime minister's former and current colleagues.

One day in 1906, thirty-two-year-old Winston Churchill told a young woman, "We are all worms, but I do believe that I am a glowworm."

"I have met a genius," the young woman exclaimed upon arriving home. Her father, Herbert Asquith, a future prime minister, listened to her gush on, but when she said the name of the extraordinary young man was Winston Churchill, his surprise dissolved into irony. "Well, Winston would certainly agree with you there, but I am not sure you will find many others of the same mind." As British historian Paul Addison has noted, one of the master narratives of British political life in the first half of the twentieth century was the "conflict between Churchill's heroic self-image, [which he] communicated to the world through a stupendous barrage of publicity . . . and the hard-bitten observations of politicians, civil servants and military men, conversing in their clubs after another difficult day with Winston." Churchill in the abstract was easier to admire than Churchill the flesh-and-blood man whose remarkable qualities of mind and heart came with a high price in the form of rashness, bellicosity, a galloping ambition, endless monologues, and a backward-looking vision. Spread end to end, the Churchill vision was as colorful as the Bayeux Tapestry, but he sought Britain's future in its past, in the late Victorian and Edwardian periods of his childhood and young manhood. Sensing this instinctively, in 1945 the British public chose someone else to lead them into the postwar future, just as in May 1940 they instinctively knew that Churchill was the right man to lead them through the war and rallied around him. "If I had to spend my whole life with one man," wrote Nella Last, a plainspoken North Country woman, "I'd choose Mr. Chamberlain, but I think I'd sooner have Mr. Churchill if there was a storm and I was shipwrecked. He has a funny face, like a bull dog living on our street that has done more to drive out our unwanted dogs and cats . . . than all the complaints of house holders."

"Old men forget and about Churchill they forgot by the Imperial gallon." Had it been up to what one historian has called the "respectable tendency" in the Conservative Party—the men and women who spoke of "England" rather than "Britain," put on mourning clothes when Chamberlain fell, and then wrote "Winston and Me" memoirs after the war—Churchill would never have become prime minister. "Hitler will thank Thor for our quislings [Churchill supporters]," wrote Charles Waterhouse, a "true blue" Tory, country gentleman, Life Guard in the First World War, and MP for Southeast Leicester. "I regard this as a greater disaster than the invasion of the Low Lands," wrote that shrewd political wife Nancy Dugdale after Churchill became prime minister. "The crooks are on top as they were in the last war," warned Lord Davidson, an influential political writer. A "negation of democracy" said Patrick Donner, an influential Conservative MP and a disillusioned Churchillian. In the Foreign Office, Henry Channon and Rab Butler raised a toast to Chamberlain, the "king over water," when the seals of office passed to Churchill. In Downing Street, John Colville heard whispers of a Chamberlain restoration. None of the naysaying would have posed a threat to Churchill had he come to power with a political base of his own, but he was too individualistic and idiosyncratic to attract a large following in or outside a political party. On the afternoon of the eleventh, when he told Chamberlain "to a large extent, I am in your hands," he was not just being polite. Churchill could not hold Downing

Street without the Conservative Party, and he could not hold the Conservative Party without Chamberlain, who remained its leader and commanded the support of the Conservative faithful in and outside the House of Commons. Prime Minister Churchill's first round of cabinet appointments reflected this reality.

To his own supporters, the new prime minister gave very little. Leo Amery was sent to the India Office, far from the center of power; Duff Cooper, to the Ministry of Information, closer to the center of things, but not that much closer, while stalwarts such as Harold Macmillan and Harold Nicolson had to settle for junior postings. Labour did better. Attlee entered the war cabinet as lord privy seal, and Greenwood as minister without portfolio. (Holders of this post do not oversee a ministry, as other members of the cabinet do, but, like their colleagues, they do get to vote on all decisions the cabinet makes.) Two other Labour men also received important appointments. Hugh Dalton became the minister of economic warfare, and Ernest Bevin, labour minister. Of the thirty-four ministerial posts in the Churchill government, twenty-one were filled by men who had served under Chamberlain—among them Anthony Eden, a sometime Churchill ally who became secretary of state for war, and Kingsley Wood, who was given Exchequer as a reward for his betrayal of his old master. The only Chamberlainite of consequence who failed to be reappointed was Sam Hoare, who was packed off to Madrid as ambassador to Spain. Chamberlain himself remained in the war cabinet as lord president of the council, a post whose nominal duties allowed him to focus his energy and attention on the war. Lord Halifax was reappointed foreign secretary. Unofficially, the two men were in the cabinet to ensure that Churchill did not risk the life of the nation on some rash new adventure. "The only hope lies in . . . the wise old elephants [restraining] the rogue elephant," said Lord Hankey, a senior civil servant.

The British public was more welcoming. "Good luck, Winnie!" and "God bless you!" well-wishers would shout when Churchill's car arrived at the Admiralty, where he was staying until the Chamberlains moved out of Downing Street. The new prime minister would emerge from the backseat, tip his hat, and then pose for the cameras with a group of well-wishers. The next day, a photo of a confident, smiling Churchill would be on the front page of the *Mail* or the *Express*, and no one would guess what he told an aide after one of those photo ops. "Poor people, poor people. They trust me, and I can give them nothing but disaster for quite a long time."

The closest Churchill came to articulating that thought in public was in his inaugural address as prime minister, on May 13. He told the House that, for the foreseeable future, he could promise little but "blood, toil, tears, and sweat." The May 13 speech was also noteworthy for two other things: the cool reception Churchill received from Conservative backbenchers, especially in comparison to the ovation Chamberlain received that evening, and the new war aim he introduced. Gone was the talk of inducing a "change of heart" in Germany and of teaching Herr Hitler that aggression does not pay. Now, Britain's goal was "Victory, victory at all costs! Victory, however long and hard the road may be!" Victory, even if it meant total war and all that came with total war: burned-out cities, ruined factories, and national bankruptcy. The two "wise old elephants" kept silent about the "rogue elephant's" new war aim, but events in France would not keep them silent for long.

CHAPTER SEVEN

"THERE FADED AWAY THIS NOISE WHICH WAS A GREAT ARMY"

"It went too damn well. . . . What is [Hitler] up to?"

It was May 11, two days before Churchill's inaugural speech in the House of Commons, and a *Times* of London correspondent* was standing on an unshaded road just inside the Belgian frontier, scanning the sky. Except for a few puffy white cumulus clouds, it was empty. The reporter was puzzled. The BEF unit he was attached to had been on the road for nearly eight hours and, other than the occasional visit by a curious Storch, a German reconnaissance aircraft, the Luftwaffe had yet to appear.

Hundreds of other British and French units were also on the march that morning, and they were all converging on the same point. After examining the documents in Hoenmanns's plane, General Gamelin had concluded that Case Yellow, the Germans' offensive plan, would unfold like the Schlieffen plan of 1914: a thrust through Belgium into northern France, then a swing southward toward Paris. The only notable variant in Yellow was that it included an attack on Holland, which had remained neutral in the Great War. Looking for a place to break the German drive,

---

*The *Times* reporter was Kim Philby, who would later earn notoriety as a Soviet spy.

Gamelin's eye fell on the Dyle, a river east of Brussels. The north–south direction of the Dyle made it a natural defensive line, and the Belgians had already built a network of antitank positions along its banks. The Dyle's position, well east of the Channel coast, would also make London happy. In a fit of solipsism, the British had convinced themselves that Britain, not France, was the target of the Case Yellow offensive. After seizing air bases along the Dutch and Belgian coasts, the Germans planned to bomb Britain into submission. As a defensive position, the Dyle possessed only one drawback: it was in Belgium—and Belgium was neutral, and its new young king, Leopold, was determined to keep it that way.

After the capture of the German plan the previous January, the Allies and the Belgian High Command did hold secret staff talks, but when the Luftwaffe blew Clare Boothe out of a Brussels hotel bed in the early hours of May 10, Belgium was still neutral and the French and British troops tasked with defending the Dyle line were asleep in base camps many miles away, in northern France. As bugles blared and rifles and backpacks were examined and reexamined, there was much nervous talk among the troops about air attacks. The French and British units marching up to the Dyle would be moving along open roads under an unclouded sky. General Alan Brooke, the dour Ulsterman who commanded the BEF's Second Corps, was as surprised as the *Times* reporter by the Luftwaffe's absence. "Everything so far has been running like clockwork with less interference from bombing than I had anticipated," Brooke noted in his diary.

The Second Corps' experience was not unusual. On May 11, the only thing awaiting most of the British and French troops entering Belgium were grateful Belgians. "In towns and villages," said one British captain, men and women "lined our route and little children ran along [beside] the trucks, throwing flowers to the troops. . . . People in motorcars drove up and down the convoy, distributing cigarettes and chocolate, and whenever we stopped, women came out of the house with hot coffee." For the veterans of the Great War—the colonels, majors, and senior sergeants who had friends buried at Dickebusch Old Military Cemetery, Dickebusch New Military Cemetery, Kemmel Château Cemetery, Kemmel Churchyard Cemetery, and a dozen other British and Commonwealth burial sites in Belgium—the return to the country of their early manhood occasioned a somber remembrance of things past. The veterans seemed to be "retracing steps taken in a dream," as if "they saw again faces of friends long dead and heard the half remembered names of towns and villages," wrote Drew Middleton, an American war correspondent.

The ferocious air battle in Holland, which drew in hundreds of German aircraft on May 10 and 11, was widely credited for the safe passage. But Paul de Villelume, a French colonel, thought that explanation was nonsense. The Germans are luring the Allies into a trap, he told Gamelin during a visit to the French High Command. Gamelin shrugged and said even if de Villelume was right, it was too late to do anything about it. "When we took the decision to go into Belgium, we decided to take all the risks." The German planners had modeled their offensive on the bullfight, and, in a sly piece of typecasting, they had assigned Gamelin—fatalistic, rigid, and unimaginative—the role of the bull. The Wehrmacht attacks in central Belgium and southern Holland were the matador's cape. They would draw the best French and British infantry and armored units north to meet what appeared to be the main German thrust; the matador's sword were the Panzer divisions hidden in the high forests of the Belgian Ardennes, the weak center of the Allied line. As the French and British rushed north to take up positions on the Dyle, the Panzers would burst out of the Ardennes and spear Gamelin in the flank.

"I could have wept with joy," Hitler said of the moment he

learned the Allies had adopted the Dyle plan; and on May 13, when he learned that the Panzers had pierced Gamelin's flank along the Ardennes, for once the Führer was speechless. "It's a miracle! It's a miracle!" is all he could say.

General Irwin Rommel began May 13 crouched in a ditch in Dinant, a picturesque little Belgian river town that sits in a low valley between a high rock face and the Meuse River, the last natural barrier before the rolling tank country of eastern France. Behind Rommel, men and equipment were massed in rows back to the high woods of the Ardennes east of Dinant. In front of him, a column of Mark IV Panzers was creeping along the eastern bank of the river at walking speed, firing their guns point-blank into the French positions on the other side of the Meuse. Overhead, a squadron of Stuka dive bombers assembled into attack formation. The planes dipped their noses toward the river; the screech of sirens rent the air and silvery geysers of water erupted on the surface of the Meuse. Simultaneously, a stream of field-gray uniforms and rubber dingies rushed past Rommel's position and down to the water's edge. Firing from the French side of the river intensified, "then a rubber [raft] came drifting down [river] toward Rommel. The badly wounded soldier clinging to the side of the raft shouted 'help!'" Rommel ignored his plea. "The enemy fire was too heavy."

First-class French units might have been able to hold the western bank of the Meuse on the morning of the thirteenth; but, not expecting a major battle in the Ardennes, Gamelin had put most of his Class A divisions on the Dyle. With the exception of two Class A reserve divisions, the Meuse front was defended by undertrained, underequipped Class B units who were quickly overwhelmed by the professionalism of the German troops. French gun crews fled blockhouses; French officers abandoned their commands; panicked privates and corporals turned their helmets backward—a sign of Communist sympathy—and ran through the French positions, shouting "Beat it! Beat it!" By the evening of the thirteenth, there was a German bridgehead on the western bank of the Meuse at Dinant, and a second, more threatening lodgment downriver, around Sedan. The exhausted French troops in the eighty-four-kilometer gap between the two towns spent the night of May 13–14 listening to the intermittent shellfire from the Germans' side of the river and wondering what the morning would bring.

When Captain Beaufre arrived at the headquarters of the Northeast Command at 3:00 a.m. on May 14, General Alphonse Georges, commander of the northern front, was seated in a cone of light under a chandelier in a huge salon. Georges's gloved left hand, paralyzed during an assassination attempt in 1934, hung limply at his side; his right hand, a good, strong soldier's hand, was tracing the gap in the Meuse front on a table map. Behind him, a group of senior commanders were following the hand's progress across the map from Dinant to Sedan. In the gap between the two towns, several hundred thousand French soldiers awaited orders from this room, yet except for the muted voice of the general describing the situation along the river, and the chirping of the crickets outside in the spring darkness, the salon was quiet. Beaufre was surprised. He had expected to hear telephones ringing, clerks shouting—the pandemonium of a command in crisis. The quiet continued for a few moments. Then, abruptly, Georges rose from the map table and announced: "Our front ha[s] been pushed in at Sedan." His soldier's discipline broke, and he fell into a chair and "a sob silence[d] him."

Twelve hours later, Churchill received an urgent call from Reynaud, who requested that an additional ten RAF fighter squadrons be sent to France "at once, if possible today." (A squadron contains twelve to twenty-four aircraft.) Churchill hesitated. A new Air Staff report estimated that sixty fighter squadrons would be necessary "for the adequate defense of this country," and the chief of the Air Staff, Cyril Newall, believed that if Holland fell and the Luftwaffe could operate from bases on the Dutch coast, even sixty squadrons might be insufficient. The Air Staff report also contained another important number: twenty-nine. That was the number of fighter squadrons currently available for home defense. If ten squadrons were sent to France, Churchill knew there was a good chance that most of them would never see Britain again. The wastage rate in the combat zone was ferocious. In the past four days, the RAF had lost almost two hundred planes, including more than half the seventy British bombers sent to attack the German lodgment at Sedan. He sent Reynaud a soothing but ambiguous reply: "No time is being lost in studying what we can do to meet the situation."

Later that evening, in a conversation with Ambassador Kennedy, Churchill became the supplicant. Britain, which ended the First World War with 433 destroyers, had entered the Second World War with 200, and the night Kennedy visited, seven of them were sitting at the bottom of Norwegian fjords under a thin sheet of spring ice, and four others had been so badly damaged in the campaign, their future as fighting ships was in question. As the British destroyer fleet shrunk and the U-boat threat rose, Churchill had fixed his attention on the United States. At the beginning of the war, 170 American destroyers had been in drydock or otherwise out of action; 68 had since been returned to active duty, but that still left 102 destroyers unemployed. Churchill wanted the United States to loan Britain 40 or 50 of the old destroyers for convoy duty.

However, the road to Washington led through Joe Kennedy,

and few men were more ill equipped to understand Churchill, a romantic if there ever was one (in the old-fashioned sense of having an emotional attraction to the heroic), than Joe Kennedy, a man without a romantic bone in his body. In a cable to Roosevelt after the meeting, Kennedy argued against the destroyer request. "I asked [Churchill] . . . what could we do if we wanted to help you all we can? . . . The bulk of our navy is in the Pacific, and we have not enough planes for our own use and our army is not up to requirements. So if this is going to be a quick war, all over in a few months, what could we do?" Unusually, in this instance, Kennedy confined his observations about Churchill's personal behavior to his private diary. "I couldn't help but think how ill conditioned Churchill looked and the fact that there was a tray with plenty of liquor on it alongside him and he was drinking a Scotch highball, which I felt was indeed not the first one he had drunk that night. . . . The affairs of Great Britain might be in the hands of the most dynamic individual in Great Britain, but certainly not in the hands of the best judgment in Great Britain."

The next morning Reynaud called again. This time he sounded hysterical. "We are beaten. We have lost the battle." The official French communiqué for May 15 was more restrained, but for the half of Paris who had lived through the Great War as adults, the use of the phrase "particularly desperate" to describe the fighting around Sedan and Dinant evoked memories of September 1914 and the news that the Germans had reached the Marne, only eighty-seven miles east of the capital. But if the experience of war had taught Parisians anything, it was that, in the shadow of the apocalypse, the only way to retain one's sanity was to live in the moment. That afternoon Picasso and his "jealous, dark mistress" could still be found seated at their usual table at Café Flores; statues of an Aberdeen terrier urinating on a copy of *Mein Kampf* continued to fly off the shelves of the stores on the rue de Rivoli;

there were Punch-and-Judy shows in the parks, honking taxicabs on the streets. "The air was sweet, the unstartled birds sang," and the laughter of children sang through the Bois and Luxembourg Gardens. Still, in the back of everyone's mind was the awareness that, 130 miles to the east, French soldiers were marching into captivity, hands over their heads, the "dim candle of fear burning in their eyes." At six that evening, Reynaud called Churchill again: "The road to Paris is open. Send us all [the] aircraft and troops you can."

The next morning (May 16), when Panzer units reached Laon, a town seventy-five miles east of Paris, General Gamelin announced that as of midnight he would disclaim any responsibility for the safety of the capital. Gamelin's decision was kept quiet, but the rumors about Laon could not be suppressed. Walking to the National Assembly at 10:30 a.m., Achille Bardoux, a French senator, thought "Paris seemed normal." When Bardoux left the Assembly at a quarter past twelve, the Laon rumor was everywhere and the atmosphere in the city had become "frantic." The police were requisitioning buses in the streets; soldiers were unloading antitank guns from flatbed trucks outside the Bois. The railway stations were under siege by the frightened, the desperate, the determined, and the hopeless; and police with tommy guns patrolled the streets. At Galeries Lafayette, there was a run on walking shoes and suitcases. And at the headquarters of the French High Command in the Paris suburb of Vincennes, a group of young secretaries was taken out to the courtyard in their summer dresses and shown how to load and fire a 75-millimeter cannon. A visiting French staff officer wondered if the High Command had "completely lost their heads." Inside the main headquarters building, General Gamelin, who had delegated the closing of the broken Meuse front to his subordinates, sat in his office, "sad and unoccupied."

At midday, Reynaud called an emergency meeting at the Quai d'Orsay and summoned General Pierre Héring, the military governor of Paris; Roger Langeron, the prefect of police; Édouard Daladier, the minister of defense; Jules Jeanneney, the leader of the French Senate; and Édouard Herriot, the leader of the Chamber of Deputies. When the meeting convened at 1:00 p.m., the French bureaucracy had already answered the first question the officials addressed: Could Paris be saved? Outside the window, enormous columns of black smoke were billowing skyward from courtyards in the government quarter. None of the defense measures proposed at the meeting would have extinguished the fires. One involved sending a flotilla of shallow-bottomed warships up the Seine to Paris to bombard the Germans; another involved blowing up French factories, though how that would save the capital was never clearly explained. General Héring seemed to interject a note of reality into the discussion when he described his plan for defending Paris; but then he admitted that he did not have enough explosives to implement the plan. The second question the officials addressed—should the government evacuate Paris?—produced a sharp exchange between Reynaud, who had already drawn up a plan to evacuate the government to Tours, a town 149 miles south of the capital, and Daladier, who believed the evacuation of Paris would have a devastating effect on national morale. The two men argued back and forth until another minister, Anatole de Monzie, pointed out that they were arguing about nothing. There was not enough transportation available in Paris to support a large-scale evacuation.

In London, May 16 also began with troubling news. Earlier in the morning, a "very seriously alarmed" Reynaud had told Ronald Campbell, the British ambassador, that German armored units could be in the capital by nightfall. There were also reports that some French units were abandoning their positions on the Dyle line and retreating westward behind Brussels. Churchill, who found the Belgian news "extremely grave," proposed that "he himself should go to France that very afternoon" and assess the situation personally. As his fat-bodied De Havilland Flamingo rose into the London sky at 3:00 p.m., Reynaud was addressing the French National Assembly. "We shall fight before Paris; we shall fight in Paris if need be," he declared.

An hour later the Flamingo was circling above the runways of Le Bourget Aerodrome, which cut diagonally across a sprawl of suburban homes and stores. Off in the distance, the Eiffel Tower stood, serene and confident in the clear air of the day. The mood at Le Bourget was neither of those things. As General Hastings Ismay, who had been appointed Churchill's chief military adviser, was walking into the reception area, Colonel Harold Redman, head of the British military mission at Gamelin's headquarters, pulled him aside and said that Paris could fall within the next few days. Ismay was "flabbergasted." "They never got here last time in four years. . . . You will find things are different this time," Redman said. Stepping out of the Flamingo, Churchill immediately sensed that the situation was "incomparably worse than we imagined."

When the British party arrived at the Quai d'Orsay, Reynaud, Daladier, and Gamelin were already seated in the conference room, where the meeting was to be held. The expression of "complete dejection" on each man's face said all that needed to be said. "The French High Command is already beaten," Ismay thought. Like the Halifax-Churchill meeting on May 11, there are several versions of the Allied summit at Quai d'Orsay on May 16. Churchill has "everybody standing," Reynaud has everybody "seated," and a number of the incidents mentioned in the French accounts are absent from the British and vice versa. However, everyone agrees that a situation map rested on an easel in the meeting room and that the most dominant feature of the map was the "small but sinister bulge" that extended from Sedan to Laon. After Churchill said a few words, Gamelin placed himself in front of the easel and "like a good lecturer . . . gave an admirable discourse, clear and calm, on the military situation. . . . His ladylike hand marked here and there on the map the positions of our broken units and our reserves. . . . He explained but he made no suggestions. He had no view on the future." This account by Paul Baudouin, Reynaud's *chef de cabinet*, also includes the observation that during the lecture, Daladier, the general's chief patron, "sat in the corner like a schoolboy in disgrace."

The room was quiet for a moment after Gamelin finished. Then Churchill asked how large the French Army's strategic reserve was. Gamelin shrugged and said: *"Aucun"* (none).

"Aucun?"

Churchill got up and walked to the window. The French bureaucracy was still in the grip of pyromania. Below, in the courtyard, "venerable officials [were] pushing wheelbarrels of archives into [large bonfires]." Gazing down at the scene, Churchill realized that no matter what the French said about defending Paris, they were preparing to evacuate the capital. When he returned to the table, Gamelin was saying that he intended to abandon the Dyle line and fall back behind Brussels. The general concluded his presentation with an interesting new hypothesis. He said that the Channel coast, not Paris, might be the German objective. A German corridor between the Meuse and the sea would cut the Allied army in half and trap the French and British units in Belgium, the best equipped and trained Allied troops, in a giant pocket, where they could be destroyed piecemeal. Gamelin's new hypothesis also explained the mysterious absence of the Luftwaffe during the march up to the Dyle: the French and British were being lured into a trap.

Reynaud, who spoke next, disagreed with his general. The German target is Paris, he said, pointing to the "sinister" red bulge. "I assure you that in this bulge there is at stake not only the fate of France but also that of the British Empire." Reynaud repeated the sentence for emphasis.

Churchill turned to Gamelin: "When and where [did the general] propose to attack the flanks of the bulge?"

Gamelin shrugged. "Inferiority of numbers, inferiority of equipment, and inferiority of method." Outside, columns of smoke were still rising into the early evening sky. Churchill got up and walked over to the window again. "The old gentlemen were [still] bringing up their wheelbarrows and industriously casting their contents into the flames."

A debate about the air war brought the meeting to an acrimonious conclusion. The previous day (May 15), the RAF had sent four of the ten squadrons Reynaud had requested. Now the premier was insisting that the other six were needed immediately to stop an expected German drive on Paris. Churchill refused. The twenty-nine RAF fighter squadrons still in Britain "were the life of the country and guarded our vitals from attack. We must conserve them." As the evening wore on, however, another consideration began to press on Churchill. The German attack on Paris would give the French Army "a last chance to rally its bravery and strength. It would not be good historically if [French] requests were denied and their ruin resulted." Later that evening, he sent the war cabinet a cable endorsing the French request for the additional squadrons. In Downing Street, minds accustomed to the dry, crisp minutes of British officialdom read the prime minister's rich, rolling Gibbonesque prose with mounting surprise and alarm. The "moral gravity of the hour"; "allow France to find her bravery and strength." As he scanned the cable, an aide said, "Churchill is still thinking of his books." "Blasted rhetoric!" said another. John Colville was too transfixed by the "terrifying" math in the cable to notice the prime minister's prose. On May 14 alone, the RAF had lost seventy-one planes. Now Churchill was proposing to pledge a quarter of Fighter Command's remaining aircraft to France, and the only safeguard imposed on this precious gift was that six of the newly pledged squadrons would operate from bases in southern England.

At about ten, the war cabinet telegraphed its assent to Churchill in Hindustani. Ismay, an old India hand, had suggested the idea, knowing the language would befuddle the German code breakers. As the teletype machine printed out *"h-a-n"*—Hindustani for "yes"—Churchill decided he must tell Reynaud the good news in person and commandeered Ismay for driving duties. The city the two men drove through that night was engulfed in a "wind of panic." The singing of drunken soldiers echoed through the blacked-out streets; in the crowded railway stations, passengers strained to hear the departure announcements over the crying of children and the shouts of the gendarmes; and on the westbound roads, drivers stood next to their automobiles in the spring darkness, wondering whether the traffic would move before the dive bombers returned at first light.

In Reynaud's quarter, one of the wealthiest in Paris, there was no sign of expectant life behind the shuttered windows above the deserted streets. Most of the residents were in Brittany, Provence, or another province far from the war, and those who remained were observing the blackout. At Reynaud's apartment, Churchill and Ismay were greeted by a maid, who said that the premier was in the bedroom and deposited the English visitors in a sitting room. Ismay noticed that a woman's coat was slung over one of the chairs. Presently, Reynaud appeared in a dressing gown, and Churchill received his grateful smile. Phone calls were made, the doorbell began to ring, and the apartment filled with cigarette smoke, the clink of glasses, and French and English voices. Daladier, who arrived at about midnight, clasped Churchill's hands in his when he was told that France would receive the additional six squadrons. But the restorative effect of the British gift was short-lived. A half hour later, Daladier was slouched in a chair, looking "crushed and bowed down with grief." One guest described Reynaud as looking "like some small broken piece of machinery."

"You must not lose heart," Churchill told him, then launched into a remarkable soliloquy about honor, redemption, and Armageddon. "Crowned like a volcano by the smoke of his cigars," said the poet laureate of May 16, Paul Baudouin. Churchill told his French colleagues "that even if France was invaded and vanquished, England would go on fighting until the United States came to her aid, which she would soon do in no halfhearted manner. . . . Until one in the morning, he conjured up an apocalyptic vision of the war. He saw himself in the heart of Canada, directing over an England razed to the ground by high-explosive bombs and over a France whose ruins were already cold, the air war of the New World against the Old dominated by Germany."

Returning to London the next morning, General Ismay was comforted by the orderliness and calm on the streets. The city "seemed like a much loved old nanny gathering me to her bosom and saying: 'Don't fuss and budget, dearie, it will all come out all right.'" Ismay's observations said more about his state of mind than the state of British morale. That comforting old cliché—Britain loses every battle except the last one, a cliché that had sustained the nation through two centuries of crises—was losing its power to reassure. Holland, Belgium, France: what a French officer had said about the Allied campaign in Norway seemed even truer now. Against the German Army, the French and British were "the Zulus." "We are living in a new phase of history, the course of which no man can foresee," General Ironside wrote. "Nobody believed that we should be in a war, certainly not in a death struggle, so soon. We made no preparations, even for a war industry . . . and we cannot catch up now. It is too late. The year may yet see us beaten." That thought had also occurred to many ordinary Britons. On May 13, the day the Germans breached the French defenses on the Meuse, two workmen in the yard below Muriel Green's home were discussing the possibility of a German invasion. Two weeks earlier, Muriel would have considered such talk seditious. Now most of the people she knew—friends, family, even her deliveryman—were expecting a German invasion, or something worse. During a tennis match at a local park, Muriel overheard the deliveryman say to his partner, "I think they are going to beat us, don't you?" "Yes," the partner replied, but "if they do win, [we'll] still be able to play tennis.'" The Nazis were sports enthusiasts. In Norfolk, a housewife told an official from Mass Observation, "Oh Lord. This is serious. I think we are going to lose the war."

During the third week of May, Mass Observation and the Home Intelligence Service, a new survey organization, both noted a dramatic change in the public mood. Unmoored from the old certainties and assumptions about British power, people were cycling daily, sometimes hourly, from anxiety to optimism to pessimism to bewilderment, depending on the latest news from France. On May 18 the *Evening Standard* proposed an antidote to the unsteadiness. The paper urged readers to embrace a belief in ultimate victory, though, as the title of the *Standard*'s editorial, "Faith," acknowledged, at present there was almost nothing to sustain that belief but faith. Public perceptions of Hitler were also changing. The old view of the Führer as a clownish Charlie Chaplin figure had been washed away by the remarkable German victories in France and the Low Countries; in place of the clown there was now a wizard. Mass Observation reported that many people had developed an "autosubconscious tendency to think of Hitler as wonderful" and of his advances "as inevitable." Mass Observation noted that women, in particular, were inclined to view Hitler as "a somewhat mystical astrological figure" who does whatever he says he will do. Proof of the observation came when the *Evening Standard* published a cartoon of Hitler peering across the English Channel from a tour bus emblazoned with the placard "London, August 18." The cartoon, intended to ridicule Hitler's invasion threat, had "precisely the opposite" effect, noted Mass Observation. Anti-American feeling was also growing. On the Dover–London train, an MO official overheard a man reduce his fellow passengers to giggles with the latest joke about the Americans. "A Yank ship left the other day," the man said. "You know what it was called? *Gone with the Wind.*"

Churchill briefly discussed morale at the war cabinet on May 17, but mostly he talked about France. He had been deeply impressed by the pessimistic atmosphere in Paris the day before, and saw little prospect of a sudden French revival. Gamelin and Daladier were "depressed"; the French Air Force had been reduced to a quarter of its preoffensive strength; and the French Army was showing signs of instability. There was no talk of a French defeat that morning, but in the days that followed Churchill began to act like a man who believed it had become a serious possibility. He suspended all further aircraft deliveries to France, ordered Britain's domestic defenses strengthened, had an emergency evacuation plan drawn up for the BEF, and requested an "emergency powers" bill that would give the government "totalitarian powers."

He also approached Roosevelt again. The president, who had said no to his first request for the loan of forty or fifty destroyers for convoy duty, said no again, citing congressional opposition and US naval needs in the Pacific. But domestic concerns were not the only reason for Roosevelt's reluctance on the destroyer issue. The president's personal knowledge of Churchill was limited to the letters the two men had exchanged since the beginning of the war. Most of what Roosevelt knew about Churchill he got secondhand from the reports of officials in his administration, and much of it concerned Churchill's alcohol consumption. Joe Kennedy frequently enlivened his cables to Washington with colorful descriptions of Churchill's drinking; but, aware of Kennedy's defeatism, Roosevelt did not attach much importance to the ambassador's views. Roosevelt did listen to Adolf Berle, a strait-laced corporate lawyer who was an assistant secretary of state, and to Sumner Welles, also an assistant secretary of state. On May 5, five days before Churchill became prime minister, Berle wrote: "The rumor . . . going around here is that [Churchill] is drunk all the time. Welles says on the first two evenings he saw Churchill, he was quite drunk. I asked [Welles] whether he saw any indications of clear cut leadership [in Churchill] and Welles answered that he saw none." Over the summer, Churchill's heroic leadership would put Roosevelt's reservations about his drinking to rest, but not the president's reservations about bringing the US into the war. Roosevelt knew it would take a year or more to train and equip an American army up to a European standard; and like Lincoln, who waited for the South to fire the first shot, he may have felt the only way to ensure a divided America entered the war united was to await an unprovoked attack by Germany or Japan.

"Victory! Victory at all costs!" Churchill's war policy had a thrilling ring to it; it was almost an epic poem in itself. But was it a realistic policy for a nation with a small endangered army (which could mobilize only ten divisions for the defense of France) and an overextended navy—a fragile empire with an ally who had begun the war with more than ninety divisions and whose surrender would remove from battle a force that was still many times larger than Britain's? Chamberlain and Lord Halifax, who thought in prose, not poetry, believed it was not. While Churchill was in Paris, Chamberlain told Joe Kennedy that without France, an Allied victory was impossible. The next day, in a conversation with Sam Hoare, the air minister, Chamberlain sounded even more defeatist. Hoare told friends that Chamberlain was claiming that "everything [was] finished," that "the USA [was] no good," and that "we could never get our army out, or if we did, it would be without equipment." General Ironside was also pessimistic about Britain's prospects if France fell. "Could we maintain the Air Struggle?" he wrote in his diary after the cabinet meeting on May 17. "Could we get enough machines to continue? Could we keep our industry going under Nazi bombardment from so close as Holland and the Channel ports? Could I get enough of the B.E.F., men and equipment, back to England to ensure security against air invasion?" The *Evening Standard*'s May 18 editorial "Faith" was well timed. That was also the day it became clear that Gamelin's hypothesis was correct: The Germans planned to trap and destroy the British and French troops in the North—the cream of the Allied Army—before turning on Paris. "A miracle may save us," Alex Cadogan wrote. "Otherwise we're done."

By the third week of May, several leading members of the old British ruling class—men who bore historic titles such as the Duke of Wellington, the Duke of Westminster, the Duke of Buccleuch, and Lord Tavistock—were quietly agitating for a compromise peace. "If the Germans received fair peace terms, a dozen Hitlers could never start another war," Tavistock insisted. Indeed, in the House of Lords, the political home of the old ruling class, appeasers were so thick on the ground that before giving an address to the Upper House in mid-May, Lord Hanky said he would be speaking to "most of the members of the Fifth Column" in Britain. In addition to Lloyd George, who still appeared to be holding himself in readiness to parley with the Germans, the list of prominent commoners who favored a compromise peace included Richard Stokes, an influential Labour businessman; and the thirty MPs and ten peers who belonged to the Stokes group and who, like Stokes, looked to Lloyd George to negotiate an end to the war. Other opponents of Churchill's "Victory at all costs!" policy included Basil Liddel Hart, the most influential British military writer of the interwar years; Montagu Norman, governor of the Bank of England; the prominent actors John Gielgud and Sybil Thorndike; the playwright George Bernard Shaw; and a significant minority of ordinary Britons. In April, Mass Observation estimated that 10 percent of the population continued to oppose the war, but in some localities the percentage was higher. In early May, a pacifist candidate named Annie Maxton won a surprising 25 percent of the vote in a solidly conservative Scottish constituency, running under a slogan that slyly mocked the bellicosity of her opponent, a retired army major:

"1918, Never Again, 1940, Oh yeah!"

However, only the two "wise old elephants"—Chamberlain and Halifax—were in a position to influence British war policy. Both men were prepared to keep fighting even if France fell, if the only alternative was unconditional surrender and a German occupation. But was that the only alternative? While Chamberlain was prepared to explore the question, it was Halifax who—untainted by a recent political disgrace—emerged as the principal spokesman for testing the possibilities of a compromise peace. With everything Britain possessed, the work of centuries at stake;

with the life of the nation at stake, the foreign secretary felt it was the duty of the war cabinet to do so. This put him at odds with Churchill, who felt Hitler and the German aggression had put everything Britain stood for in the world at stake. Thus were set the terms for one of the most historic debates of the twentieth century.

CHAPTER EIGHT

A CERTAIN EVENTUALITY

On the morning of May 19, a British staff officer, sturdy of build and hard of eye, arrived in Dunkirk, a resort town on the Franco-Belgian border. Normally, at this time of year, the local shops and beaches would be crowded with tourists from Brussels and Lille, but the morning General Henry Pownall arrived, the only civilians in view were a packet of refugees huddled near the Leughenaer, a medieval tower and, in better times, a popular tourist attraction. The Luftwaffe had been over at first light, and the refugees were scavenging through the rubble of a bombed-out building for foodstuffs and household goods. Most of the scavengers had been on the road for days and looked it. They were unwashed and exhausted, but even in their present disheveled state notably better dressed than the Chinese, Spanish, and Polish refugees who had been tramping through newsreels for the past decade. That was one of the novelties of war in middle-class countries—well-dressed refugees. When Pownall's staff car arrived at the French command post near the harbor, silos of angry black clouds were billowing up from the docks—another reminder of the Luftwaffe's early morning visit. A French soldier at the gate examined Pownall's ID, then waved him through. When his staff car stopped at a communication center a few hundred feet away, Pownall was still rehearsing what he would tell the War Office.

During the first days of the German offensive, the French and

Belgians had borne the weight of the battle and had sustained casualties commensurate with that distinction. Then, in the second week, the German trap snapped shut, and the BEF, which had suffered only five hundred casualties in the first seven days of fighting, found itself confronted with the prospect of annihilation. One German army was approaching from the east, another from the south. "I am afraid I am not at all feeling optimistic today," Sir John Gort, the BEF's commander, wrote his wife on the morning of the nineteenth. Then he dispatched Pownall, his chief of staff, to Dunkirk, the nearest town still in telephone contact with London. When the director of military operations came on the line, Pownall said Gort wanted to retreat to Dunkirk and "fight it out with his back to the sea." The word "evacuation" was not mentioned, but Gort's request to fall back to a Channel port indicated that that is what he had in mind.

Until Pownall's call, the prime minister's Sunday had been relatively peaceful. When Mrs. Churchill came home complaining about the pacifist sermon her vicar had preached, Churchill briefly lost his temper and bellowed, "You ought to have cried, 'Shame, desecrating the House of God with lies!'" But then the soothing rhythms of a Sunday morning reasserted themselves, and the prime minister's mind filled with thoughts of Chartwell, his country house in Kent. A few hours later, he was standing by a pond on the estate, about to feed a bag of ant eggs to his one remaining black swan—the local foxes had claimed the others—when the phone rang in the main house. It was an indication of the concern Pownall's call had aroused at the War Office that the police car sent to pick up Churchill ran all the red lights between Chartwell and London and kept the siren on for the entire trip.

General Ironside's day had also been disrupted by the Pownall call. Two plans had been drawn up to meet the eventuality facing the BEF: the one that Gort favored, an evacuation by sea, and the one Ironside favored, the BEF fights its way out of the northern pocket and rejoins the Allied armies to the south. Even a successful evacuation would be costly, Ironside knew. Most of the BEF's heavy equipment—tanks, trucks, and artillery guns and probably most of its troops—would have to be abandoned on the beaches. The political consequences of an evacuation would also be tremendous. The French would cry "betrayal!" and "perfidious Albion!" American skepticism about an Allied victory would deepen, and opinion in the dominions, Canada, Australia, South Africa, and New Zealand, would be badly shaken. When the war cabinet convened that afternoon, Churchill endorsed Ironside's view. A BEF retreat to the south would put the Belgian Army on the British flank in jeopardy, he acknowledged; however, this was no time for sentimentality. Britain was in a war of national survival, and "we should do [the Belgians] no service by sacrificing our army."

That evening, in a radio broadcast, Churchill returned to the theme of national survival.

I speak to you for the first time as Prime Minister in a solemn hour for our country, for our Empire, for our Allies, and, above all, for the cause of freedom. A tremendous battle is raging in France and Flanders. The Germans . . . have broken through the French defenses north of the Maginot Line, and strong columns of their armored vehicles . . . have penetrated deeply and spread alarm and confusion. Behind them are now appearing infantry columns, and behind them again the large masses are moving forward. We must expect that . . . soon . . . the bulk of that hideous apparatus of aggression . . . will be turned on us. . . .

Centuries ago words were written to be a call and a spur to

the faithful servants of Truth and Justice: "Arm yourself and be ye men of valour, and be in readiness for the conflict; for it is better for us to perish in battle than to look upon the outrage of our nation and our altar. As the Will of God is in Heaven so let it be."

The next morning, when Ironside arrived at Gort's headquarters in northern France, he was reassured by the sense of good order in the camp—staff officers darting into and out of tents, the other ranks assembling for breakfast, mess kits in hand. Except for the faint rumble of artillery fire from the north, the only sounds heard were the low murmurs of morning voices and birdsong from a grove of trees near the mess tent. Inside the headquarters building, a note card tacked to a door announced: "Office of C-in-C." When Ironside entered, John Standish Surtees Prendergast Vereker, the sixth Viscount Gort, was seated behind a makeshift desk—a plank supported by two trestles—examining a map. Gort had as many medals as he had names (six), a mixed reputation as a commander, and the distinction of being among the handful of men who could lose the war for Britain in a week. The BEF not only represented the flower of the British army but also "its root, branch, and stem." Its destruction would leave no cadre of experienced officers and NCOs to train the new conscript army; of more urgent importance, it would leave no cadre of trained men to meet a German invasion.

After explaining the advantages of a breakout, Ironside asked Gort if he saw the plan as a "possible solution." Gort said he did not. Most of the BEF was heavily engaged behind Brussels. "A withdrawal south . . . however desirable in principle, was not in the circumstances practical." The most Gort would commit to was a limited attack south by two divisions. As Ironside was leaving, Gort said he still favored his "last alternative." Events were quickly making that alternative—evacuation—the only alternative. On the morning of the twentieth the Panzer columns that breached the Meuse a week earlier reached the Channel. From one end of France to the other, a fifteen-mile-wide German corridor filled with tanks, tank destroyers, mobile artillery units, and infantry divisions now separated the Allied armies in the north from those in the south. The next day the Panzers would swing north and drive up the coast. A week hence, the Channel ports of Boulogne and Calais would be in flames, and suntanned German soldiers would be posing for newsreel cameras in front of abandoned British tanks with names such as "Excalibur," "Valiant," and "Indomitable." Two weeks hence, the newsreels would be flickering across movie screens in the United States, Sweden, Argentina, and other neutral nations.

On May 22, Reynaud appointed two Great War heroes to his government. He introduced Philippe Pétain, who needed no introduction, to a somber National Assembly as "the Victor of Verdun," and General Maxime Weygand, who had been recalled from North Africa to replace Gamelin, as the man "who had halted the German onslaught . . . in 1918." Pétain's remit was to restore public confidence in the Reynaud government; Weygand's, to reproduce the "Miracle on the Marne," the Allied victory that had checked the German drive on Paris in 1914. A military miracle was a great deal to ask of a seventy-three-year-old man; but as the small, physically elegant Weygand lost no opportunity to demonstrate, he was not a typical seventy-three-year-old. On his first day as commander in chief, he astonished the staff at Vincennes, by bounding down a flight of stairs, four at a time, then vaulting out to the lawn and running a hundred-yard dash. "Instead of ectoplasm, we [have] a man!" exclaimed one young French captain.

Churchill was no less impressed by France's miraculous septuagenarian. "The only fault with you—you are too young," he told the general when he visited Vincennes on the afternoon of the twenty-second to be briefed on the "Weygand plan." In a swift, daring pincer movement, the general planned to reunite the Allied armies in the north and south and to blunt the Panzer spearhead by punching a hole through the German corridor. "At the earliest moment—certainly tomorrow," the British and French units in the northern pocket would attack southward into the corridor and "join hands" with a new French Army group of eighteen to twenty divisions, attacking northward from bases outside the pocket. In London, reaction to the Weygand plan ran the gamut. Churchill was excited. "Provided the French fought well, there seemed a good prospect of success," he told the war cabinet. Ironside was lukewarm. "When it came down to things, the plan was still all *projets* [projects]." Gort hated the plan. Upon receiving a copy, he exploded, "How is an attack like this . . . to be staged in an hour's notice?. . . . The man [Churchill] is mad. I suppose these figments of the imagination are telegraphed without consulting his advisers." Alec Cadogan of the Foreign Office suspended judgment. "Counter offensive should start tomorrow," he wrote in his diary on the night of the twenty-second. "But will the French fight?"

The next day Churchill called Paris several times to inquire about the progress of the Weygand offensive, but he was unable to get a clear answer. No one seemed to know what had happened to the eighteen to twenty divisions the general had promised for the attack in the south. Finally, a little before five, Churchill called Reynaud and said that perhaps it would be "better if the British army fought in retreat toward the coast." *"We must go on!"* [italics in original] Reynaud insisted. An hour later, Weygand called Churchill. The attack was not only in progress, the general said; three key towns—Amiens, Albert, and Perrone—had been recaptured. Weygand was even more expansive in a conversation with Ironside. Not only had Amiens, Albert, and Perrone been recaptured, but also "the maneuver was continuing under good conditions." The most charitable thing that can be said about Weygand's report is that it was wildly misleading. As yet, Churchill had no way of knowing that, but he seemed to sense the general was dissembling—maybe a little, maybe a great deal. He could not be sure yet, but during a visit to Buckingham Palace on the evening of the twenty-third, he told the king that an evacuation of the BEF by sea might still be necessary.

"I suppose you're pretty busy just now, plenty of people sailing and all that." It was the morning of May 23, and a British officer on his way to Calais was talking to a transport sergeant in Portsmouth Harbor. "Not many sailing," the sergeant said, "but they'll be plenty coming home. If you ask me, [your] regiment is going the wrong way." Of the three Channel ports with the facilities to support a large-scale evacuation, Boulogne was only a few hours away from falling on the morning of the twenty-third, and Calais, nineteen miles north of Boulogne, maybe a day or two away. British soldiers were shooting French soldiers in cellars; decomposing bodies were stacked like cordwood under billboards for Dior perfumes and Renault automobiles; and panicked refugees were pushing cars into the harbor. At 3:00 a.m. on the morning of the twenty-fourth, Brigadier Claude Nicholson, the British commander in Calais, was notified that his units would be evacuated "when you have finished unloading MTs [motor transports]." A few hours later, the evacuation was postponed. Calais would be defended to buy time for the BEF's last potential evacuation site, Dunkirk.

"The final debacle cannot be long delayed," General Ironside wrote when the news from Calais came through. No "more than a minute portion of the BEF . . . [can be evacuated and they will have to abandon] all the equipment we are so short of in this country. . . . We shall have lost practically all our trained soldiers in the next few days unless a miracle appears to help us. . . . Horrible days we live through."

The loss of the BEF was one of the two existential threats facing Britain in the final week of May 1940. The other was a French surrender. Churchill first realized that that had become a serious possibility during his visit to Paris on May 16. Those old gentlemen in the courtyard of the Quai d'Orsay were not burning documents to keep warm. Upon returning to London, he asked Chamberlain to form a study group to examine "the situation in which we might find ourselves obliged to continue our resistance single handed in this country." Inside of that tortured sentence was a simple question: what resources would Britain require to carry on the battle alone? The Chamberlain study group took only twenty-four hours to arrive at an answer. Britain would need massive amounts of American aid and a "form of government which would approach totalitarian."

On May 25, the Chiefs of Staff also presented the war cabinet with an appreciation of Britain's prospects in an Anglo-German war. Called *British Strategy in a Certain Eventuality* (the eventuality being the fall of France), the report had the same lineage as Chamberlain's study. It grew out of a request by Churchill, who gave the chiefs the same remit he had given Chamberlain: examine the resources Britain would need to carry on the war alone. However, *Eventuality* was so intelligent and comprehensive, it indirectly answered a question Churchill had reserved for himself: *should* Britain continue to pursue war on its own?

Eventuality opened on an apocalyptic note. Upon the collapse of France, it asserted, "the main objective of German policy [would be] the rapid elimination of resistance in the United Kingdom," either by:

(a) unrestricted air attack aimed at breaking down public morale;

(b) starvation of this country by attack on shipping and ports;

(c) occupation of the United Kingdom by invasion.

Or by some combination of the three.

"From the very first weeks of a French collapse," the report noted, "the United Kingdom and its sea approaches will be exposed at short range to the concentrated attack of the whole of the German Naval and Air Forces operating from bases extending from Norway to the North West of France." In the event that Germany chose the third option, a land invasion, the thirteen and a half British divisions—all but three partially trained and partially equipped—available for home defense would face an invasion force of seventy or more well-armed German divisions. *Eventuality* came to two conclusions about Britain's prospects. The first: In the long term Britain did not have "any chance of success" unless "the United States of America is willing to give us full economic and financial support." The second conclusion addressed Britain's short-term prospects. In the year or so it would take the United States to mobilize its war machine, four factors would determine national survival. These were:

(a) "whether the morale of our people will withstand the strain of air bombardment;

(b) "whether it will be possible to import the absolute essential minimum of commodities necessary to sustain life and keep our war industries in action;

(c) "our capacity to resist invasion;

(d) "whether our fighter defense are able to reduce the scale of attack."

The four standards provided a reasonably objective way to assess whether Britain possessed the capacity to bear the struggle alone for an extended period. In the Chiefs' view, if morale held, the RAF maintained air superiority over the home island, and their other criterion were met, there was a good chance Britain would still be standing when the US, the dominions, and the empire were fully mobilized. The dangers enumerated in *Eventuality* also left little doubt about Britain's fate if the criterion could not be met.

The British people knew nothing of *Eventuality*, of course, but the human mind can understand without knowing. And the desperate battles in Calais and Boulogne, the sound of the heavy guns echoing across the Channel, the new wave of evacuations to the countryside, the tank traps and parachute traps, the suddenly vanished road signs, the sixty-year-old privates and corporals guarding checkpoints all said the situation was desperate. Even many committed optimists were shaken by the *Evening Standard*'s change of tune in a May 24 editorial. "Faith" in ultimate victory was apparently no longer sufficient. "Prepare for the worst," the paper counseled. The war felt very near now, and the danger, personal. Mass Observation's morale report of May 24 spoke of rumors of midnight German parachute landings and fifth columnists, of secret weapons caches, and of last good-byes. Henry Channon, determined to preserve his diaries for posterity, buried them in a local churchyard. One trend MO failed to pick up was the funny tricks the war was playing on people's minds. Attending a memorial service for a friend on May 23, Vera Brittain imagined herself at a requiem for "European civilization, suicidally destroying itself and now unable to arrest the fearful tide of slaughter," while Margery Allingham found herself unable to compose a simple letter anymore. Would the person Margery was writing to still be alive when the letter arrived? Would Margery still be alive when her letter arrived? The questions put her in a terrible muddle.

Nonetheless, public expressions of fear remained rare. On the afternoon of May 24, Chiswick High Street in southwestern London was crowded with shoppers and young mothers gossiping in outdoor cafés; Margate, with day-trippers; and the lawns of Hyde Park, with secretaries, their skirts rolled up to their knees to catch the noonday sun. At kiosks and newsstands across Britain, twelve- and thirteen-year-old boys ogled "Jane," the *Daily Express*'s pretty young secret agent (depicted in the cartoon of that name) who daily saved the British Empire in her underwear. Visiting Regents Park in London, one woman was surprised by the prewar atmosphere. "A few elderly people . . . sit on chairs, a few young ones sailing in boats with striped sails . . . a vast green field very vivid." It's just like a prewar Sunday, she told her husband. As the summer progressed, the propagandists at the Ministry of Information would weave the tranquil parks, the sunning secretaries, and the Margate day-trippers into a narrative of an Eternal England, where fortitude and a stiff upper lip were part of the national heritage. To Margery, that was just another example of the ministry talking out of its hat. In her village, stiff upper lips were the rule, but they reflected not an imperviousness to fear but a desperate attempt to control it. "The danger was so close, the appalling size of the smash up so apparent that the only thing to do was to do what everyone else was doing, keep . . . steady eyes front. Once you looked sideways, once you looked around, once you let your imagination out, you knew you might lose your head. Clearly the thing to do was to get yourself into a definite frame of mind and keep it, even if it made you slightly stupid."

———

On Saturday, May 25, Britain awoke to a set of alarming headlines in the *Daily Express*:

GERMAN TROOPS REPORTED IN CALAIS
SMOKE THREE MILES HIGH DRIFTS OVER THE CHANNEL

and a sermon in the *Times*:

> In every crisis of their fate, [the British people]
> Have . . . never placed their trust in
> Their strength alone. The nation is called . . . to seek
> the ultimate
> Support where our fathers sought it, from the right
> hand
> of God.

Despite the alarming headlines, the war seemed very far away during Edward Spears's flight to Paris that morning. The sea below the two-engine Blenheim was as "blue as the Mediterranean"; the sunlight on the wing, as golden as an ear of June corn. Until an RAF sergeant ordered him to "keep a sharp lookout" for enemy aircraft, Spears could almost imagine he was flying to Paris for a holiday weekend. Half an hour later, the French coast came up, and the Blenheim passed over a patchwork of neatly squared fields of gold and green, then over church steeples, rooftops, and village squares. Toward Paris, the war reappeared. The roads were pockmarked with bomb craters and dense with refugees—hundreds at first, then thousands; then, toward the western approaches to Paris, tens of thousands.

In his youth, Spears had known France as a student and soldier; later, as a businessman and politician (and, it was rumored, as an intelligence agent). This morning he was returning as Winston Churchill's personal representative to Reynaud, and he was taking up the post at a delicate moment in Anglo-French relations. Paris and London had spent the better part of the previous day blaming each other for the failure of the Weygand offensive. In the French version, the plan failed because Gort had pulled the BEF back toward the Channel coast instead of attacking the northern side of the German corridor. "Many people now quite openly blame the whole horrible fiasco on the British High Command," said Clare Boothe, who was in Paris that May. In the British version, the plan failed because the eighteen to twenty French divisions Weygand promised never materialized. The Mass Observation report for May 24 had noted a "great increase and sometimes intense violence of criticism against the French." Officially, Spears's remit was to promote Anglo-French understanding by serving as a conduit between Churchill and Reynaud; unofficially, it was to keep France in the war as long as possible.

In Paris as in London, there were barrage balloons overhead, antiaircraft guns in the parks, and sandbags surrounding government buildings. But in London it was still possible to catch glimpses of the prewar city beneath the battle dress. In Paris, it was not. The sparkle and vivacity were gone. When Spears arrived in the city at about noon on the twenty-fifth, Paris was entombed in a somber Good Friday quiet. There were no buses on the streets and barely any taxicabs. On the Seine, empty tourist boats sailed back and forth under a May sun, and on the empty quays above the river booksellers sat in collapsible chairs, napping. A good part of the city had melted away to the roads and railway stations, and the residents who remained seemed listless and depressed. Attending a prayer service at Notre Dame, the French senator Achilles Bardoux was struck by the apathy of the congregants. The "stricken and silent crowd has lost its voice so that it can no longer even sing the 'Marseillaise.' The shadow of 1870 [the year

Prussia defeated France] is spreading over the country." In a Paris
bistro, two women listening to Reynaud's radio broadcast burst
into tears and shouted *"les salauds! les salauds!"* (the bastards! the
bastards!).

Spears's first stop that afternoon was the Ministry of Defense,
where Reynaud kept an office. (Like Churchill, he was his own
defense minister.) The premier greeted Spears with an accusation: "British generals always made for harbors." Next, the
"harmonium-like" telephone on Reynaud's desk rang; after that,
it never seemed to stop ringing. Several of the calls were from the
Comtesse de Portes; several others, from favor seekers. Between
calls, Spears tried to tell a story about a childhood incident to
illustrate the dangers of Allied disunity. "Once, as a boy," he told
Reynaud, "I had seen a large cage full of rats thrown into water.
After trying madly to escape, their last choking action had been
to tear each other apart. I have never forgotten the horrible sight.
Later...I understood the lesson." It was a good story, but it would
have had a greater impact if the phone had stopped ringing and
Spears had controlled his anger. Fourteen years later, he was still
complaining about the incident in his memoirs. "The Chairman
of a reputable Board in the City of London would never allow
himself to be interrupted at a meeting where he was discussing
the price of soap. [And] here we were, when the fate of France
hung in the balance, interfered with in this way."

An hour later Spears was seated in the elegant, high-ceilinged
salon with several members of the French War Committee (the
rough equivalent of the war cabinet). The first speaker that afternoon was a feral-looking French major named Fauvelle. General
Georges Blanchard, the commander of the Allied forces in the
North, had sent Fauvelle to Paris to brief the War Committee
on conditions in the pocket. Fauvelle's appearance almost made
the briefing superfluous. "I have seen, in my time, broken men,"

Spears wrote later, "but never before one . . . fit to be scraped up by a spoon or mop." Fauvelle, who seemed oblivious to the effect he was having on his listeners, began bluntly. "I believe in a very early capitulation. The troops have no bread . . . the heavy artillery has been lost. Horse drawn transport no longer exists as all horses have been killed by air bombardment. There is little ammunition. There are no armored vehicles left [and] troop movements have been incredibly hampered by the flow of refugees." When Fauvelle finished, General Weygand turned to Reynaud with "a look of absolute exasperation" and said, "This war is sheer madness; we have gone to war with a 1918 army against a German army of 1939. It is sheer madness." Visiting the British embassy that evening, Spears told Oliver Harvey, a Foreign Office official, "Gort's only hope is to get to the coast."

In London, there was no talk of capitulation on May 25, but there was a serious discussion about negotiating an end to the war. That the testing began on May 25 was not happenstance. Halifax had been shaken by *A Certain Eventuality*, and, quite by chance, the cabinet's itinerary that morning included an invitation from Signore Paresci, the press secretary at the Italian embassy in London. The invitation was unexpected. All hope of reaching an Anglo-Italian concord seemed to die on May 17, when Mussolini responded to a conciliatory note from Churchill with bared teeth: "The Italian-German Treaty guides Italian policy today and tomorrow in the face of any event whatsoever." Now, Paresci appeared to be reopening the door to talks. Through a Foreign Office official, the press secretary intimated that a new British approach to Italy would not be unwelcome.

Probably nothing would come of it, Halifax told Churchill at the morning cabinet meeting, but Halifax said that about almost everything. For a man of his class, it was common and a bit low to appear anything but disinterested. Nonetheless, Halifax was interested in the invitation. That same day, the twenty-fifth, or possibly the day before or after, he drafted a cable to Roosevelt in Churchill's name. Either because Churchill objected to it or for some other reason, the cable was never sent, but it offers a glimpse into Halifax's state of mind in late May. The cable requested that in the event of a complete Allied collapse, America intervene with Hitler on Britain's behalf. Halifax may have seen Paresci's invitation as another avenue of approach to Berlin, but at the morning cabinet meeting on the twenty-fifth he made a case for accepting the invitation on the grounds that Anglo-Italian talks would encourage the French, and even if the talks went nowhere, they would buy the Allies a little time. Churchill, who had more pressing matters on his mind that morning, said he had "no objections" to talking to the Italians. A few hours later, Giuseppe Bastianini, the "well mannered and conciliatory" Italian ambassador, visited the Foreign Office. The brief of their meeting that Halifax drew up later shows that fairly quickly he steered his Italian visitor away from the subject Bastianini wished to discuss—preserving Italy's neutrality—to the topic Halifax wished to discuss: Italy mediating a settlement between Germany and the Allies. Fluent in the elliptical language of diplomacy, Halifax used illusion and implication to say what could not be said openly. He quotes himself as proposing that Mussolini reprise the "honest broker" role he had played at Munich and almost played again at the outbreak of the war the previous September. At another point, he has himself telling Bastianini, "If any discussions were to be held with a view to resolving European questions and building a peaceful Europe . . . matters which caused anxiety to Italy must certainly be discussed as part of a general European settlement." According to Andrew Roberts, Halifax's biographer, "general European settlement" was code for a quid pro quo. Britain would consider Italian claims on Suez, Gibraltar, and Malta and encourage Paris to consider Italian claims on Algeria and Tunis in return for Italian help in facilitating a negotiated settlement with Germany. Bastianini, who was also fluent in the elliptical language of diplomacy, seemed happy to play the game. "If such a conference were held," the ambassador asked, would His Majesty's government "consider it possible to discuss general questions, involving not only Great Britain and Italy but other countries?" Halifax said it was difficult "to visualize . . . a widespread discussion [of international concerns] while the war was still on."

"Once such a discussion began, the war would be pointless," Bastianini replied.

Halifax left the meeting feeling it had been "not unsatisfactory." Bastianini left it feeling that the foreign secretary had been a little too elliptical. Later that afternoon Paresci told a Foreign Office contact that Lord Halifax had not advanced any specific proposals and that his discussion of the territories Italy might receive in a general settlement lacked "geographical precision." The meeting had *"rated"* (miscarried), Paresci said. Paresci's Foreign Office contact was sent back to the press secretary with orders to make a better impression.

How much Churchill knew about all this is unclear. He may have read Halifax's report on the Bastianini meeting and the cable Halifax had written in his name, but on a day that Alec Cadogan described as "black as black," it is unlikely that Churchill gave much thought to anything except the war. The previous day, the twenty-fourth, a series of ferocious German attacks had brought the Panzers so near to Dunkirk that General Wilhelm von Thoma, chief of the Panzer section at the OKH (German Army High Command), could see the town from his staff car. It should have been a moment of triumph for von Toma; one last push and the British and French would be on the beaches, trapped between the Panzers and the Luftwaffe. But all he felt was frustration. Just before noon on the twenty-fourth Hitler had ordered the Panzers to halt in place. "You can't talk to a fool," Toma told a colleague when Hitler ignored his protest. Seventy years on, historians still debate why Hitler issued the order. At different times, he offered different explanations. At one point he said that he "did not want to send the tanks into the Flanders marshes"; another time, that the British were finished and "would not be back in this war."

Whatever the reason, the order confronted Gort with a decision. Should he take advantage of the order and fall back to Dunkirk? Or should he honor his pledge to the French and provide two BEF divisions for a revised version of the Weygand plan? On the afternoon of the twenty-fifth, a firefight near Menen, a Belgian town on the French border, settled the issue. A German map captured in the fight indicated that the Führer order would be lifted the following morning, the twenty-sixth, and that an attempt would be made to close the road to Dunkirk. Acting on his own recognizance, at six thirty on the evening of the twenty-fifth, Gort ordered the BEF units in the northern pocket to begin falling back to the port.

Half an hour after Gort issued the order, the French War Committee convened for its second session of the day; this time the meeting was held in a half-lit Élysée Palace, whose gloomy atmosphere reminded one committee member of a "spa on the day the baths shut down." Except for the occasional whoosh of an automobile on the Avenue de Marigny, the twilight city outside the palace was quiet. When General Weygand rose to open the meeting, hope got up and left the room. Straightening his young man's body to its full height, the general said in an old man's voice, "It is my duty to prepare for the worst." Then Weygand described the catastrophic sequence of events about to befall

France. The catastrophe would commence with the annihilation of the Allied pocket in the North and end with the destruction of the last large body of intact French troops, the forty-three to fifty divisions (estimates vary) holding the Somme–Aisne line south of the pocket. They would be obliterated by a German force "three times their own strength" (150 divisions). Facts must be faced, Weygand told the committee: All chance of victory or even of survival has passed. Now France fights only for reputation. It would be the duty of the army "to fight until the [Somme–Aisne] line [is] completely broken in order to save our honor."

Should the national government retreat to the provinces if the Germans drive on Paris? Reynaud asked.

No, said Weygand, who had no idea he had just stepped into a trap. The answer confirmed Reynaud's suspicion that the general's sudden fondness for a Roman ending—for days Weygand had been urging the government to emulate the Roman Senate, which had continued to deliberate when the barbarians reached the gates of Rome—was a ruse. If the government remained in Paris as Weygand wanted, once the city was occupied, the ministers would have no alternative but to sign an armistice, and that would give Weygand what he wanted—a quick end to the war— and what he perhaps wanted even more: a quick end in which no blame attached to his name.

Albert Lebrun, the president of the French Republic, also had a question. Would it not be better for France to initiate talks now, while its army and navy still existed? Before Weygand had a chance to reply, Reynaud answered Lebrun. The decision to leave the war was not up to France alone, he said. The agreement that Britain and France signed the previous March required each party to get the other's permission before seeking a separate armistice.

Now it was Weygand's turn to interrupt. Yes, he told Lebrun. France would have to consult England before accepting a German peace offer, but, faced with the threat of invasion and the loss of the BEF, he believed that London would be prepared to accept—perhaps even to solicit—a German peace offer.

It was Pétain's turn next.

After spending some time with the marshal earlier in the day, Spears had pronounced Pétain "dead in the sense that a figure that gives no impression of being alive can be said to be dead." That was a serious misjudgment. Pétain might be old, but he was aware of the power his name carried. To millions of his countrymen, the name Pétain was inseparable from the name Verdun, and that association gave his word a unique weight, especially when giving voice to a feeling shared by the French nation as he was that night. Pétain's theme was that perennial French crowd-pleaser "perfidious Albion." He said each ally's obligation under the March treaty should be commensurate with each one's contribution to the war, and he left his colleagues to do the math. France had begun the war with more than ninety divisions in the line; Britain, with the promise to deliver ten divisions to the Western Front within nine months.

César Campinchi, the minister of the navy and a little terrier of a man, seemed appalled by Pétain's cynicism. "A peace treaty must never be signed by France without a previous agreement with England." Brave words, but they would have been braver still had not Campinchi immediately walked them back. Of course, he said, a new government might not feel bound by the no-separate-peace pledge signed by the present government. Later in the meeting the observations of General Joseph Vuillemin, chief of the French Air Staff, set off a brief round of British-bashing. Some of the complaints voiced could be put down to vindictiveness; ever since the breakthrough on the Meuse, the British had been vocal in their criticism of the French Army and the French soldier—but some of the criticism directed at Britain was not only justified but echoed the views of officials far more sympathetic to Britain than Vuillemin, Pétain, and Weygand. Among them was Lord Davies, a former parliamentary secretary to Lloyd George, who said, "Things must go better now . . . after all we've made every bloody mistake that can be made," and the Canadian diplomat William Patterson, who told a colleague, "If I ever have to go through another war, let it not be with the English—their slowness drives me mad." Weygand's observation about France fighting a 1939 German army with 1918 methods was also true for Britain. In the kind of war Germany was waging, both Allies were out of their depth.

Before the committee dissolved at 9:30 p.m., it was decided that Reynaud should fly to London the next day to talk to Churchill, but members of the war committee left the Élysée Palace with different ideas of what Reynaud planned to tell the prime minister. Paul Baudouin, Reynaud's chef de cabinet, imagined he would ask Churchill to release France from the no-separate-peace agreement. Generals Weygand and Guillemin imagined that the premier would demand an increase in British military aid. They were wrong. Reynaud already knew what he wanted to talk to Churchill about, and it was not any of those things.

One night toward the end of the war General Alan Brooke, who had commanded the BEF's Second Corps in May 1940, heard Churchill give a disquisition on the human brain's capacity to "register catastrophe"; the prime minister likened the brain's absorption ability to that "of a three-inch pipe in a flood." The "pipe will go on passing water through under pressure, but when a flood comes, the water flows over [and around] the pipe whilst [it] goes on handling its three inches." Similarly, said Churchill, "the human brain will register emotions up to its three-inch limit;

additional emotions flow past unregistered." Listening to the disquisition, Brooke was brought back to May 25, 1940, the day he read a translated version of the captured German battle plan and the day the Luftwaffe bombed the mental hospital in Armentières, a French town near the Belgian border. When Brooke arrived in Armentières at about five that afternoon, the town looked like a scene from the medieval *Dance of Death*. Except instead of smiling skeletons, there were smiling "lunatics in brown corduroy suits . . . grinning at one another with a flow of saliva running from the corner of their mouths and dripping noses." After a bitter day of fighting, bombarded by rumors of every description, flooded by refugees, the "lunatics . . . were the last straw." "Had it not been that . . . one's senses were numbed with the magnitude of the catastrophe . . . the situation would have been unbearable," Brooke wrote later.

On the evening of the twenty-fifth, some of the German units on the Belgian side of the Allied pocket were close enough to Dunkirk to see the Leughenaer and the other town landmarks. But Armentières, on the French side of the pocket, was part of an archipelago created by the fortunes of war. It sat at the southern end of a forty-mile corridor that was one of the last open escape routes to Dunkirk. Farther up the corridor, retreating French and British troops shared the roads with "lame women suffering from sore feet, small children . . . hugging their dolls, and . . . the old and maimed struggling along." Still farther up the corridor, the roadside cafés were filled with drunken Belgian soldiers who had "given up any idea of fighting." Before retiring on the night of the twenty-fifth, Churchill, aware that General Time was fighting on the German side at Dunkirk, issued a final order to Gort: "March north to the coast in battle order."

Earlier on the twenty-fifth, near Whitehall, the American journalist Edward R. Murrow saw a young woman "crying very quietly" at a bus stop. There were several other people at the stop, but the woman was either indifferent or oblivious to them. "She didn't even bother to brush her tears away," Murrow noticed. When he turned the corner, the woman was still weeping, and the other passengers were staring into the street. Abrupt changes in public opinion are uncommon, but on May 25, through some mysterious human instinct, millions of individual Britons seemed to collectively focus on the "smash up" that Margery Allingham had written about. Murrow sensed the change, as did the *New Yorker* correspondent Mollie Panter Downes. The London that Panter Downes described on the twenty-fifth was not as bleak as Paris, but the shops and stores were empty, the streets half empty, and everyone seemed gripped by the "horrifying sense of living the same old nightmare again." Like Murrow, Panter Downes also had an eye for the telling detail. That year, she told *New Yorker* readers, the tulips outside Buckingham Palace were "the color of blood." The Mass Observation report for May 25 confirmed what was apparent on the streets that afternoon: "On the whole, the quality of optimism has violently declined and the quality of pessimism deepened. The public mind is in a chaotic condition and ready to be plunged into the depths of an utterly bewildered, shocked, almost unbelieving dismay. The whole structure of national belief would seem to be rocking gently." Home Intelligence, the Ministry of Information's survey unit, picked up many of the same changes but described them in more temperate language. "Depression is quite definitely up. . . . Even working class men, [hitherto] the strongest optimists, are often qualifying their remarks with slight suspicion or doubt about the way things are developing. . . . Morale among women is . . . considerably lower than that of men." Perhaps sensing this, Mrs. Robert Noble, a columnist for the *Essex Newsman*, urged her female readers toward "cheerfulness and practical common sense . . . two qualities that the home front cannot do without."

The sharp decline in morale had many sources. Every night now, the French coast was flashing on and off like a neon sign as German and French gunners exchanged rounds. And everyone knew that the bombers would be coming soon. "It was just like expecting the end of the world," wrote the historian Arnold Toynbee. "In a few minutes the clock was going to stop and life as we have known it was coming to an end." A hundred generations had passed since England had last experienced invasion, but now people awoke each morning in expectation: Would the wireless announce a landing, a parachute assault? Would the bombers be over today? "The threat to this island grows nearer and nearer," said the *Daily Express*. Warned the *Daily Mail*: "If Hitler consolidates his hold on the Channel Ports, the onslaught on these shores will be at hand." Headlines such as AMERICANS, GO HOME also made people feel downhearted and isolated.

In *The End of the Affair*, Graham Greene described the summer of 1940 as "sweet with the smell of doom." For most people, probably nothing contributed more to that sense of doom than the reappearance of that palmist of the Great War, the newspaper lists of the dead and missing. The *Times* of London's list for May 25 included a young American, twenty-one-year-old RAF sergeant Alfred Cuthbert Thompson, of Bayonne, New Jersey. The paper also noted that the young men who would be lining up to register for conscription that day belonged to the 1912 to 1920 class. Perhaps not entirely coincidentally, on May 25 the *Daily Express* published an article titled "Go home, hint to British film exiles in America." Among the prominent British actors and directors the *Express* accused of sitting out the war in Hollywood were Cary Grant and Errol Flynn, both thirty-one, prime fighting age; Laurence Olivier, thirty-three; Ray Milland, thirty-five; and Alfred Hitchcock, thirty-nine.

In an analysis of morale published on June 1, Mass Observation would note that raw fear alone was insufficient to explain the emotional volatility and confusion of the previous two weeks. Another factor was at work, one that MO had touched on in earlier reports: the collapse of a belief system that in previous crises had steadied public opinion. Things formerly taken for granted—Britain always won the final battle; God was on Britain's side; Britain fights with strong allies—could no longer be taken for granted. In the coming weeks, MO noted, the great task for Churchill and his government would be to create a new national narrative, one that inspired courage and hope but was also plausible. The narrative had to be forthright in acknowledging the dangers facing the country and it had to provide a credible explanation of how the dangers would be met and overcome.

There could be no more talk of "Peace in our time" or "Hitler missed the bus." The public had had enough of fairy tales.

CHAPTER NINE

THE ITALIAN APPROACH

On Sunday morning, May 26, William Shirer, the Berlin correspondent for CBS News, visited a company of German engineers outside Lille, a French city on the southern side of the Allied pocket. Lille had seen some of the bitterest fighting of the campaign, but when Shirer arrived that morning, the engineers, who were scheduled to lay a pontoon bridge under fire in a few minutes, were lying on the edge of a wood reading *Western Front*, the German army newspaper. Shirer was stunned. Except for the dirty jokes and the rumbling of passing ambulances, the scene was as idyllic as any he remembered from his Midwestern boyhood. He took out his notebook and wrote: "Morale of German troops fantastic."

The most charitable thing that can be said about the mood in London that Sunday morning is that after weeks of brilliant weather, nature had finally produced a day in tune with the national temper. The rain started a little after 5:00 a.m., and it was still raining at 7:00 a.m. when church bells began pealing across the city. A little later that morning, Harold Nicolson turned on the BBC to hear the war news. When it was over, he sat down and wrote his wife a letter. The Nicolsons were planning to commit suicide when the Germans invaded, and, as invasion now appeared imminent, Nicolson felt it was time to begin thinking about the practical aspects of the suicide pact. "You really ought to have a 'bare bodkin' [poison pill] handy so that you can take your quietus when necessary," he told his wife. "I shall have one also. I am not in the least afraid of such a sudden and honorable death. . . . But how can we find a bodkin which [works] quickly and . . . is easily portable? I shall ask my doctor friends."

Despite the rain, the city below Nicolson's rooms at 4 King's Bench Park was up early that morning. Across the empire, May 26 had been designated National Prayer Day. In India, tens of thousands of His Majesty's Hindu and "Mohammedan" subjects had gathered in temples and mosques. In Australia, "overflow congregations" had attended services in Sydney and Melbourne; and in New Zealand, a crowd of three thousand, including the prime minister and his cabinet, had attended a service at Wellington town hall. And as Sunday morning made its way westward across the globe, there were prayer services in British Columbia, Manitoba, the Canadian Arctic, and at the World's Fair in Flushing Meadows, New York.

In London, the churches and synagogues were particularly full. By 9:00 a.m., the streets in Whitehall had disappeared under a canopy of dripping umbrellas, and under the umbrellas marched representatives of every segment of British society: City stockbrokers in black bowlers; plump, pink-cheeked Colonel Blimps in uniforms "gorgeous with medals"; gossipy East End housewives; unemployed West End actors (four plays had closed and two openings had been canceled in the past week); shop girls in cheap Woolworth's dresses; repentant ex-Mosleyites (their former leader, the fascist Oswald Mosley, had been arrested on May 23); pacifists from the Peace Pledge Union; society women in bellboy hats, their minds moving restlessly back and forth between the national crisis and lunch at the Dorchester or Carleton that afternoon; and Great War veterans, wondering why and how it had all gone so wrong so quickly.

An hour before the start of the Westminster Abbey service, the war cabinet convened for a morning session. Except for the twenty-five-foot-long cabinet table, the only notable decoration in the sparsely furnished cabinet room was the portrait of Robert Walpole, an eighteenth-century statesman, hanging over the fireplace. On this morning, as on every other morning for the past hundred or so years, Walpole was gazing across the room, at the plane trees in St. James Park. Below him, Churchill was briefing the cabinet on the overnight news. Spears had cabled a depressing account of Major Lavelle's report, rumors were circulating of a Belgian surrender, and Reynaud was flying over for lunch that afternoon, probably to say that France was leaving the war. Churchill's final announcement produced a protest from Cyril Newall, the chief of the Air Staff. Newall could not understand why the prime minister had commissioned another paper on Britain's prospects in the event of a French surrender.

There was some discussion about how the new report, *British Strategy in the Near Future*, differed from the day-old *British Strategy in a Certain Eventuality*. Then, almost imperceptibly, the war cabinet slipped into one of the most consequential debates in British history. It is time to "face the facts," Halifax told the cabinet as the city outside the window gathered for prayer. "It is no longer a question of imposing complete defeat on Germany but of safeguarding our own empire and, if possible, that of France." This was a long way from "Victory! Victory at all costs!" In so many words, Halifax was saying if the only choices available to Britain were invasion or a compromise peace, a compromise peace might be preferable, even if it involved some territorial concessions. Halifax also told the cabinet that during his talk with Signore Bastianini the day before he had informed the Italian ambassador that "Britain would . . . be prepared to consider any proposal that led to a secure peace in Europe, provided our liberty and security were assured." Churchill pounced on that last sentence.

Peace and security were insufficient, he said. "We must ensure our complete liberty and independence. Any negotiation which might lead to a derogation of our rights and power" would be unacceptable. Despite the emphatic tone, Churchill was not saying that he opposed a negotiated settlement; only one that "might lead to a derogation of our rights and power." In part, the note of ambiguity may have been a ploy by a politically vulnerable prime minister. A very hard line could incite a cabinet revolt by Halifax and the other "wise old elephant," Chamberlain.

After Churchill concluded, the conversation wandered off in other directions, but Halifax was not finished yet. He had been particularly struck by one of the observations in *Certain Eventuality*: the RAF's ability to defend the British sky would be the most vital element of national survival. Toward the end of the cabinet, Halifax turned the observation into a question. If the Chiefs of Staff were right about airpower, he asked, how would the RAF's ability to maintain air superiority be affected if France and Belgium capitulated and Germany was left "free to switch the bulk of her efforts to air production"? The question highlighted what would emerge as a fundamental point of difference between the prime minister and the foreign secretary in the coming days. Halifax believed that if there were to be a negotiation, better to hold it now while Britain's military assets were still largely intact and could be used as a bargaining chip, while Churchill wished to demonstrate Britain's resolve and strength in a final Götterdämmerung battle that would put those assets at risk.

The other members of the war cabinet contributed little to the morning debate. A few days earlier, Chamberlain had noted in his diary that if France fell, "we should be fighting only for better terms, not for victory." But this morning all he had to offer were random observations. At one point he noted that Mussolini "might send an ultimatum to France very shortly, saying that unless she would agree to a conference, Italy would come in on Germany's side." At another point he wondered if it was "possible to ask the French whether Italy could be bought off." The lack of focus might have been health-related. In late May, Chamberlain was experiencing the first symptoms of what would prove to be terminal cancer.

When the cabinet meeting ended a little before ten o'clock so the ministers could attend the Prayer Day service at Westminster Abbey, no one except Halifax had spoken in favor of a negotiated settlement, but no one, including Churchill, had firmly closed the door to negotiation.

Despite the rain, the police predictions of a large turnout for the Prayer Day service proved accurate. By the time the service began at 10:00 a.m., the nave of Westminster Abbey was full and the crowd had spilled out of the abbey's great west front, down the stairs, and across the street to the old Westminster Hospital, which had recently been converted into a YMCA and was now guarded by machine guns. The increasing militarization of the imperial capital depressed Vera Brittain, who felt the "barricades and heaps of sand bags . . . barb-wire entanglements and machine gun emplacements [had] transformed familiar streets dominated for centuries by peace and prosperity" into battle stations.

"Hullo, Winnie"'s and "Good luck"'s greeted Churchill outside the abbey, but the shouts quickly died away. The rain, the war, the fear for friends and loved ones in France—people were in a somber mood that morning. Inside the abbey, the congregants took their seats amid stained glass windows, the tombs of the good and great, and the mildewy odor of damp clothing. The king, sleek and handsome in a midnight-blue Royal Navy uniform, sat in the chancel (a section of the altar) between his plump little Scottish queen and the royal couple's guest, the exiled Queen Wilhelmina of Holland, whose bourgeois habit of wheeling her own baby carriage had recently produced snickers in certain quarters of London. The suave air chief Cyril Newall, Admiral Dudley Pound—his jacket sleeves spangled with gold service stripes almost all the way up to the elbows—and a dozen other prominent military and civilian dignitaries took their places in the choir stalls adjacent to the chancel. Surveying the congregants amid the swelling choral music, Churchill "could feel the pent-up, passionate emotion, and also the fear, not fear . . . of death or wounds or material loss, but of defeat and the ruin of Britain." The observation probably said more about Churchill's state of mind than the British people's on May 26. Nonetheless, Prayer Day did produce many memorable and moving scenes: industrial workers in the Midlands and North of England, praying on loading docks and at lathes; and in front of the abbey itself, several hundred people standing in light spring rain, singing the national anthem. The next day the papers would say that the worshippers had prayed "for the men of the Allied forces . . . for the peoples on whom the terrors of invasion have fallen, for the victory of right and truth," and most of Britain did pray for those things, but not all of Britain. Even in the most solemn hours of national life, human nature is never entirely righteous.

This observation inspired poet John Betjeman's "In Westminster Abbey," an ode to the London society woman at prayer in wartime.

> Gracious Lord, oh bomb the Germans
> Spare their women for Thy Sake
> And if that is not too easy
> We will pardon Thy mistake.
> But Gracious Lord, what'er shall be,
> Don't let anyone bomb me.
>
> Keep our Empire undismembered
> Guide our forces by Thy Hand,

Gallant blacks from far Jamaica,
Honduras and Togoland;
Protect them Lord in all their fights,
And even more, protect the whites.

. . . Now I feel a little better,
What a treat to hear Thy Word,
Where the bones of leading statesmen
Have so often been interr'd.
And now, dear Lord, I cannot wait
Because I have a luncheon date.

About an hour after the Westminster Abbey service, a large black automobile appeared in the courtyard of Admiralty House, the rear door opened, and Paul Reynaud stepped out and into the beating heart of the British Empire. Directly to the north, Nelson's Column rose above Trafalgar Square; directly to the south lay Downing Street, the Foreign Office, the Cenotaph, and the Horse Guards Parade Ground; and looming up before Reynaud, in all its somber majesty, was Admiralty House. Four stories high and nearly a city block long, the building, which spoke of power, but in a low, cultivated voice, came as close as any physical structure could to embodying the amour propre of the British Empire.

There are three versions of why Reynaud visited London on May 26. In the French War Committee's version, the purpose was to seek France's release from the no-separate-peace agreement with Britain. In Reynaud's version, the visit was prompted by a telegram from the French ambassador in Rome, François Poncet, who had warned that Mussolini was preparing to march but might still be dissuaded by territorial concessions. The third explanation comes from Reynaud's military aide, Colonel de Villelume. De Villelume claims the trip was made at his suggestion and that Reynaud's intention was to propose that the Allies ask Italy to mediate an armistice agreement with Germany. All three accounts contained a measure of truth, though when Reynaud arrived in London on the late morning of the twenty-sixth only the second version was completely true.

Over lunch with Churchill at Admiralty House, Reynaud painted the Allied position in the blackest of colors: Paris under assault by 150 German divisions; Britain pummeled night and day by massive German bomber fleets based on the Channel coast only forty or fifty miles from southern England; the blockade weapon fatally compromised by German conquests and the Nazi-Soviet pact; an isolationist United States unwilling and unable to provide military assistance. Finally, Reynaud came to Italy. He said an Italian attack would be fatal for France, which had lost its best divisions and most modern equipment in the battle in the North. Then Reynaud presented what amounted to the Reynaud plan: The Allies would offer Mussolini a quid pro quo. In return for territorial concessions, Italy would pledge to remain neutral. The point of the deal was to free up troops. The Germans were certain to turn on Paris once Dunkirk fell, and the agreement would allow France to move ten divisions from its border with Italy north to meet the expected assault. Before rising from the table, Churchill asked Reynaud, who had "dwelt not obscurely upon [a] possible French withdrawal from the war . . . if any peace terms had been offered him." No, Reynaud said, but the French "knew they could get an offer, if they wanted one."

When the war cabinet convened a little after 2:00 p.m. on the afternoon of May 26 Churchill briefed his colleagues on the Reynaud plan. The advantage of the plan was that it would provide more divisions for the defense of Paris; the disadvantage was the price. In return for a neutrality pledge, the Duce would probably demand British as well as French concessions, including "the neutralization of Gibraltar and the Suez Canal, the demilitarization of Malta, and the limitation of naval forces in the Mediterranean." Just describing the concessions was so unbearable that Churchill suddenly swelled with emotion and swore that Britain "would never give in. We would rather go down fighting . . . than be enslaved by Germany." He went on in this vein for several minutes; then the outburst ended as abruptly as it had began, and he asked Halifax to visit Reynaud at Admiralty House. At this point the recording secretary drew a veil over the cabinet's deliberations, noting simply that "a further discussion ensued on whether we should make any approach to Italy." When the veil lifted, Halifax was still in his seat and was telling the cabinet, "The last thing Mussolini wanted was to see Herr Hitler dominating Europe. He would be anxious, if he could, to persuade Herr Hitler to take a more reasonable attitude." This was the closest Halifax had come to saying what had been implicit in his earlier discussions of the Italian approach: it was a pathway to talks with Germany.

Churchill, whose subtlety is often overlooked, chose not to challenge the foreign secretary. On a day when the BEF was facing annihilation and France was near collapse, he seemed to sense it was best to keep his pitch low. After Halifax finished, Churchill said that he "doubted whether anything would come of the approach to Italy but . . . the matter was one which the war cabinet would have to consider."

Halifax remained in his seat long enough to hear Arthur Greenwood give the cabinet a wildly inaccurate analysis of Germany's economic weakness. Then he excused himself and went to Admiralty House to talk to Reynaud. The only record of that conversation is the summary Halifax prepared later, and nowhere to be found in it is the Reynaud who had come to London seeking a way to keep Italy neutral. Indeed, Halifax's Reynaud sounds remarkably like Halifax. The most probable explanation for this is that, during their talk, Halifax described his version of the Italian approach, and Reynaud found it superior to his, in which France grants large territorial concessions simply for the right to move ten divisions from its Italian front. Reynaud's use of the term "just and durable peace" also betrays the hand of Halifax, who had used that phrase in his talk with Signore Bastianini.

In fairness to Halifax, he was not the only cabinet member guilty of manipulation on Prayer Day. As Air Chief Cyril Newall had noted at the morning cabinet, the new Chiefs of Staff paper commissioned by Churchill, *British Strategy in the Near Future*, was essentially a redo of the barely day-old *Certain Eventuality*. But there was an important difference between the two papers. Military reports are often based on a set of assumptions—for example, the enemy will deploy X number of divisions in battle. In *Near Future*, Churchill asked the Chiefs of Staff to factor into their analysis several assumptions that they did not use in *Certain Eventuality*, among them that the BEF reached Dunkirk safely (far from certain on the afternoon of May 26) and that "prolonged British resistance might be very dangerous for a Germany engaged in holding down the greater part of Europe." (This was very close to a pipe dream. By late 1940, Germany headed an economic bloc of 290 million with a GDP greater than either that of the United States or the British Empire.) The new assumptions did not change the chiefs' conclusions about Britain's prospects, but they did give the new report a different tone. In *Eventuality*, the most the chiefs were prepared to offer was pinched hope: "It is impossible to say whether or not the United Kingdom could hold out in all circumstances. We think there are good grounds for the belief that the British people will endure the greatest strain, *if* they realize as they are beginning to do—that the existence of the Empire is at stake." In *Near Future*, the hope is unqualified and the chiefs' tone, personal. "Prima facie Germany has most of the cards, but the real test is whether the morale of our fighting personnel and civil population will counterbalance the numerical and material advantages Germany enjoys. We believe it will."

But was that "We believe it will" the Chiefs' unbiased military opinion, or was Churchill hiding behind the curtain, playing ventriloquist?

According to Christopher Hill, professor of international relations at Cambridge, Churchill knew that if he hoped to "lead the Cabinet toward the unbending resistance [to Germany]" he'd had in mind since the outset, he could not allow doubts to grow. He thus employed the classic political tactic of asking for another paper when the first did not come up to his expectations and loaded the dice in the language of his brief (a reference to the positive assumptions in *Near Future*). This episode also highlights some of the other ways Churchill kept the senior military men in line. "The COS [Chiefs of Staff] had reserved their right to change their view when they saw the paper," notes Professor Hill, but it was too late, "given its presentation to the Cabinet, which was the purpose from Churchill's point of view. This and the fact that the Confidential Annexes to the paper went missing shortly after the war suggest that the PM had maneuvered his military advisors for political purposes."

On occasion, Churchill also used manipulation to keep his Cabinet colleagues committed to the war. For example, he took the somewhat unusual step of circulating his correspondence with Roosevelt to the cabinet. The president had no intention of bringing the United States into the war, but, reading his words of support, the other members of the cabinet could be forgiven for thinking otherwise. The prime minister's maximalist, never surrender! rhetoric also had the effect of committing his cabinet colleagues to a policy that had never been formally agreed upon. With everything at stake, Churchill was playing the deep game.

The final event of this momentous afternoon was the informal cabinet meeting Churchill convened at Admiralty House after Reynaud left. Unusually, the first fifteen minutes were not recorded; allegedly, the secretary, Edward Bridges, arrived late. When the cabinet did go back on the record, Churchill was defending the proposition that a Britain alone could survive. "We [are] in a different position from France. In the first place we still [have] powers of resistance and attack which [the French] had not. In the second place, they would be likely to be offered decent terms by Germany, which we should not. If France could not defend herself it was better that she should get out of the war rather than that she should drag us into a settlement which involved intolerable terms. There was no limit to the terms which Germany would impose on us if she had her way." Halifax, who found Churchill's analysis unconvincing, said he "was not quite sure it was in Herr Hitler's interest to insist on outrageous terms." After all, he knew his own internal weaknesses. Then Halifax brought the discussion back to the Italian approach, which he "could see no harm" in testing. With reservations, Attlee and Chamberlain agreed.

Churchill, who had been left spinning in the air by Halifax's maneuvering, restated his position more forcefully. "The suggested approach to Signor Mussolini . . . implied that if we were prepared to give Germany back her colonies and make certain concessions in the Mediterranean, it was possible for us to get out of our present difficulties." That was an illusion. "For example, the terms offered us would certainly prevent us from completing our rearmament." For the rest of the afternoon cabinet Churchill was like a dog with a bone, returning again and again to the negotiation issue. At one point he warned, "We must take care not to be forced into a weak position in which we went to Signore Mussolini and invited him to go to Herr Hitler and ask him to treat us nicely"; at another, "We must not get entangled in a position like that before we had been involved in any serious fighting." Still, he remained mindful of his political vulnerability. At the conclusion of the cabinet, he told his colleagues he had no objection "to an approach being made to Signore Mussolini."

Greenwood said a few words; then Churchill told the cabinet that nothing should be decided "until we [see] how much of the Army we could re-embark from France." The request would be ignored; the peace debate would resume the next day and spill over into May 28. However, by the evening of the twenty-sixth, a few things had become clear. Though he had not had a particularly brilliant day, Churchill still held most of the cards. His executive powers gave him some control over the reports his colleagues saw and what they read in the reports. More important, he was the only cabinet member—indeed one of the few men in Britain in May 1940—who had a war strategy that offered a credible hope of survival and, perhaps, eventually victory. A Britain alone stays in the war, fights a great air battle with Germany (which became the Battle of Britain), and, enjoying the home advantage, prevails because it can rescue more of its downed pilots, exploit its lead in radar technology and fuel considerations, and limit the German fighters to twenty-two to twenty-five minutes' flying time over Britain. The plan would not bring victory, but it would bring what in the late spring and summer of 1940 was almost as valuable to Britain: time. Time to rebuild its shattered military and put its industries on a full wartime footing, and time for the dominions to mobilize their resources. Fighting Germany to a standstill might also persuade the Americans to offer unrestricted military aid and perhaps eventually bring them into the war.

Halifax had a better debate than Churchill on the twenty-sixth, but as the days passed, the weaknesses in his argument would become apparent. Though peace was a more attractive commodity than war, he was advancing a controversial position—a negotiated settlement—against an unusually forceful prime minister with his own strategy, and, in the sudden rush of tumultuous events, Halifax had not had time to develop a simple, cogent argument that distinguished clearly between what he was saying—Britain should test the possibility of a compromise peace—from what he was not saying—Britain should surrender. When Churchill spoke of fighting on alone, the mantle of history—Agincourt, Waterloo, Trafalgar, the Armada—sang through his sentences. When Halifax spoke of achieving a new "European arrangement," he sounded like a nervous solicitor reading from a half-thought-out brief. Still, the foreign secretary was not without advantages. He was a popular figure in the Conservative Party, and his resignation would damage the prime minister, and if the other "wise old elephant" in the cabinet, Chamberlain, resigned in sympathy, the Churchill government could fall—and Churchill was aware of this.

Of the three other members of the war cabinet, Greenwood and Attlee leaned toward the Churchill position; Chamberlain, at times, toward Halifax's; but during the debates all three men would occasionally contradict themselves, as would Churchill, who, at various points, could be heard saying if "we could get out of this jam by giving up Malta and Gibraltar and some African colonies, he would jump at it." A number of historians have pointed to such remarks as proof that Churchill was prepared to accept a negotiated settlement, and he may have been, though it is difficult to conceive of any German terms he would have found acceptable and, if he did accept, would honor. By temperament,

Churchill was a maximalist and a romantic. "The Gatling gun is jammed and the colonel is dead" was not a schoolboy poem to him, it was a life plan. However, in late May 1940, a war policy based on "Vitaï Lampada" would have been very hard to sell to a frightened, confused British public. The most Churchill could hope to win in the debates with Halifax was a sanction for his plan—Britain stays in the war to fight its battle. He did not state his view that baldly, but his frequent assertions that Britain's position could change in the next two or three months were code for the big battle. What else could change Britain's position so quickly and so dramatically? For the most part, Churchill's twists, turns, and contradictions can be dismissed as the verbal equivalent of rope-a-dope by a vulnerable politician.

Reynaud, the other major figure in the events of May 26, returned to Paris infused with a convert's zeal. "The only one who truly understands is Halifax," he told a colleague. "[Halifax] is clearly worried about the future and realizes some European solution must be reached. Churchill is always hectoring and Chamberlain undecided." Unlike most of the other parties to the peace debate, Mussolini, the ghost at the table on May 26, exhibited the virtue of consistency. On May 17 he had rudely rebuffed a moving and elegant appeal for Anglo-Italian comity by Churchill, and on May 26, fearful Germany would claim all the spoils, he was even more eager to bring Italy into the war. That afternoon, as the Italian approach was debated in London, in Rome Count Ciano, Mussolini's foreign minister, was noting in his diary that "the Duce . . . plans to write a letter to Hitler announcing our intervention for the latter part of June." And the following day, May 27, Mussolini would rebuff yet another peace appeal from President Roosevelt. All of this was or would soon be known to the Allies, as would the Duce's muzzling of the Italian ambassadors in Washington, Paris, and London, who were under orders not to engage in substantial negotiations with British and French officials, which is why one of the most interesting things about the debates over the Italian approach is what they said about the level of fear and desperation in Allied capitals.

The British public, unaware of the great issues being debated in their name, and braced by the Prayer Day observances, achieved a steadiness of mood on the twenty-sixth that had eluded them the previous two days. From Manchester came accounts of "an excellent spirit in the factories"; from London, of "more cheerfulness" on the streets; and from Oxford, of more "optimism." However, the analysts at Mass Observation were loath to credit the Almighty for the improvement. The twenty-sixth fell on a Sunday, and even in wartime Sunday was a slow news day, which meant less exposure to disturbing headlines. The analysts also gave the government's new censorship program some of the credit for the improvement in morale, though they were of two minds about the program itself. Unquestionably, softening and/or holding back bad news for a few days did help stabilize public opinion, but was it a devil's bargain? A fair amount of evidence suggested that censorship could intensify the impact of bad news when it was finally released. This insight was particularly relevant on the evening of May 26. Earlier in the day, Hitler had lifted his Panzer halt order, ensuring that another large packet of dreadful news would shortly be making its way across the Channel.

In Calais, which guarded the southern flank of the Allied corridor, the German assault began in a light rain at about 9:00 a.m. on the twenty-sixth, two days after Brigadier Nicolson learned that the British garrison would not be evacuated. News of the decision arrived in a most unlikely manner. On the afternoon of the twenty-fourth, Lieutenant Hugo Ironside was in the Citadel, a British stronghold in Calais, when the phone rang. When Ironside picked up the receiver, there was a familiar voice on the other end of the line. He was speaking to General Edmund Ironside, chief of the Imperial General Staff and a family relation. The elder Ironside said that to relieve the German pressure on the Dunkirk perimeter, the British garrison was being ordered to mount a last-man-last-round stand in Calais. As he wrote down the message, Lieutenant Ironside must have had mixed feelings about his esteemed relative: he was in the army rather than the air force because General Ironside had told him his chances of survival would be better as a soldier.

On the evening of the twenty-fifth, a small armada of British yachts and trawlers had appeared off Calais, briefly rekindling hopes of an evacuation. But the ships were freelancing and only a few dared the harbor to evacuate troops. The only vessel with official business in Calais that evening carried a message for Nicolson: "Hold out at all costs." At eight the next morning, London received a desperate situation report from Nicolson. "Quays and harbor under MG [machine gun] fire. . . . Troops dead beat, no tanks left . . . reinforcements would have to be on a considerable scale . . . [and] probably a forlorn hope." An hour later, the sound of tank engines could be heard toward the east; then a wall of artillery fire descended on the Old Town (the ancient part of Calais). After the barrage ended, Airey Neave, a British captain wounded earlier in the day, heard the crunching sound of hundreds of feet running over a field of rubble. Then other sounds drifted down to the cellar where Neave was hiding: the crackle of gunfire; the "hoarse shouts of German under officers" entering the first floor of Neave's building; the heavy thud of boots rushing down the cellar stairs; and, finally, "field gray figures waving revolvers" in his face. "It was a sad ending," Neave wrote. At about three in the afternoon of the twenty-sixth, Anthony Eden sent a message to the Citadel: "Am filled with admiration for your magnificent fight"; but by the time the cable arrived, the "every man for himself" order had been given and no one was in the Citadel to read the message. An hour later, Brigadier Nicolson surrendered. Shortly thereafter, all organized British resistance in the town ended.

At six that evening, the Admiralty signaled Vice Admiral Bertram Ramsay, the flag officer, at the Dover station: "Operation Dynamo is to commence." Dynamo was the code name for the seaborne evacuation of the BEF, and the naval high command was not optimistic about its prospects. On the open beaches and shallow waters around Dunkirk, men and ships would be vulnerable to air attack, and now that Calais had fallen, the sea route between Dunkirk and Dover (the latter, the landing site for evacuated troops) would be within range of German artillery. Best estimates were that forty-five thousand men, or about a fifth of the BEF's quarter-million-man force, could be rescued before German shelling and bombing made the beaches unapproachable. To Patrick Turnbull, a British transportation officer, even that estimate sounded optimistic. Turnbull was not a religious man, but the scene framed in the windshield of his truck as he drove into Dunkirk on the evening of his evacuation—silos of heavy black smoke billowing up into a blood-red sky—had such an Old Testament power that for a moment Turnbull imagined he was viewing "a giant funeral pyre on which was being consumed the corpses of French and British military might."

Later that night, after the news from Calais had come through, Churchill asked John Martin, one of his secretaries, to look up a passage in George Borrow's prayer for England at Gibraltar. The passage read: "Fear not the result, for either shall thy end be majestic and an enviable one or God shall perpetuate thy reign upon the waters."

Prime Minister Chamberlain arrives in Munich on September 29, 1938, for a conference with Hitler and Mussolini. Chamberlain came to Munich determined to defend the Never Again pledge the publics of the West made after the carnage of the Great War; Hitler and Mussolini arrived at the conference equally determined that there should be an Again.

Prelude to Munich: Chamberlain visits Berchtesgaden on September 15, 1938, to discuss German demands that the Sudetenland, the ethnically German region of Czechoslovakia, be granted self-determination. Chamberlain left the meeting thinking Hitler was "a man who could be relied on"; Hitler left it thinking Chamberlain was "a silly old man with an umbrella."

Hitler and Chamberlain at the Berchtesgaden meeting on September 15, 1938.

The famous photo of Chamberlain promising "peace in our time" on his return from the Munich conference. Within days of his return, streets in Britain were being named after him, and Chamberlain dolls and Chamberlain bouquets peeked out from a thousand shop windows, proclaiming, "We are proud of you."

The Chamberlain Cabinet in November 1939, the second month of the war. Standing from left to right are Sir John Anderson, home secretary; Lord Hankey, minister without portfolio; Leslie Hore-Belisha, secretary of state for war; Winston Churchill, first lord of the Admiralty; Kingsley Wood, secretary of state for air; Anthony Eden, secretary of state for dominion affairs; and Eric Bridges, Admiralty. Seated from left to right are Lord Halifax, secretary of foreign affairs; John Simon, chancellor of the Exchequer (Treasury); Chamberlain; Samuel Hoare, lord chancellor; and Lord Chatfield, minister of defense.

King George VI visits Washington in June 1939. Personally arranged by President Roosevelt, the tour was intended to make an isolationist American public more sympathetic to the British cause, but the royal charm did not work on everyone. "The English soap is being poured over Uncle Sam's devoted head and lathered into his ears and eyes," warned the antiwar press baron William Randolph Hearst.

Churchill and Halifax on a London street in March 1938. In the summer of 1940, as the fall of France became inevitable, Halifax and Churchill would engage in one of the most consequential debates of the twentieth century: should Britain fight on alone, or seek a compromise peace with Germany?

Lord Halifax and Sir Alexander Cadogan, permanent undersecretary at the Foreign Office, on their morning walk to work. The buttoned-down Cadogan had a bit of Dorian Gray in him. By day, he was a reserved and impeccably correct diplomat; by night, an often vicious diarist whose withering portraits of the good and great of his time have proved a treasure trove to generations of historians.

Joseph Kennedy, shortly after his appointment as ambassador to Great Britain in 1938. A State Department official who worked closely with Kennedy believed his greatest flaw as a diplomat was short-sightedness. Because Kennedy was "primarily interested in the financial side of things," wrote the official, "he cannot, poor man, see the imponderables which in a war . . . will be decisive."

The price Britain paid for victory in the Second World War is reflected in the life of Sir Harold Nicolson, diplomat, author, politician, and leading opponent of appeasement. Nicolson was born in 1886 into a Britain supreme in all things, and he died in 1968 in a Britain whose greatest boast was that it was the home of the Beatles.

German Messerschmitt 110s bombing gasoline dumps in the Calais-Dunkirk region in early June 1940. Employing the Luftwaffe as flying artillery worked brilliantly in the Battle of France, but it left German pilots ill prepared to fight a strategic air war such as the Battle of Britain.

British soldiers in Calais march into captivity. To keep the twenty-four-mile road between Calais and Dunkirk open for evacuation, the British garrison in the town was ordered to sacrifice itself in a last-man, last-round defense.

Evacuation of British troops from Dunkirk. Dunkirk's resort-town atmosphere created surreal scenes, such as a five-mile column of men marching through a forest of Ferris wheels and merry-go-rounds down to the sea.

British soldiers wading through the shallows to waiting ships. About the scene on the evacuation ships, one man wrote, "The men lying on the decks looked like sea creatures crawled up to the shore to die."

Three hundred thirty-eight thousand men, including well over a hundred thousand French troops, were evacuated from Dunkirk at a cost of two hundred twenty-six ships, most of them British. The RAF also lost one hundred forty-five planes during the evacuation, thirteen more than the Germans, who lost one hundred thirty-two.

Paul Reynaud, premier of France, in 1940. Able and intelligent, Reynaud was a true French patriot, but he lacked the spark of greatness that enabled Churchill and Clemenceau, France's First World War leader, to mobilize the national will and sustain it through a long season of setbacks and defeats.

Comtesse Hélène de Portes's (here shown posing for Spanish painter Fredrico Masses) flirtation with fame and power ended tragically. She was killed in June 1940 while fleeing the Germans with her lover, Paul Reynaud, the premier of France. Reynaud, who was at the wheel, survived the crash.

General Maxime Weygand assumed command of the Allied armies on May 20, 1940, at the age of seventy-three. Weygand's greatest talent, however, was for survival, not war. He emerged from two world wars unscathed, despite being arrested by the Nazis during—and by the French after—the Second World War. He was released both times, and died in his bed in 1966 at the age of ninety-eight.

Hitler tours Paris on June 23, 1940. After visiting Napoleon's tomb, the Führer told a companion that was "the greatest and finest moment of my life."

After Dunkirk, Britain had only three and a half fully equipped and trained divisions to meet a German invasion. Here Churchill inspects a few of the few on the coast of southern England.

This *Daily Mirror* headline underscores Churchill's greatest achievement in 1940: his ability to infuse what one historian has called his "indomitable stoutness and unsurrendering quality" into the British people.

Churchill and Vice Admiral Bertram Ramsay, August 25, 1940. The previous June Ramsay had overseen the Dunkirk evacuation; in this photo, he shows Churchill his plan for defending Dover, which, because it is only twenty miles from the French coast, was thought a likely German invasion site.

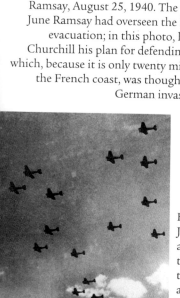

Heinkel 111 bombers over Britain at the end of July 1940. The He 111's heavy bomb load capacity and ability to absorb punishment made it among the most effective of the German bombers; but, at this early stage of the war, it was already becoming apparent that, even with a fighter escort, daylight bombing was an extremely hazardous enterprise for the attacker.

Hawker Hurricanes rising to meet a German attack, July 1940. During the Battle of Britain, the slower Hurricane would typically attack the German bomber stream, while the faster, more nimble Spitfire went after the bombers' fighter escort.

A dogfight over London in September 1940. In the final stage of the Battle of Britain, the Luftwaffe attempted to break the will of the British people by pulverizing London and other major metropolitan areas.

Heinkel 111 bombers over London, September 1940. In the first thirty days of the Blitz, which began on September 7, 1940, almost thirty thousand bombs were dropped on London. Six thousand Londoners were killed, and twice that number seriously wounded.

Churchill visits a bombed neighborhood in Bristol. Bristol's large concentration of war industries made it the fifth most bombed city in Britain during the Second World War.

CHAPTER TEN

"GOOD MORNING, DEATH"

I said, "Any ideas how we shall win?"

"Oh, the usual formula," said Carter. "Mastery of the air with American help. Bomb their factories to blazes. Stir up trouble in the occupied countries, and there you are."

"Time factor for the process?" I said.

"Oh, God knows," said Carter with a grin. "We leave that bit out."

I said, "Oh, well, we usually do win things."

"Yes," said Carter. "Between us I think that's really the best argument at the moment."

Visiting the pediatric ward of a London hospital on the morning after the Prayer Day, a visitor found the silence deafening. "The children had no heart for the rocking horse [and] the mothers talked . . . in low voices." By the final week of May, the war had overwhelmed every aspect of British life. It was the bride at every wedding, the corpse at every funeral, the song in every music hall, the subject of every conversation, the first thought every morning, the last thought every night. It was the postman on his bike with a satchel of death notices and the soldier in the *Evening Express* cartoon standing on Dover's cliffs proclaiming "Very Well Alone." The war was everywhere now and all-encompassing; it disrupted the settled rhythms of thought and feeling and insinuated itself into the most intimate precincts of private life, making conversations previously heard only in the films of Ronald Colman and Greta Garbo a part of daily life. "Every time we meet now," Harold Nicolson told his wife, "it must be in both our minds that we may never meet again."

The physical geography of the war was as extensive as its emotional geography. It encompassed the fishing villages of coastal England, where government men walked the wharves and piers, inquiring about the local supply of small boats, and Claridge's and the Ritz, where men "unshaven and still covered with [the] mud" of France lunched on partridge and champagne. At the beginning of June, a major just back from France told Clare Boothe (who had just arrived in London herself): "In the last war I used to sleep at the Ritz in Paris every night and barge out to the front right after breakfast. Queer . . . I should now be coming back from the front to Claridge's." The geographical reach of the war also extended to the Home Office, where plans were made to evacuate a hundred thousand British children to the United States and the dominions. "It is a portent of things to come," Vera Brittain said upon hearing of the plan. "The Government would not organize so large a scheme unless it was convinced that horror and dislocation would come to this country with the downfall of Europe." The war's geographic domain also intruded into the private lives of Winston and Clementine Churchill. On the evening of May 30, the Churchills were summoned from the living quarters at Admiralty House (the Chamberlains had not yet vacated Downing Street) to the reception area, where the prime minister's nephew, Johnny Churchill, awaited them "in full battle kit" and "soaking wet."

"Johnny, I see you have come straight from battle."

The younger Churchill told his uncle he had been "sent . . . to say that [there was a] most urgent need for small boats to get the troops off the beaches and out to the bigger ships."

The prime minister examined his nephew's battle kit. "Have you come straight from the sea?"

"Yes," Johnny said, "and I will be pleased to go back in again in a fast motor boat to give everyone encouragement."

On the morning of May 27, all of the war's various emotional and geographic matrices intersected at the point Johnny Churchill would return to later in the day, the Dunkirk corridor.

In the closing days of May, the German advance had become so rapid that the image of the corridor on Allied situation maps changed almost daily. On the twenty-seventh, it suggested a vise crushing a metal pipe. The southern side of the corridor was under attack at more than half a dozen points, and on the northern side at at least four. Mindful that the decisive air battle would be fought over Britain, not Dunkirk, on May 27, the RAF put only sixteen fighter squadrons over the beaches, insufficient to blunt the ferocious attacks of the Germans, who won the day in the air and on the ground. Only 7,700 men were evacuated on the twenty-seventh, and almost all of them arrived in Dover (the main reception area for evacuees) complaining about the RAF. But at least they were home. The root, branch, and stem of the Allied army was still inching its way through the treeless, marshy flatlands of Flanders toward the beaches, machine-gunned from the air, shelled from the ground, and stumbling across trench lines dug sometime between the First Battle of Ypres and the Fourth. Of this army, one man wrote, "It looked like a lava of mud crawling slowly towards the sea from a far off eruption":

Every road was packed with Lorries, mobile search lights, Bren-gun carriers, fifteen hundred weights. Ambulances, broken down Lorries, anything on wheels. . . . Everywhere . . . fluttered from the little brick-house villages through which [the soldiers] crawled. . . . Tokens of surrender—sheets, towels, table cloths, even handkerchiefs. It would be five long years before some of [the soldiers] would see this kind of abject, total surrender—that would be Germany in 1945. Most of the houses were barricaded behind their wooden shutters, though the anxious soldiers could sense the tense . . . life behind those shutters. Here and there, little groups of women stood, arms crossed over their aproned bosoms, watching the defeated army go by without any feeling, as if it were no concern of theirs; as if these beaten young men in khaki might be aliens from some other and remote world.

Oppressed by the pervasive atmosphere of the war the previous day, while the rest of Britain knelt in prayer, John Colville, the young Downing Street aide, slipped away to Oxford with a lady friend. Colville's diary entry for May 26 reads like a lyric from "These Foolish Things Remind Me of You." Lunch on a river bench, "the laughter of the children along the tow path," Christchurch Meadows under "the setting sun. I have never felt greater serenity or contentment." But the next morning, Monday, May 27, when Colville returned to Downing Street, the war was standing at the door waiting for him. There were rumors of an imminent Belgian surrender and of cabinet discussions about a negotiated settlement. "We have reached all but the last ditch," Colville thought. "A timely miracle would be acceptable." But the only miracle May 27 had to dispense was another day of "king's weather."

In the unusually long, contentious cabinet meetings of the twenty-seventh, the afternoon session would be devoted to a second debate about a compromise peace; the morning session to a related issue, the possibility of a Belgian surrender. Just before dawn on the twenty-seventh, the counselor at the Belgium embassy in London informed the Foreign Office that King Leopold was contemplating a separate peace with Germany. The counselor said the Belgian Army was ruined, which was true, and left the Foreign Office to sort out how that would affect Britain's military position. Spears's little fable about drowning rats clawing each other to death as they tried to escape was beginning to acquire the character of a prophecy. Two days earlier, the British had considered sacrificing the Belgian Army to save the BEF. Now King Leopold was proposing to sacrifice British and French troops—a Belgian surrender would leave portions of the Allied corridor undefended—to save his army. Churchill asked Admiral Keyes, his personal representative in Brussels, to impress upon the king the "disastrous consequences" of a capitulation on the Allies and on Belgium; Keyes said he would try but was not optimistic; the king's mind seemed made up. Oddly, given Belgian strategic importance, when the cabinet convened at 11:00 a.m., none of the ministers pressed for details about Leopold's decision; even more oddly, Sir John Dill, who had just replaced Ironside as chief of the Imperial Staff, reported that the Calais garrison, which had surrendered sixteen hours earlier, was still "holding out with great gallantry."

The air estimates, the next topic on the cabinet's agenda, produced a more lively discussion. Both *Certain Eventuality* and *British Strategy in the Near Future* had cited airpower as the essential element in Britain's short-term survival, and the Air Ministry's current estimates, which gave Germany a four-to-one advantage in aircraft, called into question the RAF's ability to defend the home island. Aware of this, Churchill opened the morning cabinet with a magic trick even Houdini would have admired. He began by citing the aircraft production numbers from the past three years that showed Germany had produced twenty-five thousand military aircraft and Britain fifteen thousand, which meant, at a bare minimum, the Luftwaffe enjoyed only a five-to-three (not a four-to-one) advantage in the air. Next, Churchill cited a new study by the vice chief of the Air Staff, Richard Peirse. Peirse's figures reduced the Luftwaffe's advantage in aircraft to two and a half to one. Then, by factoring in the British kill ratio—which Churchill claimed was three to one in Britain's favor—he made the German advantage disappear. In terms of number of aircraft, he told the cabinet, the "balance was on our side."

The air minister, Archibald Sinclair, immediately challenged the analysis. The "figure of fifteen thousand . . . referred to aircraft without their full equipment. The German figures of twenty-five thousand . . . covered aircraft complete in every respect."

Churchill, who had been Sinclair's superior officer in France during the Great War, held his ground. "From [Peirse's] table," he said, "it appeared that the odds against us were only two and a half to one and our airmen were shooting down [German planes at a ratio of] three to one; the balance was on our side."

Cyril Newall, the chief of the Air Staff, said the prime minister was overstating the kill ratio. It was "very much less favorable for us at night. It was only in the day fighting that we were able to inflict such heavy losses on the enemy."

Churchill changed the subject to France.

Chamberlain still wanted to talk about airpower. The warnings in *Near Future* about the British aircraft industry's vulnerability to attack were alarming, he said. "If the enemy pressed home night attacks, he was likely to achieve such material and moral damage . . . as to bring all work [at the factories] to a standstill. The prospect of . . . the aircraft industry being brought to a complete standstill was extremely dangerous."

Newall said Chamberlain had highlighted "the kernel of the whole problem"—the danger of an attack on the aircraft industry. "Even on dark nights the Germans would be able to find big areas like Coventry [an important center of aircraft production in the Midlands] and bomb them indiscriminately. If the Germans succeeded in gaining complete air superiority, it might not be necessary for them to invade us at all."

Chamberlain still wasn't finished, but now he wanted to talk about the United States, the factor the Chiefs of Staff considered the most important to Britain's survival. Chamberlain said it was "perhaps not unjustifiable to assume that America would offer its full support." But "we might not obtain this support in the immediate future." This hypothesis Churchill did not challenge. On May 15, his eloquent plea to Roosevelt—"I trust you realize, Mr. President, that the force and voice of the United States will count for nothing if they are withheld too long"—had produced an expression of sympathy, a promise to cut some red tape, and little else. Though Britain's survival was a vital national interest of the United States, in late May Roosevelt was not convinced Britain could survive, which meant American weaponry could end up in German hands.

Churchill made a second request for American aid on the twentieth; this time the request included a threat—though it was so eloquently stated that two readings were required to hear the low growl in the prime minister's voice. "If members of the present administration were finished and others came in to parlay amid the ruins, you must not be blind to the fact that the sole remaining bargaining counter with Germany would be the [British] fleet, and if this country was left by the United States to its fate, no one would have the right to blame those then responsible if they made the best terms they could. Excuse me, Mr. President, for putting this nightmare bluntly. Evidently, I could not answer for my successors, who in utter despair and helplessness might have to accommodate themselves to the German will." The warning about the Royal Navy made an impression. The one-ocean US Navy and the second-rate US Army Air Force would find the defense of the Eastern Seaboard very difficult against a combined naval force that included a German-controlled Royal Navy, and the 6 battleships, 19 cruisers, and 116 submarines of Mussolini's Regia Marina. On May 24, Roosevelt urged Mackenzie King, the Canadian prime minister, to ask the other dominion prime ministers to join him in making a joint plea to London to transfer the British fleet to North America. Coming from an American president, Roosevelt felt the request could be misinterpreted. Churchill knew about the secret approach to Canada, but he kept his anger in check until a proposal to lease British territories in the Americas to the United States came up at the morning cabinet on the twenty-seventh. Churchill told his colleagues he found such a prospect unbearable. "The United States has given us practically no help in this war, and now that they saw how great the danger was, their attitude was that they wanted to keep everything which would help us for their own defense."

A discussion of Stanley Bruce and his transgressions brought the cabinet back to common ground. Bruce was the Australian high commissioner, and his "gloomy view" of Britain's prospects had produced a sensation at a meeting of the dominion high commissioners the previous evening. When the incident came up at the morning cabinet, Chamberlain offered to reassure Bruce and the other high commissioners that "we resolve to fight on,"* even if

---

*In the transcript of the morning cabinet on the twenty-seventh, Chamberlain's statement—"we resolve to fight on"—is followed by a mysterious note in parentheses: *"This statement would apply of course to the immediate situation arising out of the hypothetical fall of France. It would not mean if at any time terms were offered they would not be considered on their merits"* [italics added]. It is unclear what the statement refers to,

France surrendered. A. V. Alexander, Churchill's successor as first lord of the Admiralty, favored a sharper response. He said Bruce should be given a good talking-to, but the dominions secretary, Viscount Caldecote, felt that was unnecessary. Bruce answered to the prime minister of Australia, Robert Menzies, and Menzies had "pledged all of Australia's resources in the event of France going out of the war." Caldecote was not as informed about Menzies's thinking as he imagined. At the end of May, Menzies would suggest approaching Roosevelt about a peace conference, and in July he would propose that Britain lay out her war aims as the starting point for a peace conference.

Churchill said he would "issue a general injunction to ministers to use confident language" to avoid any more incidents like Bruce's outburst. Then the cabinet broke for lunch, and the debate about war and peace shifted to Rome and Paris.

By the final week of May 1940, the European diplomatic community was divided about Italy's entry into the war. One school held that Mussolini's refusal to meet with high-ranking French and British officials and the gag order he had placed on his ambassadors meant Italy would march. A second school, composed largely of British and French diplomats, disagreed. Members of this group held that, in the case of Mussolini, character was destiny. The Duce's avarice ensured that he would see the war as an opportunity, and his cunning assured that he would wait until he sensed an intervention would command the very highest price, then jump in and offer his services to the belligerent powers as a mediator and a peacemaker.

---

how it got into the transcript, or who put it there. But its placement after the declaration "we resolve to fight on" suggests that despite the decision to fight on, Britain would still be prepared to consider any terms that might be on offer.

The Italian foreign minister, thirty-seven-year-old Count Galeazzo Ciano, belonged to the first school of thought. Ciano "could not fix the exact moment of Italy's entry into the war," he told an acquaintance. But he was sure "it would be soon." Ciano was arguably the second most interesting man in Italy in 1940. He had a physical glamour more often associated with Italian race-car drivers than Italian foreign ministers; he was a war hero, having commanded La Disperata, a renowned Italian bomber squadron, during the Abyssinian campaign. He was married to Mussolini's daughter Edda and his private life had launched a thousand rumors. What makes Ciano more interesting than the playboy who got daily rubdowns at the Rome Golf Club and could not keep his hands to himself around an attractive woman and the gangster who had been implicated in several murders is that he was also an authentic Italian patriot. Ciano believed Mussolini was leading Italy into the abyss, and in time he would turn against his father-in-law; but on May 27, a day all roads led to Rome, that time was still some years off.

One of Ciano's first visitors that morning was William Phillips, the American ambassador. Phillips announced that he was carrying a "message of the greatest importance from President Roosevelt" and had been instructed to deliver it personally to the Duce. Ciano said that was out of the question. Mussolini was not receiving visitors that day. If Mr. Phillips would give him the gist of the message, he would make notes and pass them on to his chief. The Roosevelt plan Phillips presented that morning sounded remarkably like the plan Halifax had proposed to Bastianini for a reason: it had been inspired by London and Paris. It read:

> In the hope of helping your Excellency to prevent [the] extension of [the war] to the Mediterranean theater and perhaps to other zones, I would like to submit to you certain considerations . . .

I am prepared to inform the governments of Great Britain and France of Italian aspirations in the Mediterranean zone, if you desire to make them known to me.... If you did wish to use my offer of mediation, it would be understood, should the three powers come to an agreement, that France and Great Britain would be deemed ipso facto, pledged to carry out immediately, at the end of the war, the conditions which had been agreed upon, and to accept the participation of Italy in peace negotiations on the same footing as that of the belligerent countries.

Ciano's unenthusiastic reaction annoyed Phillips. Didn't he understand? Phillips was speaking on behalf of the president of the United States! Ciano said he "understood completely, but nothing could now change the course of events. . . . Mussolini wants a war, and even if he were to obtain by peaceful means double what he claims, he would refuse."

A few hours later, André François Poncet, the French ambassador, visited Ciano. In the wrong light, it would have been easy to mistake François Poncet for a waiter at one of the better Parisian restaurants. But, along with the large nose, the neat mustache, the predilection for bow ties, and the air of perennial attentiveness, the ambassador also possessed a subtle feline intelligence and a talent for collecting information. When he was stationed in Berlin, William Shirer, the CBS correspondent, considered François Poncet the best-informed diplomat in the German capital. Over the past few weeks, the ambassador's visits with Ciano had acquired the character of a flirtation. Ciano, the suitor, would ask what territorial concessions Italy could expect in return for a pledge of neutrality, and François Poncet, the shy but coy damsel, would reply that he was not at liberty to reveal such information. Usually Ciano would press, though never very hard. Amoral in the big things, he was a gentleman in the small things. That day was a little different.

Ciano began as he had begun the Phillips interview, with a warning: Italy would march, and even "the richest gifts" could no longer dissuade Mussolini. Then, not really expecting an answer, he asked François Poncet, as a matter of personal curiosity, "what kind of presents" would France have been prepared to offer? Unexpectedly, this time Poncet exposed a little leg. "Tunisia and perhaps even Algeria." That night Ciano wrote in his diary: "My conference with Poncet is . . . important . . . as a psychological indication. . . . He made some very precise overtures [but] . . . he is too late." The Duce "is convinced that things are now coming to a head, and he wants to create enough claims to be entitled to his share of the spoils."

At about the time that François Poncet was telling Ciano "Tunisia and perhaps even Algeria," in Paris, Reynaud was telling Spears about his conversation with Halifax the day before: he said the foreign secretary had told him if Italy agreed to "collaborate in establishing a peace that preserved the independence of Great Britain and France" he, Halifax, would tell Mussolini that "the Allies would . . . discuss Italian claims in the Mediterranean, including those connected with the access to that sea."

Spears was shocked by Halifax's indiscretion but kept his surprise to himself. "The only way to keep the Italians out" of the war, he told Reynaud, "is to make it clear to them that if they do come in, they will be hit so hard that they will be only too glad to scuttle out again. To bribe them at this stage will only encourage them, and I cannot see the British people giving up Gibraltar and Suez."

Reynaud said the Panzers could take Paris whenever they wanted, but he said it in a way that sounded more like a pout than a warning.

Spears stood up and put his hands on Reynaud's shoulders. "These are tales for frightened children. The . . . lines of advance [into Paris] are comparatively narrow. They could be mined wholesale." Reynaud did not look reassured.

Spears left the meeting depressed. How could little Reynaud, with his toy soldier courage, stand up to Pétain: spectral, emotionally detached, and prepared to use his immense prestige to bring about an armistice; to Weygand, obsessed by the desire to emulate the Roman Senate and putting it about that Dunkirk was an "English defection"; to the Comtesse de Portes, who shared his bed, poisoned his mind, and "hated the English"; and to the comtesse's protégé Paul Baudouin, Reynaud's *chef de cabinet*, who was rumored to be working closely with "financial groups dead set against the war"? The premier possessed many virtues, Spears knew—intelligence, industry, patriotism—but lacked the strength of character and visceral courage of a Clemenceau or a Churchill.

Toward the end of May, Clare Boothe was sitting in Le Bourget Aerodrome, awaiting a flight to London, when a "little Frenchman" in a homburg and spats took the seat next to her. When they got to talking, Boothe discovered that her companion was a diplomat and a veteran of Verdun, the bloodiest battle of the Great War. For 299 days in 1916—through winter snow, spring mud, and summer heat—300,000 German artillery shells had daily poured into Verdun. When the shelling stopped on the 300th day, between 340,000 and 378,000 French soldiers were dead, and hundreds of thousands more were maimed. Boothe, who had read about Verdun as a schoolgirl, asked the diplomat how he had endured such carnage. "Let me tell you a story," he said. "The first day [I] was in the trenches, the barrage was so frightful it made the heavens tremble, and the next dawn it began again and the following day it was the same. . . . The third night, of my regiment, thirty men were left, and I said to myself, the battle is lost and I will die. . . . Then as the fourth dreadful dawn began to break, [I] told myself, 'Ah, but tomorrow, not even tomorrow can I live *forever*. . . . So although it was not easy, [I] decided when the sun lit the summer horizon to rise from the trench, [and] turn my rifle to the sound of the guns, saying, 'Good morning, death.'"

On the morning of May 27, 1940, Patrick Turnbull entertained a similar thought as he sat under a poplar tree outside Armentières, counting the twin-engine Dorniers and the Heinkel bombers forming up on the horizon. Turnbull counted 120 planes, then stopped. This morning, for the first time since the start of the German offensive, he was feeling something like relief. His transportation unit had been ordered to Dunkirk for early evacuation. As he was contemplating this happy thought, the driver in the lorry next to his shouted, "Who are the poor sods who are going to cop it this time?" and pointed to the sky. Turnbull looked up; the Dorniers and Heinkels had turned south and were headed toward him. Over Armentières, the planes opened their bomb bay doors, and columns of five-hundred-pound bombs whistled downward through the morning sky. Turnbull waited for Armentières to disappear in a cloud of black smoke; instead, jets of flames shot up from the town. The Germans were using incendiaries today. Death by explosives at least had the virtue of quickness; death by incendiaries did not. You burned and burned before you died. This thought brought to mind an ancestor of Turnbull's, one of the St. Giles martyrs, who had been burned at the stake. Turnbull took out his map and searched for an alternative road to the beaches. There were none. The only road to Dunkirk led through Armentières.

Five minutes later, Turnbull was "crashing down the main street [of the town] at sixty or seventy miles an hour." The heat from the burning buildings on either side of the street was so intense, the steering wheel was "burning in his hands," his face felt as if it had "been shoved in an overheated oven," and "stinging globules of plastic were dripping onto his trousers" from a melting plastic ornament on the dashboard. Turnbull was waiting for the petrol tank to explode and kill him or the flames from the buildings to engulf the lorry's cabin, when the street took a sharp turn and the holocaust abruptly gave way to "the blessed sight of green fields." Turnbull pulled over onto the grass and collapsed.

Earlier that morning, representatives of the French and British High Commands had met in Cassel, a town nineteen miles north of Armentières and one of the last outposts of seminormalcy along the Franco-Belgian border on May 27. Except for the columns of men and matériel passing outside the window, the occasional unburied body, and the distant sound of artillery fire from the town of Hazebrouck, where the Germans were attempting to break into the southern flank of the Allied corridor, the war was a relatively discreet presence in Cassel that morning. When the meeting convened at a local school, there was some talk of how to respond in the event a Belgian surrender suddenly left the northern side of the corridor undefended, but Dunkirk dominated the discussion.

In his memoirs, Churchill claims that Reynaud was told about the British evacuation during his visit to London on May 26. If so, Reynaud did not inform his generals, or, if he did, the information got garbled in transmission. Weygand's orders only authorized a French withdrawal to the port, not an evacuation. On the morning of the twenty-seventh, the French troops moving up to the corridor were under the impression that they would make a final stand in Dunkirk with their backs to the sea. Some historians have suggested that the British were deliberately vague on the "touchy subject" of evacuation, leaving the French to infer what was happening from events. Whatever the reason, on May 30 Gort's chief of staff, General Pownall, who, like his superior, was inclined to view perfidy as a uniquely French affliction, noted in his diary, "The French and British government were none too well *d'accord* over the business [of evacuation]."

Though there were many instances of bravery, the retreat

up to the beaches that morning had a chaotic, ragged character. Many of the troops, French and British alike, were very young—in their late teens or early twenties—new to combat, and led by officers often as inexperienced as they were. The troops were hungry, tired, and frightened; and, day and night, they marched toward an unseen sea, under a sky embroidered with silvery tracers, through a flat, featureless landscape offering little protection from shell fire or air attack, in boots sodden by marsh water. Inevitably, morale fell and incidences of indiscipline rose. Returning to his headquarters in the French town of Lomme, General Brooke of the Second Corps saw the body of a French soldier lying in the street. "Who shot him?" he asked. "Oh, some of these retreating French soldiers," his adjutant replied. "They said he was a spy, but I think the real reason was that he refused to give them cognac!" In another incident, a British officer had to draw his pistol to prevent a truck full of panicked French troops from driving his lorry off the road. In British units, acts of indiscipline were more infrequent but far from uncommon. Under the strain of exhaustion, fear, and hunger, inevitably some men broke. In one incident, an apparently shell-shocked officer refused to leave his hole, insisting he had to protect his eggs; he had no eggs. In another, a major jumped the line on the beaches and rushed a waiting boat. A naval officer shot him dead in the surf. Feeling betrayed by "the Frogs" and "the Belgies," who had "jacked it in, [leaving them] to carry the can," the retreating British troops pillaged shops and looted wine cellars. And, not infrequently, an officer or military policeman who challenged the looters would find a half-drunk nineteen-year-old waving a pistol in his face.

For Patrick Turnbull, the most vivid memories of the retreat were the enormous piles of abandoned British vehicles and heavy equipment he passed on the way to the beaches. "They boarded the road, they were in ditches, scattered over the sad flat fields.

They lay on their sides, stood forlornly on their wheels like lost dogs imploring adoption, were upturned, their wheels sticking up in the air like petrified limbs, twisted by bomb blasts, backed by fire, forming a seemingly unending and melancholy Guard of Dishonor." During the final week of May, when the government men appeared in Marjory Allingham's village to commandeer small boats for the evacuation, she thought, "Things [are] as bad as that, are they?"

Halifax's and Churchill's divergent views on that question produced some very sharp exchanges during the afternoon cabinet of May 27. "At the moment," said Churchill, who spoke first, "our prestige in Europe [is] very low. The only way we could get it back is by showing the world that Germany could not beat us. If after two or three months we could show that we were still unbeaten, our prestige would return. [Moreover,] even if we were beaten, we should be no worse off than we should be if we were now to abandon the struggle. Let us therefore avoid being dragged down the slippery slope with France."

Cabinet transcripts rarely convey the emotional atmosphere of a meeting. But after Churchill said "If worse came to worst, it would not be a bad thing for this country to go down fighting for the other countries which have been overcome by Nazi tyranny," one can almost sense Halifax's agitation swelling until, finally, the man Hitler once called "Christ's brother" seems to lose his composure entirely.

The day before, Halifax reminded the Cabinet, the prime minister said that if he was "satisfied that matters vital to the independence of this country were unaffected, he would be prepared to discuss terms." Now he "seemed to suggest that under no conditions would we accept any course except fighting to a finish." Halifax said he found this position unacceptable. He also took issue with Churchill's statement that "two or three months would show whether we were able to stand up to the air risk." Was the prime minister proposing to gamble "the future of the country on whether the enemy's bombs happened to hit our aircraft factories"? He would be prepared to take that risk if "our independence was at stake," Halifax said, "but if it were not . . . he would think it right to accept an offer which would save the country from avoidable disaster."

Churchill took half a step back. "If Herr Hitler were prepared to make terms on the restoration of German colonies, and the overlordship of Central Europe, that was one thing, but it was quite unlikely that he would make such an offer."

"Suppose Herr Hitler . . . offered terms to France and England," Halifax said. Would the prime minister "be prepared to discuss them"? It was a trick question, and it got a trick answer. Churchill said he "would not join the French in asking for terms, but if he were told what the terms offered were, he would be prepared to discuss them."

Chamberlain intervened at this point to put a question to the entire cabinet: What if Hitler offered France terms, and "when the French said they had Allies, Hitler said, 'I am here, let them send a delegate to Paris'"? Should Britain comply? The cabinet was unanimous: "The answer to such an offer could only be 'No.'" Despite the show of support for Churchill's no-surrender position, the two wise old elephants won the day on points. After further deliberation, the cabinet agreed to follow Chamberlain's suggestion and go a little farther with the Italian approach "to keep the French in good temper."

That morning, Stanley Bruce had brought the cabinet back to common ground. In the afternoon, Franklin Roosevelt would. After a discussion of the president's proposal to station the British fleet in "Canada or Australia," there was general agreement; Roosevelt "seemed to be taking the view that it would be very nice of him to pick up the bits of the British Empire if this country were overrun."

Rumors about the afternoon cabinet began to circulate almost immediately upon its conclusion. Colville heard that Halifax had said, "Our aim can no longer be to crush Germany but rather to preserve our own integrity and independence." Broadly correct though it was, the rumor omitted a significant detail: Halifax had played his trump card that afternoon, a resignation threat. "I can't work with Winston any longer," he told Cadogan when they talked a few minutes after the cabinet ended. "Nonsense," Cadogan replied. Winston's "rodomontades probably bore you as much as they do me, but don't do anything silly." There was no danger of that; Edward Halifax was the least silly man in England. The "apologies" Churchill offered Halifax when they spoke later that evening in the Downing Street garden restored their working relationship, but did not end their policy differences—nor take Halifax's resignation threat off the table. The foreign secretary's diary entry for May 27 reads, "I thought Winston talked the most frightful rot"—this was probably a reference to Churchill's "go down fighting" remark—"and Arthur Greenwood as well. I said exactly what I thought of them, adding that if that was their view . . . our ways must separate."

This long, tumultuous day was still not quite over. At 10:00 p.m., Churchill told an emergency meeting of the war cabinet that Belgium had capitulated, imperiling the BEF, whose northern flank was now unguarded and vulnerable to immediate attack. Prepare yourselves for "heavy tidings," the prime minister told his colleagues. In Paris, where the Belgian news was greeted with despair and desperation, elements in the Reynaud government argued for an approach to Mussolini independent of Britain.

When the ten o'clock cabinet meeting concluded, Colville walked Churchill back to Admiralty House, his residence until the Chamberlains vacated Downing Street. During the walk, Churchill said he "did not think [the French] would give in and at any rate, they ought not to do so." When he arrived at Admiralty House, Churchill was too restless to go to sleep. He read papers in his office for a while, then asked Colville to "pour me out a whiskey and soda, very weak, there's a good boy." Churchill was planning a surprise for the following day, but for now he was keeping it a secret.

At the American embassy in Grosvenor Square, Joe Kennedy was also up late, composing a cable to Washington about this eventful day. "My impression of the situation here is that it could not be worse. Only a miracle can save the British Expeditionary Force from being wiped out. . . . I suspect the Germans would be willing to make peace with both the French and British now—of course on their own terms, but on terms that would be a great deal better than they would be if the war continues. . . . I realize this is a terrific telegram but there is no question that it is in the air here . . . Churchill, Attlee, and others will want to fight to the death but there will be other numbers [political figures] who realize that the physical destruction of men and property in England will not be a proper offset to a loss of pride. In addition to that, the English people, while they suspect a terrible situation, really do not realize how bad it is. When they do, I don't know which group they will follow—the do or die or the group that wants a settlement. It is critical, no matter which way you look at it."

CHAPTER ELEVEN

"WE WERE NO LONGER ONE"

Early on the morning of May 28, a sultry Tuesday of low clouds, tropical temperatures, and intermittent showers, the bulk of the Belgian Army assembled in one of the last remaining unoccupied sectors of the country, a forty-eight-mile pocket that stretched westward from Menan to Cadzand, a coastal town on the Dutch-Belgian border. (There was a second pocket, around Bruges.) Many of the soldiers knew this region well. They had ridden the Ferris wheel in Dunkirk or honeymooned in Nieuport, a beach town north of Dunkirk. In the 1920s and 1930s, the coast of Belgium and northern France had been a popular resort area; now it was about to become the final resting place of the Belgian Army. Per the German surrender instructions, at first light Belgian troops had begun lining up along the puddled roads of the pocket. Once in position, hushed conversations could be heard here and there along the line, but many of the men were quietly staring at the ground, thinking of better days. This army of stumpy little chocolate makers, bakers, brewers, and ironworkers had gone to war with 1,338 artillery pieces but just 10 modern Renault tanks, 200 tank destroyers, 180 serviceable aircraft, and 42 armored cars—the legacy of King Leopold's failed neutrality policy—and had suffered in proportion. Between May 10 and May 28, the daily

Belgian casualty rate rarely fell below 1,000, and on bad days, such as May 24, the number of killed and wounded was closer to 2,000. The men standing by the road with four- and five-day beards and dazed expressions were what remained of that army.

Around 8:00 a.m., the hazy morning mist was illuminated by what looked like the lights of a distant city. The German staff cars were followed by a Panzer column, the young tank commanders standing erect in the open turrets as if posing for a photograph for *Der Sturmer*, the Nazi propaganda magazine; next came an infantry formation; then more Panzers. The stream of men and matériel continued through the morning to the muffled sound of artillery fire: the Germans moving west toward Nieuport and Dunkirk, their faces hidden under coal scuttle helmets; the Belgians, in their French-style Adrian helmets, marching east toward an uncertain future under white flags of surrender.

When the wireless announced the Belgian surrender later that morning, Jane Pratt, a Buckinghamshire woman, was typing a summary of the morning's events for her diary. Jane's first entry, an account of a dawn visit to her garden, was more a meditation on life in wartime than a report on plant life. "Rhododendrons, tulips, violets, white lilies . . . are still in flower but little else. . . . Spring came late this year. Summer is here now. Early, hesitant summer." Later that morning, the Belgian news produced another meditation, this one on duty. During the Great War, Jane had experienced death almost daily—the death of cousins, uncles, former schoolmates, tradesmen, teachers; but then she had been armored by the resilience of youth; now she was approaching late middle age. Could she go through all that again? "I . . . see what I must do," she wrote, "but I don't want to do it. . . . I don't want to do it." Overwhelmed, Jane began to cry. "This is a very dramatic moment. Am weeping all over my typewriter. Perhaps I shan't have to go. Shall I wait a little longer? But isn't that what we've all been doing—*hoping*, and we and the French are all alone against the Nazis . . . and they are at our doorstep." Jane rose from her writing desk resolved to join the Civil Nursing Reserve, but later in the day changed her mind and decided she could make a greater contribution to the war if she remained in Buckinghamshire and joined the staff of a local newspaper. That evening, Jane changed her mind again and was back where she started in the morning: hoping "something may happen to turn the tide of events and deliver me from the need of this sacrifice."

Because news of the surrender did not come through until late morning on the twenty-eighth, the morale reports for the day have a sketchy, anecdotal feel: "A woman weeping in a market place"; another woman describing herself as "furious" and "wildly annoyed" at King Leopold; strangers gathered around a wireless in stores and pubs, discussing the surrender. But the random observations all pointed to the same conclusion: the news had "given the British public a great shock," though that was not immediately apparent from the morning papers. It could be argued that the lateness of the Belgian announcement—4:00 a.m. on the twenty-eighth—caught the newspaper unprepared, but given the British press's addiction to sensationalism, that proposition could not be argued entirely convincingly. The *Star*, a popular London tabloid, devoted six pages to the racing results and two to the Belgian news on the twenty-eighth. The *Daily Mirror*'s coverage was more extensive, but sandwiching the surrender between ads for laxatives and a cartoon of "Jane," girl spy and "Queen of the Undie World," was tasteless. The BBC, which also wove the surrender into its usual light morning fare, got a sharp rap in the knuckles for it in the House of Commons that afternoon. "There is something wrong with the BBC today," S. Reed, a Labour MP, told the House. Have "we fallen so low that statements of national importance . . . [are to be] followed by the most trivial trash it was possible for a man to listen to?" Among the notable exceptions to the tabloid coverage was an editorial in the *Daily Express*: "The news is grave. It grows graver by the hour. There can be no pretence about the serious position of the BEF."

For obvious reasons, the *Express* did not elaborate on what made the BEF's position serious, but it was clear enough on the War Office maps. Against a determined infantry attack, the thin screen of British troops defending the twenty- to thirty-mile gap in the Allied corridor created by the Belgian surrender might be able to hold for a day—perhaps a day and a half—but no more. Then the Germans would break through the screen, set up a defensive perimeter across the corridor, and close the road to Dunkirk. "All this day of the twenty-eighth, the escape of the British army hung in the balance," Churchill recalled in his memoirs. "It was a severe experience for me, bearing so heavy a responsibility, to watch . . . flickering glimpses [of] this drama in which control was impossible and intervention more likely to do harm than good."

That evening, William Shirer, CBS News's Berlin correspondent, ended his day at the German Propaganda Ministry. The ministry was showing a new documentary, *The German Triumph in the West*, and as ruined town after ruined town flickered across the screen, Shirer noticed that the raspy-voiced German narrator was becoming more and more excited until finally he seemed to almost swoon at the carnage. " 'Look at the destruction, the houses going up in flames. . . . This is what happens to those who oppose German might!'" When the screening room lights came up, Shirer was momentarily frozen in his seat. On several occasions since May 10 he had wondered: "Is Europe soon to be ruled by such a people, by such sadism?" That night the answer seemed clearer than it had been a week ago.

———

The MPs who gathered in the House on the afternoon of the twenty-eighth to hear the prime minister's formal announcement of the surrender were expecting tales of measureless perfidy and threats to rip out Leopold's heart. Instead, they got the somber, measured words of a statesman acquainted with the sorrows of war. "I have no intention of suggesting to the House that we should attempt at this moment to pass judgment on the king of the Belgians. . . . The [Belgian] Army has fought very bravely and has both suffered and inflicted heavy losses." The response of the French, who shared a common border with Belgium, was less empathic. In a morning broadcast on the twenty-eight, Reynaud described the surrender as "a deed without precedent." By late morning, thousands of Belgian refugees were being thrown into the streets by their French hosts, and thousands more were taunted and heckled at French train and bus stations or attacked because their cars bore Belgian plates. Meanwhile, across the still-unoccupied regions of northern France, the cry went up "Anywhere but here!" By late afternoon of the twenty-eighth, a "polyphonic symphony of motor horns, roaring and humming engines, the thundering of heavy lorries . . . [and] the asthmatic rattle of old Citroëns" descended upon Limoges, a town 216 miles south of Paris. "All day and all night," said a resident, "the mechanized divisions of disaster passed by and the people in the streets stared at them; some pityingly, some with hostile contempt, some with anxiously thoughtful eyes, wondering when their turn would come to join the Great Migration to the south."

"A deed without precedent." For a moment that morning, Reynaud's brave speech made Spears think the French would "stand by us to the end." That illusion failed to survive a midmorning visit to the premier's office. There was no harmonium-like telephone ringing this time, just Spears, his companion; Ronald Campbell, the British ambassador; and Reynaud, who introduced his guest to two new French proposals. Spears thought the first, a direct appeal to Roosevelt for "the urgent armed intervention of the United States," gave off a fume of desperation. "We could not expect the Americans to declare war overnight," he said, ". . . and to ask the impossible, knowing it was impossible, would give the impression we had given up hope. . . . Our people would think we were clutching at straws."

Reynaud was astonished. The French people "would think he was doing exactly the right thing in appealing to the president." The premier's second proposal involved the Italian approach, which was proving a good deal more indestructible than the French Army. Reynaud said France was prepared to give Mussolini the names of the territories he would receive, in return for a pledge of Italian neutrality. Spears and Campbell knew this was a lie: Reynaud wanted the Duce to act as a mediator between the Allies and Hitler, but out of politeness—or maybe pity—they did not challenge him until Reynaud asked if Britain would match the great sacrifices France was prepared to make in its North African empire by offering concessions on Suez and Gibraltar. As Campbell tried to reason with the premier, Spears succumbed to a thought he had been resisting for days: "We were no longer one."

There were other signs of Allied discord on this cheerless Tuesday morning. During an 11:00 a.m. visit to BEF headquarters on the Franco-Belgian border, General Blanchard, commander of the French forces in the northern pocket, was "horrified" to learn that the BEF had been ordered to evacuate back to Britain. This was the first Blanchard had heard of the plan. His orders from Weygand were to fall back on Dunkirk and make a final stand. An argument ensued, Gort insisting that the Belgian surrender had left the Allies with no alternatives but evacuation or surrender; Blanchard insisting that a retreat would mean the destruction of the French divisions defending Lille. As Gort and Blanchard argued back and forth, one of those events that often happen in films and only rarely in real life occurred. An emissary from General Prioux, commander of the Lille garrison, arrived. Prioux would have to hold his position for another day, the emissary said. His men were too exhausted to retreat that night. Gort turned to Blanchard: "For the sake of France, the French Army, and the Allied cause," order Prioux to retreat now. Blanchard promised to talk to him, but he was still turning over Gort's earlier announcement. "Tell me something, General," he said. "If Prioux insists on holding his position for another day, will the BEF retreat, knowing the retreat will mean the destruction of the garrison? And leave the French units on the flanks of the BEF exposed to attack?" Gort repeated his earlier statement. His orders were to evacuate the BEF to Britain. For the next four days, the Lille garrison would defend the city and the southern rim of the corridor with such valor that, upon surrender on May 31, the Germans would afford the garrison the Honors of War. The British would be slower to publicly acknowledge the valiant French stand in Lille. In *Their Finest Hour*, published in 1949, Churchill finally gave the city's defenders their due: "These Frenchmen . . . for four critical days contained no less than seven divisions. Which otherwise could have joined in the assaults on the Dunkirk perimeter. This was a splendid contribution to the escape of their more fortunate comrades and of the British Expeditionary Force."

On May 28, the first war cabinet of the day convened at 10:00 a.m., an hour before the Gort-Blanchard meeting, and Dunkirk dominated the agenda. On the second day of the evacuation, it was still too early to foresee the immense scale Operation Dynamo would take: 861 vessels, including a cruiser; 39 destroyers; 311 small craft; 9 corvettes and gunboats; and 2,739 aircraft. But even on the morning of the twenty-eighth, it was evident that an immense and perilous adventure was in the making. Except for the evacuation figures—11,400 men rescued overnight and another 2,500 that morning—the generals had nothing but bad news for the cabinet. General Dill, the Chief of the Imperial General Staff (CIGS), reported that "Gort did not have enough troops" to close the gap [created by the Belgian surrender] and [would be unable to] prevent the Germans from breaking through to Dunkirk." Air Marshal Sir Hugh Dowding, head of Fighter Command, warned that the continuous patrols over the beaches had brought Fighter Command near to "the cracking point." "If this exceptional effort [over Dunkirk] had to be repeated on the following days," Dowding said, "the situation would be serious." "Serious" from Dowding meant the Dunkirk losses could weaken Fighter Command's ability to defend the home island. There was also a report that the SS *Queen of the Channel*, one of the ships evacuating troops, had been bombed off Dunkirk and was sinking; and that five to eight Panzer divisions, supported by several motorized units, were menacing the area around Hazebrouck, one of the last Allied strongpoints on the southern flank of the corridor.

Cassel, the hill town where the representatives of the French and British High Commands had met the day before, was not mentioned at the cabinet meeting, but on the morning of the twenty-eighth, the geography of the town—nine kilometers northwest of Hazebrouck—put it directly in the path of the German advance. The 145th Brigade, the rearguard British unit defending Cassel, was expecting an attack by evening, and it did not help brigade morale that Cassel's hill town views allowed the men of the 145th to watch the German units in the flatlands below cut off their line of retreat to the beaches. The rain and the splattering of human remains in the town square—the result of a direct hit on a personnel carrier earlier in the day—were further drains on morale.

Brigadier Nigel Somerset, the commander of the brigade, was the great-grandson of Lord Raglan, the man who had issued the order that resulted in the Charge of the Light Brigade at Balaclava. Now, unless withdrawal orders arrived soon, Somerset would be leading his own suicide mission. The London tabloids would love it, of course. Some fool of a newspaper editor would probably reprint Tennyson's "The Charge of the Light Brigade" next to his obituary.

> Half a league, half a league,
> Half a league onward,
> All in the valley of Death
> Rode the six hundred.

On another morning, Somerset might have found some black humor in the intersection of family, fate, and Fleet Street, but not on that morning. He was angry for his men and angry for himself. The destruction of an entire brigade seemed an awful price to pay to buy a few extra hours for the British and French troops moving up the corridor. "We were the 'Joe Soaps' [scapegoats] of Dunkirk," Somerset wrote later. "We were being sacrificed so that as many British and French [troops as possible] could get away from Dunkirk and get all the kudos for that. I felt very bitter about it."*

In London, the war cabinet meeting adjourned at about eleven, and Churchill attended to some business before preparing for his lunch with Lloyd George. On another day the old Welshman's wonderfully absurd white pompadour and cherubic face beaming with mischief and septuagenarian vanity would put a lift in Churchill's day; however, for him as for Somerset, May 28 was not such a day. There was some truth in the official explanation for that day's lunch and the two recent Churchill–Lloyd George meetings that had preceded it. The U-boat

---

*The 145th Brigade received a withdrawal order on the morning of the twenty-ninth.

campaign was threatening food imports, and Lloyd George had some clever ideas about how to increase domestic food production. But, mostly, Churchill used the meetings to explore the old Welshman's views on the war, which continued to be negative. In a long and cogent memorandum drawn up after the fall of France, Lloyd George would make what, in the context of summer 1940, seemed an unanswerable case for a compromise peace. The memorandum began with an audit of victory in the Great War. It had taken four years and nearly a million British and Empire dead; a million and a half French dead; nearly four million Russian dead; and hundreds of billions of pounds, dollars, francs, and rubles (in 1918 money) to defeat Imperial Germany. Against Nazi Germany, Britain would enjoy none of the advantages it had had in 1914–18. It would have no allies; it would have to fight its way back onto the Continent, then wage a trench war–style battle of attrition that could take five to ten years. Even America's entry into the war, increasingly viewed as Britain's last best hope, would not dramatically improve the situation. In the Great War, it had taken the United States two years to build an army capable of meeting a European opponent; it was reasonable to assume it would take that long again. Under such circumstances, the memorandum concluded, the best outcome Britain could hope for in a German war was an extended season of death, followed by a pyrrhic victory that left the home islands devastated and depopulated, the British economy bankrupt, and the empire in the hands of the Americans, the Japanese, and the Russians.*

---

*While the Lloyd George memorandum overstated the consequences, the damage the war did to Britain's postwar position was still significant. Gas rationing did not end until 1950, food rationing until 1954. Britain lost many of its markets and commercial airline routes to the United States, and the British economy, racked by periodic crises in the early decades of the postwar period, did not regain its equilibrium until the early 1980s. The British historians who argue that the war turned Britain into a "vassal state" of the United States exaggerate, but, as Lloyd George and many other critics of the war foresaw, it did cost Britain its position among the first rank of nations.

In late May, Lloyd George had yet to commit his thoughts to paper. Nonetheless, he had made no secret of his views. During the phony war he had argued that a compromise peace was the best path open to Britain; now, with the Germans on the French coast, he was arguing that it was the only path open to Britain.* Discretion not being among Lloyd George's undoubted virtues, Churchill was probably aware of his guest's intention to wait until "Winston went bust," then replace him. On the theory that Lloyd George's considerable capacity for mischief would be easier to control inside government than outside, over lunch, Churchill offered him a post at the Ministry of Agriculture.

Predictably, Lloyd George refused, and just as predictably, Neville Chamberlain was delighted that he did. Old men don't always forget, especially old men with egos large enough to be designated world heritage sites. Twenty-three years on, Chamberlain, whose political support was essential to Churchill, still had not forgiven Lloyd George for undermining him when he was Director of National Service in 1917.

"My Dear Winston," Lloyd George wrote the day after their lunch,

> You were good enough to ask me yesterday if I would be prepared to enter the War Cabinet if you secured the adhesion of Mr. Chamberlain to the proposal. . . . I can well understand the reason for your hesitancy, for in the course of our interview you make it quite clear that if Chamberlain interposed his veto on the ground of personal resentment over past differences you could not proceed with the offer. This is not a firm offer. Until it is definite, I cannot consider it.

---

*Lloyd George was not in favor of an immediate settlement. Like Churchill, he believed that Britain should fight its battle and demonstrate that it could not be beaten before sitting down at the negotiating table.

Before closing, Lloyd George could not resist taking a whack at Chamberlain.

Several architects of [the current] catastrophe are still leading members of your government and two of them [Chamberlain and Halifax] are in the Cabinet which directs the war.

Believe Me
DLG

Lloyd George's "no" was not the end of this particular story. Churchill was aware that if the war continued to go badly, he would be dismissed and a prominent national figure such as Lloyd George or Halifax brought in to negotiate a settlement with Germany. Churchill may also have used the luncheon on the twenty-eighth to test Lloyd George's fitness for office. The historian Paul Addison has argued that Churchill recognized that after the fall of France, Britain would be offered terms, and, as perhaps his most likely successor, he wanted to be sure Lloyd George, who was seventy-seven, still had the "root of the matter in him"—that is, he would refuse any terms that infringed on the independence of Britain.

The Churchill–Lloyd George lunch and the Belgian surrender were not the only significant events on May 28. Around three that afternoon, the 2,500 troops evacuated from Dunkirk earlier in the day boarded the London train in the port town of Dover. Five days hence, the bottom half of the sixty-six-mile London-Dover rail line would be an unbroken stream of discarded postcards, ice cream cartons, bottles, orange peels, cigarette packs, belts, and helmets; and the citizens of Kent and Surrey and London would be gathered, in their thousands, along the line, shouting, "Well done, lads!" and *"Vive la France!"* at the passing trains. But on the afternoon of May 28, Churchill had yet to issue his *bras-a-bras* (arm and arm) order, which gave French units equal priority with British units in the evacuation schedule. To the French troops in Lille facing the final extremity, the evacuation remained a rumor, if they had heard of it at all.

Ashford, one of the first stops on the London–Dover line, knew nothing about Lille or about the anger the French troops felt on the beaches as they watched BEF units disappear into the holds of the *Gracie Fields, The Maid of Kent,* and the other Channel steamers of the Southern Railway. When the London train stopped at the town station on the afternoon of the twenty-eighth, a battalion of white-haired matrons bearing fruit, biscuits, chocolate, beer, lemonade, jam, and cigarettes descended on the soldiers, who stepped off the train to stretch their legs. The low clouds and warm rain of morning had given way to an afternoon of patchy sunshine, and the station platform quickly filled to overcrowding with well-wishers. After the train left, Ashford would comment on how many of the young men had the same look about them: a disorderly face deeply browned by the French sun and bulging eyes that had "a wild or serious look"; and how they all seemed to speak of the same things: the long marches, sometimes on the double; the German ferocity; the injured civilians; the refugees obstructing the roads; the eye pain and breathing difficulties caused by the tear gas bombs the Luftwaffe was dropping on the beaches; and about the infrequent appearances of the RAF. This complaint owed something to Dowding's wish to preserve as much of the fighter force as possible, and something to the RAF's decision to intercept German air attacks before they reached the beaches, which often put British kills out of sight of the troops. The soldiers also spoke of "going to pieces a little" upon stepping back onto English soil, and of the parents, children, wives, brothers, and sisters they would visit on their forty-eight-hour leave. When the train pulled out of the station, two middle-aged railway workers gave the thumbs-up sign to the weary, unshaven young faces in the train windows.

Meanwhile, in London, members of the war cabinet were preparing for the afternoon session. Anticipating another confrontation, Churchill had used the concluding passages of his speech on the Belgian surrender to restate his argument for remaining in the war. He told the House that the Battle of France, though important, was only one battle in a contest whose decisive battle, the Battle of Britain, had yet to be fought. Then Churchill opened up his imagination and invited the House and the country in. The people of Britain, he said, were not just defending their towns and villages, not just defending the British nation and the British Empire. The sixty-year-old corporal, the nineteen-year-old mother on the lathe machine, and millions of ordinary Britons like them were defending something even more sacred, "the world cause." "I have only to add, that nothing which may happen in this battle can in any way relieve us of our duty to defend the world cause to which we have vowed ourselves, nor should it destroy our confidence in our power to make our way, as on former occasions in our history, through disaster and through grief to the ultimate defeat of our enemies." As Margery Allingham noted, Churchill's particular genius as a leader lay in his ability to make people feel they had to rise to his level, which had the effect of making them a little bigger and braver than they were in ordinary life. Deputized defenders of the "World Cause," milkmen, postal clerks, and housewives felt it a duty to fall in behind the prime minister. In this particular speech, however, Churchill was, subtly, also doing something else. By making the defense of the world cause a British mission, he was transforming the compromise peace option—historically an accepted diplomatic practice employed by many nations including Britain during the Napoleonic Wars—into an unacceptably shameful act.

The afternoon cabinet, which began promptly at four thirty, contained one new feature. The Italian approach was no longer spoken of in code as a way to keep Italy neutral or the French sweet. Everyone around the table knew the real purpose of the approach was to explore a negotiated settlement with Germany, had known it since the beginning of the debates. Now the ministers were prepared to speak openly and frankly about a subject they had mostly just alluded to in earlier discussions. Churchill was the first to rip off the fig leaf. He said the new French plan Reynaud had outlined to Spears the previous day was designed to lure Mussolini into a conversation, in hopes that it would lead to a conference along the lines of Munich. That would "put us on a slippery slope," and he was determined not to fall into that trap. "Our position would be entirely different when Germany had made an unsuccessful attempt to invade this country."

Halifax could find no sense in Churchill's argument, not on a day when Britain had only three and a half fully trained and equipped divisions to meet the invasion threat. Assuming Mussolini wished to play the part of mediator, he said, "and . . . could produce terms that would not [infringe on] our independence later, we ought to be prepared to consider such terms." Halifax admitted that "this hypothesis [enlisting Mussolini as a mediator] was a most unlikely one"; still, it was worth a try.

Archibald Sinclair, the air minister and a frequent guest at war cabinet meetings, said "there is no possible chance" of Britain receiving "acceptable terms" at the present moment.

Halifax disagreed. "We must not ignore the fact that we might get better terms before France went out of the war and our aircraft factories were bombed, than we might get in three months' time." Halifax's reference to "three months"—Churchill's time frame for bringing about Britain's deliverance—was probably not accidental.

If it was a sly dig, however, Churchill either missed it or chose to ignore it; he continued to attack the Italian approach. Mussolini "would take his whack out at us," he said, and it was naive to think that "Herr Hitler would be so foolish as to let us continue our rearmament." Then he reiterated an argument he had made several times since the start of the debate. If Britain continued the fight and was ultimately defeated, the terms offered would be no worse than the terms on offer now. He considered this point so important that he came back to it again a few sentences later. "A time might come when we felt we had to put an end to the struggle, but the terms would be no more mortal than those offered to us now."

Halifax said he still did not understand what was so wrong about testing the possibilities of a negotiation.

Churchill said he did. The real aim of Reynaud's new plan was to get us to the conference table and that, once we got there, "we should find that the terms offered [us] touched on our independence and integrity." Then he made a subtle psychological observation. "When, at this point, we got up to leave . . . we should find that all the forces of resolution which were now at our disposal would have vanished." Churchill's next point was a good debating tactic but historically questionable. He said, "Nations which went down fighting rose again, but those which surrendered tamely were finished."

Chamberlain also disliked the French plan, but fearing a flat no would weaken French resolve, he proposed that the cabinet fashion a reply that left the door open a little. "We should say to the French, 'In our view, mediation at this stage, in the presence of a great disaster and at a time when many people think we have no more resources left, could only have the most unfortunate results.'

. . . We concluded, therefore, that without prejudice to future, the present was not the time at which advances should be made to Signore Mussolini."

Toward the end of the debate, there was a sharp exchange between Halifax, who said that Reynaud also wanted Britain and France to make a joint appeal to the United States, and Greenwood, who said that Reynaud was too much inclined to hawk around appeals. A little later when Greenwood said that he did not feel this was the time for ultimate capitulation, Halifax took the statement as a personal attack. "Nothing in his suggestion [to test out the French plan] could even remotely be described as ultimate capitulation," he said.

It was nearly five fifteen now. Outside, the late-afternoon shadows were slipping across the back of the barrage balloons in Hyde Park, and the streets were filling with people returning from work. It was almost time to adjourn. But Clement Attlee, who had been silent for the past hour, wanted to say a final word about "public opinion." Attlee's statement was basically a restatement of a point Churchill had made several times. Public morale, already fragile, would shatter if word leaked out that the government was negotiating with Mussolini or Hitler. That was a real possibility, of course, but in an early June analysis of morale trends, Mass Observation found that the Belgian surrender and the other setbacks of May had, by forcing people to face the truth, created the foundation of a healthier, more resilient morale. "Roughly speaking," the MO report noted, "people are calm but exceedingly anxious. The events of the last month, while they have upset and in one sense lowered morale, have actually improved morale in the strictest sense of the word. For whereas before people were confident of victory, without a glimmering of what the struggle for victory might mean, now they realize to a considerable extent what they are up against. They don't realize it fully yet, especially the majority who left school when they were fourteen and have never crossed the Channel . . . but at least the period of wishful thinking is over." The statistical index MO used to track morale provided support for this view. In the index, 1.00 was the mean; scores above it indicated an increase in public optimism; scores below it, an increase in public pessimism. On May 10, the day the German offensive began, the index score was 0.82; on May 28 it was 2.17.

After Attlee finished, the cabinet briefly returned to Reynaud's proposal to make a joint appeal to Roosevelt, which no one liked. Then the other ministers went off to dinner, while Churchill prepared for the arrival of twenty-five members of the outer cabinet, whom he had promised to brief on the emergency in France. The meeting, which Martin Gilbert, Churchill's most distinguished biographer, called among "the most extraordinary scenes of the war," and John Charmley, another respected Churchill biographer, called "the most important meeting of 1940," was Churchill's surprise. And, whatever else the surprise was—a coup or just a briefing—it was Churchill unfettered and unbuttoned. The subjects he touched on included Dunkirk; Hitler; the fall of Paris; the invasion threat; and Oswald Mosley, leader of the British Union of Fascists. But they were woven into a narrative of valor and daring, which, in the mind of any halfway patriotic Englishman, would evoke images of national glory: Wellington at Waterloo, Chinese Gordon at Khartoum, Scott in the Antarctic, Drake sailing out to meet the Armada, the Light Brigade in the Valley of Death, and innumerable desperate last stands in the Punjab and the Khyber Pass of the "Gatling gun's . . . jammed and the colonel is dead" variety.

Churchill's guests loved every word of it.

"He was quite magnificent," wrote Hugh Dalton, the minister of economic warfare and a senior Labour politician. "The man, and the only man we have, for this hour." Dalton's notes of the speech indicate that in between the rhetorical flourishes, Churchill gave a full, frank, and completely calm account of events in France. Dalton has him saying of the evacuation that "it was necessary to fight our way through to the Channel Ports and get away all we could. How many we could get away we could not tell. We should certainly be able to get away 50,000. If we could get away 100,000 that would be a wonderful performance. Only Dunkirk was left to us. Calais had been defended by a British force, which had refused to surrender, and it was said there were no survivors.

"We must now expect the sudden turning of the war against this island," Churchill told his guests. "And we must not be taken by surprise, by any events. Attempts to invade this island would no doubt be made, but they would be beset by immense difficulty. We should mine all around our coast; our Navy was extremely strong; our air defenses were much more easily organized from this island than across the Channel; our supplies of food and oil were ample; we had good troops in this island, and others were on the way by sea, both British Army units coming from remote garrisons and excellent dominion troops, and, as to aircraft, we were now making more than good our current losses and the Germans were not.

"I have thought carefully in these last few days whether it was part of my duty to consider entering negotiations with That Man," Churchill said. "But it [is] idle to think that, if we tried peace now, we should get better terms than if we fought it out. The Germans would demand our fleet—that would be called disarmament—our naval bases and much else. We should become a slave state, though, a British Government, which would be Hitler's puppet, would be set up—under Mosley or some such person. And where should we be at the end of all that? On the other hand we had immense reserves and advantages.

"I am convinced," he concluded, "that every man of you would rise up and tear me down from my place if I were for one moment to contemplate parley or surrender. If this long island story of ours is to end, let it end only when each of us lies choking in his own blood upon the ground."

Churchill said many contradictory things in 1940, but when he spoke like this—and he spoke like this often that summer—he was speaking from convictions so deeply rooted in his being, they almost possessed a physical essence; combined with his manipulation of people and reports, it is difficult to imagine that he was capable of conceiving of any course other than victory, or a reasonable facsimile of it. He would fight on until the end, or until Parliament and the British people removed him from office.

When the war cabinet reconvened at seven, Churchill announced that, in the interim, he had briefed the members of the outer cabinet on the French emergency, and they had "expressed satisfaction when he told them there was no chance of our giving up." Indeed, said Churchill, he could "not remember having ever before heard a gathering of persons occupying high places in political life express themselves so emphatically." Toward the end of the evening cabinet Halifax brought up the Anglo-French appeal to the United States again. Should it be pursued? No, Churchill said. "At the present time [it] would be altogether premature. If we made a bold stand against Germany, [it] would command [American] admiration and respect, but a groveling appeal, if made now, would have the worst possible effect." Churchill also won the argument on the French plan Reynaud had presented to Spears. The cabinet agreed to reject it.

Not long after Germany's May 29 announcement that the British and French armies in northern France had become trapped in two pockets, a new joke circulated through Berlin. People would tell one another, "Now we have the Allies in both pockets"—and collapse in laughter. The smaller of the pockets was in the Lille region and held the remnants of the three French divisions still defending the town. The larger pocket, which ran roughly in a semicircle around the port of Dunkirk, held the BEF and a good portion of the French army sent north to defend the Dyle line. In newspaper maps, the pocket, which extended twenty-five miles inland from Dunkirk, resembled a thrusting sword and signified what was left of the Allied corridor, which was not much. On the twenty-ninth the general consensus among the troops in the corridor was that if they did not reach the beaches in the next thirty-six hours, they would never reach them.

In London that morning, Churchill issued a general injunction on morale. "In these dark days, the Prime Minister would be grateful if all his colleagues in Government, as well as officials as important, would maintain high morale in their circles, not minimizing the gravity of events, but showing confidence in our ability and flexible resolve to continue the war until we have broken the will of the enemy."

The injunction was well timed. In the final week of May, an end-of-days mood was settling upon certain members of the British political and military elite. On the twenty-ninth, another day of sun and intermittent rain, General Ironside wrote an elegy for the BEF and for Gort in his diary. "I shan't see him again. A gallant man. Little we thought a couple of weeks ago that this would be the end of the BEF." Henry Channon also felt the apocalypse approaching. "I wonder as I gaze out on the gray and green Horse Guards Parade, with the blue sky, the huge silver balloons like bowing elephants, the barbed wire and the soldiers about, is this really the end of England? Are we witnessing, as for so long I have feared, the decay and perhaps extinction, of this great island people?" Pessimism had also infected the Imperial General Staff. In a series of June reports, the CIGS, Sir John Dill, would question whether the British Home Army had the training and the steadiness to defeat a German invasion force, and at various points in June both Dill and Dudley Pound, the first sea lord, would raise doubts about the "ability of the Navy to protect us," and about the effectiveness of the RAF, which had been "greatly weakened by operations in France." "The scene continues to darken day by day," Chamberlain wrote in his diary. In public, Churchill wore his resolve like a suit of armor, but, away from the public eye, he was occasionally visited by fears that Britain's long island story had reached the final chapter. In a May 27 cable to the dominion prime ministers, he said that while Britain had every intention of remaining in the war, "this view is of course without prejudice to considerations that might hereafter be put forward for the cessation of hostilities and subject to developments in the military situation, which is now liable to change from hour to hour."

Mass Observation's morale report for May 29 provided considerable evidence for the contention that ignorance is bliss. "On the whole, morale was good today," MO noted, but the positive appraisal owed a great deal to the sizable number of people who had been confused by press accounts of the Belgian surrender and thought the Belgian government's renunciation of the king meant that the Belgian Army was still fighting, and to people who had left school at fourteen and had never been abroad. Together, the two groups offset the low morale scores of a third group, "the better off and the better educated, the students of strategy and the people who have crossed the Channel [and] see the position more clearly, or too clearly and, indeed, often exaggerate in their mental anticipation."

Clare Boothe, who had spent most of May in Paris, had a different view of British morale. "The average Englishman, while worried, was not like the average Frenchman, despairing. . . . The English were stiffening themselves for the coming struggle [but] they were still in no wise in the war the way the French people were." Leading members of London's diplomatic community, including Ivan Maisky, the Soviet ambassador; the Duke of Alba, the Spanish ambassador; and Björn Prytz, the Swedish ambassador, were also impressed by the steadiness of the British public. In a May 31 dispatch, another diplomatic admirer, Giuseppe Bastianini, reported to Rome that British morale was "up." Margery Allingham's theory about morale may explain the steadiness that foreigners found so admirable. In Margery's view, eyes straight ahead and a stiff upper lip were not totems of resolve but coping mechanisms that helped people keep their fears of a "smash-up" under control. The fear was never entirely hidden, though, not from people who knew how to look for it. Walking through a half-empty London on the afternoon of May 30, Edward R. Murrow saw signs of it in the grave faces and in the almost trance-like state of the "people walking slowly along the streets, reading their newspapers"; and in the deserted tearooms and half-empty shops in Bond Street. The fear was also apparent in the war rumors that George Orwell was collecting. On May 29 his diary contained almost half a dozen new ones, including that the Germans would inaugurate an air campaign against Britain, with a massive bomber strike on London on May 31, two days hence. "That Hitler's plan for invading England [included the] use of thousands of speed boats which can ride over the mine fields. That there was a terrible shortage of rifles"—this rumor was true. "[And] that the morale of the ordinary German soldier was pitiably low." (This rumor was untrue.)

Fear of the "smash-up" was also apparent in the offices of the Canadian High Commission, which, as the emergency in France deepened, had steadily gained favor with wealthy Britons (Canada did not yet have embassies of its own), who had hitherto regarded the office as the dull outpost of a dull colonial race. Day after day, "a stream of people press in, seeking travel visas for themselves or their children," wrote Charles Ritchie, a young Canadian diplomat. A certain "Lady B., looking radiant, comes in to ask if I would arrange for her son's prep school to be affiliated with a boys' boarding school in Canada and to migrate [her son's schoolmates] 'en masse' to Canada. The Marchioness of C., in the uniform of the Woman's Naval Auxiliary Unit, wants to get three children out to Canada at once. . . . The Austrian Rothschilds"— escaped from a concentration camp—"trying to pass their medical exams to go to Canada, ask if I would arrange a financial guarantee for them."

In early June, Ritchie, whose experience of war was limited to the German POWs he had seen on a boyhood visit to Calais in 1920, drove down to Dover. The evacuation was in full swing now, and the refuse trail on the London-Dover line, which had reached only up to Ashford on May 28, now encroached on the London suburbs. Dover's geography—twenty miles from France—gave the town an ancient knowledge of war. Dover Castle, begun as a Roman lookout post, had been built into a proper fortification by Henry II. In the nineteenth century the town acquired two new fortifications, Dover Redoubt and Dover Turret. The peculiarities of the current war had created two Dovers. One was centered around Castle Street, where rows of Union Jacks fluttered above gaily decorated tables manned by smiling young women who feigned shock at the cheeky banter of the soldiers and sailors who stopped for a doughnut, a crumpet, and something to drink. The other Dover was where the war was. The soldiers disembarking from the battered destroyers and Channel ferries had the haunted look of men who had been to places where, even in the deepest watches of the night, death had slept with one eye open. When

Ritchie arrived that morning, a British destroyer, "its stern blown clear off by a bomb, was limping home with flags still flying."

On the other side of the harbor, a group of French sailors were having an animated debate about the physical attributes of the naked woman in the photo they were passing around. Presently, a large navy tug arrived with a hundred or so German POWs. Ritchie was surprised by their appearance. The Great War POWs in Calais had had shaven heads. "These men . . . had long hair which fell over their eyes as they stumbled along the gangplank. Some were aviators and . . . had an air of arrogance." The other ranks, the privates and corporals, who ran down the gangplanks and huddled together like sheep on the pier, were hard to connect with the stories Ritchie had heard about German ferocity. Shorn of their weapons and coal scuttle helmets, the soldiers looked like "amputees [who] had been deprived of some vital limb or . . . castrated." The German wounded were the last to be unloaded. They were swung down from the tug's decks by a crane and then laid out on stretchers along the pier. Many were very young and already had the "waxen immobility" of the dead. Out beyond the harbor, a mist was forming over the smooth Channel sea, and from the direction of the Dover cliffs, sparkling under the late-spring sun, the cawing of gulls could be heard. From his vantage point on the pier, Ritchie could see "a group of old ladies coming out of church after eleven o'clock services." Several of the women stopped to chat near a field of buttercups where a gaggle of "little boys were rolling about wresting." Ritchie noticed that all the boys were wearing "a little cardboard gas mask case."

A little before 4:00 a.m. on Thursday, May 30, the telephone rang in Edward Spears's Paris apartment. An hour later, the prime minister's special representative to France was standing by a window in the British embassy on the rue du Saint-Honoré reading a cable from Churchill. Outside, the thin morning light was creeping across the embassy lawn, absorbing the dew on the freshly mowed grass. Over the past thirty-six hours, Spears's frustrated outburst about the state of the Anglo-French alliance—"We were no longer one"—had gone from a premonition to a truth foretold. The day before, Reynaud did not complain about the war cabinet's rejection of the new French peace initiative when Spears visited him, but that was about the only British action he did not complain about. London's mild response to the Belgain surrender, the BEF's precipitous withdrawal to the beaches, and its by-product: dozens of French units left with their flanks flapping in the air, including the three French divisions trapped in Lille: Reynaud had a large collection of British perfidies on hand, and he held each one up to the light and invited Spears to inspect it with him.

Churchill's cable was intended to address the complaints. Henceforth, French troops would "share in evacuation to fullest possible extent"; the Admiralty would aid the French Navy, as required; and upon its reconstitution the BEF would return to France. The cable also included an instruction to Spears; he was to deliver it "forthwith to Reynaud." But where to find the premier at five o'clock on a Thursday morning? A duty officer at one of the French ministries suggested Reynaud's apartment at the Palace du Palais Bourbon. When Spears arrived at 7:00 a.m., there were no female garments hanging about, as there had been on previous occasions—just Reynaud in a kimono, doing his morning exercises. It says something about Spears's state of mind that morning that he found nothing odd about that.

The first point in the Churchill cable—"French troops to share in evacuation to fullest possible extent"—occasioned a sharp exchange. "Sourly, almost sarcastically," Reynaud said that he was very glad Churchill had emphasized that "the French would be evacuated in equal numbers"; otherwise, it would be necessary to *déchaîne* (unleash) French opinion against Britain. Spears, who was still more soldier than diplomat, did not help the cause of Allied unity by replying that only Churchill's "strong hand [had] prevented British opinion being *déchaîne* against the French Command and the French generally." The two men stared at each other for a moment; then Reynaud said, in "a tone [Spears] had never heard him use [before] when talking of Churchill . . . that his resentment was as deep as was his incomprehension of the Prime Minister's attitude toward the King of the Belgians."

At the morning meeting of the French War Committee, which convened two hours later, General Weygand appeared in a new role. He was now the mortician who, having prepared the grave site, was anxiously awaiting delivery of the corpse. He told the committee that once the Germans turned south and pushed through the French defenses on the Somme–Aisne line (the last major defensive line before Paris) the army "would go on fighting, but he could not see where organized resistance could take place." Leaving the meeting, Spears felt a hand on his arm. When he turned around, Weygand was staring at him. "Send us everything you've got," he whispered. When the Germans turn south after the Dunkirk operation, the 43 to 50 French divisions defending the approaches to Paris would be facing 150 divisions. That night, Spears wrote in his memoirs, "I was overcome . . . by a feeling akin to despair. . . . It seemed suddenly unbearable to see at close hand the France I had cared for so much collapsing before my eyes. For a moment, I felt the madness that would come to a living being chained to the body of a loved creature dissolving in death."

In London, the absence of further debate on a negotiated settlement after Churchill's performance before the outer cabinet on May 28 became a source of rumor, innuendo, and speculation. Had the debate just petered out of its own accord? Had the war cabinet reached a secret accord? Or did the hiatus foreshadow a purge of Halifax and Chamberlain? Henry Channon's theory was that the silence presaged "a definite plot . . . to oust Halifax and all the other gentlemen of England from the Cabinet." Alec Cadogan was agnostic about the reasons for the cabinet's silence, but during "a horrible discussion of what instructions to send Gort" on the twenty-ninth, he had noticed a lot of tension among Churchill, Halifax, and Chamberlain. "W.S.C. [Churchill] rather theatrically bulldoggish. Opposed by N.C. [Chamberlain] and H. [Halifax]. Fear relations will become rather strained. That is Winston's fault, theatricality."

May 30, like every other day since May 10, began in crisis. By noon, 80,000 men had been evacuated, a better-than-expected result. But Fighter Command's decision to put larger but fewer air patrols over Dunkirk had made the already perilous air situation more perilous. At 8:15 a.m. the destroyer *Vimy* on station off Dunkirk cabled London: "Request continuous fighter action in the air. No more Beauforts [a slow, porky twin-engined torpedo bomber] left. If these conditions [are] . . . not complied with, a scandal, repetition, scandal, reflecting on the present British Cabinet will pass to History." Thirty-five minutes later, the Admiralty Operations center in Dover received a request from Lieutenant Fletcher, a naval officer in Dunkirk: Small "boats urgently required. Only two whalers, one cutter, one motor boat, and about 60,000 soldiers to embark. Matter most urgent."

Stories like Fletcher's would not find any place in the saga of the "little boats" created by the writer and broadcaster J. B. Priestley, whose cozy Yorkshire voice had the same effect on his wartime audience as warm milk on a cold night. "We've known them and laughed at them, all our lives," Priestley said in an early June broadcast, praising the role of the small boats in the evacuation. "We've called them the 'shilling sicks.' We have watched them load and unload their crowd of holiday passengers—the gents full of high spirits and bottled beer and the ladies eating pork pies, the children sticky with peppermint rock." When the ferry steamer *Gracie Fields* was sunk, Priestley gave it a Viking funeral. "But now—look—this little steamer, like all her brave and battered sisters, is immortal. She'll go sailing proudly down the years in the epic of Dunkirk. And our great-grandchildren, when they learn how we began the war by snatching glory out of defeat, may also learn how the little holiday steamers made an excursion into hell and came back glorious." The RAF would enter the ventricle of national memory during the Battle of Britain later in the summer, but in the final days of May few of the men on the beaches had a good word to say about the airmen. Boarding a destroyer in Dunkirk Harbor, Alan Deere, a Spitfire pilot shot down outside Dunkirk, was stopped by an army major who told him, "For all the good you chaps seem to be doing, you might as well stay on the ground." When Deere finally did get aboard a ship, "he was greeted in stony silence by a crowd of . . . army officers. 'Why so friendly?' he asked. 'What have the RAF done?' 'That's just it,' said one of the officers. 'What *have* they done?'"

When the afternoon war cabinet convened a little after five o'clock on the thirtieth, the ministers received a rare piece of good news: according to the latest War Office estimates, thus far 105,000 men had been taken off the beaches; the Admiralty estimate, 101,000, though slightly lower, was still well above the original estimate of 40,000 to 50,000 men. The other topics on the cabinet agenda that afternoon included a report that the senior French officers in Dunkirk still "had received no orders at all about evacuation," that Count Ciano had called in the British ambassador to discuss the evacuation of British nationals from Italy, and that Reynaud wanted to make yet another approach to Mussolini.

Air Chief Newall's warning of a large-scale German airborne and seaborne raid on Britain prompted a discussion of the invasion threat. Dudley Pound, the first sea lord, said the recent intelligence pointed to a heightening of the threat. German activity along the Norwegian coast had increased notably, and the Kriegsmarine was collecting motorboats in Hamburg, Bremen, and other German port towns. When Pound said the Germans had also left one line of approach to the coast open when they mined the coastal waters of southern England, Churchill became agitated: "We should not hesitate to contaminate our beaches with gas if this course was to our advantage. . . . We have the right to do what we want with our territory."

Pound sounded less than enthusiastic about Churchill's proposal. If the Kriegsmarine made a determined night attack, some vessels would probably get through, he said.

Toward the end of a discussion on the new French appeals for troops and aircraft, for "concessions to Italy," and for an Anglo-French approach to President Roosevelt, Churchill said that "when we refuse these requests, the French would use these refusals as an excuse for giving up the struggle." Then he announced that he would fly to Paris the next day to speak to Reynaud.

The next morning, when the prime minister's 10:00 a.m. arrival time came and went with no sign of his plane, the dignitaries on the tarmac at Villacoublay Aerodrome began whispering to one another. An indeterminate number of minutes passed; the whispers grew louder, the speculations more ominous; then a particularly "keen-eyed" dignitary pointed to the sky; almost immediately other hands were pointing upward. Against the gray cloud bank over Paris, the tiny silver speck to the north of the aerodrome was easy to pick out. A few minutes later, a smiling Churchill was poking a playful finger into Spears's belly. The other members of the British party included Attlee, who, in a display of proletarian solidarity, had left his new black homburg hat uncreased; the CIGS, John Dill, a tall, slim man with an elegant manner and a distant air that made him seem never entirely present; and Pug Ismay, Churchill's military adviser and a man of steadiness, good temper, and good sense.

Arriving at the French Ministry of War on the rue Saint-Dominique a little before 2:00 p.m., the British party was ushered into a large, sunlit conference room on the first floor. An immense baize-covered conference table dominated the room, which looked out on a lovely garden in the courtyard. The French delegates, who had arrived a few minutes earlier, had commandeered the side of the table with garden views, leaving the British guests with nothing to look at but their French opposite numbers across the table. They did not look very welcoming. Across from Churchill sat a sulking Reynaud; across from Dill sat Weygand, wearing an enormous pair of riding boots that gave him a certain resemblance to an aging Puss 'n' Boots. Pétain, who "look[ed] particularly somber," was sitting off by himself, having no opposite number. The marshal fascinated Spears. He never displayed any signs of "broken morale" that Spears could detect. He "had none of Weygand's ups and downs, no wild alterations between 'We will manage somehow' and 'All is lost.'" Pétain was detached but not in the way Dill was. His remoteness seemed to say: "I, Philippe Pétain, hero of Verdun, bear no personal responsibility for the sordid mess the current war has become. My war was the Great War; I had been one of the architects of the glorious victory France had won in 1918." As far as Spears could tell, Pétain viewed the current war as "a rather tiresome . . . almost boring drama taking place in a distant branch of the family from which his attention could not be entirely withheld." The only Frenchman in the room whose resolve Spears fully trusted was Georges Mandel, but Mandel was a Jew, and in the France of the Third Republic it was best to keep that kind of thing to oneself.

Churchill opened the thirteenth meeting of the Supreme War Council with an announcement: As of noon that day, May 31, 165,000 men had been evacuated from Dunkirk, including 10,000 wounded.

"How many French?" Weygand asked.

"So far only fifteen thousand."

"The French are being left behind?" Weygand's voice was "querulous and aggressive." Spears looked over at Churchill, expecting one of those Churchillian "sentences that hit like a blow." To his surprise, "the light had died out of [the prime minister's] face. It was evident that he [believed] every indulgence must be shown to people so highly tried, undergoing so fearful an ordeal." "We are companions in misfortune," Churchill told the French delegates. "There is nothing to be gained from recrimination over our common miseries." The stillness that followed this observation was "something different from silence," Spears recalled. "It was like the hush that falls on men at the opening of a great national pageant."

Weygand's question had disrupted the conference schedule. Three subjects were to be discussed that afternoon, and Dunkirk was the second. The first, Narvik, now seemed as remote as the Punic Wars. Having finally captured the town a few days earlier, the members of the Supreme War Council concluded that the British brigade and the fifteen to sixteen thousand French and Polish troops occupying Narvik, and the hundred antiaircraft guns they had brought with them, could more profitably be employed on the Somme–Aisne line or defending the beaches of southeastern England against invasion.

After the council agreed to evacuate Narvik on June 2, the discussion returned to Dunkirk and the British and French evacuation numbers. Churchill said the principal reason for the large disparity in the figures was that, "up to the present, the French troops [in Dunkirk] had received no orders to evacuate." Here Weygand interrupted to say that an evacuation order had been issued to General Blanchard, who had possessed no such order when he spoke to Gort on May 29. The conversation wandered off in other directions for a few minutes; then Reynaud brought it back to the evacuation numbers. His voice was pleasant, calm, and even, but his words were not. "Out of two hundred and twenty thousand British troops, a hundred and fifty thousand had been evacuated," he said, "whereas out of two hundred thousand Frenchmen, only fifteen thousand had been taken off. This was bound to evoke extreme and possibly dangerous repercussions in [French] public opinion, should it become known."

After noting that he was anxious that France be left with no further grounds for complaint, Churchill said, "Today, May 31, had been designated French day [at Dunkirk]; the French had absolute priority over the British." Spears noticed that Churchill's jaw thrust forward noticeably when he said the British rear guard at Dunkirk would "fight to the water edge, even though they may be *assommé*" ("wiped out").

Pétain's ancient face, pockmarked with brown age spots, remained expressionless during Churchill's speech.

Reynaud said he hoped that upon completion of the Dunkirk operation, the full strength of the RAF and the BEF would be transferred to the Somme–Aisne line to help defend Paris. This would not imperil Britain, as "the Germans would [not] attack Great Britain until the French had been liquidated."

The BEF would have to be rebuilt first, Churchill replied. "Our army will have lost everything but its rifles. We shall have lost a thousand [artillery] guns, which is extremely serious; there are not more than five hundred guns in England today. [And] we have lost thousands of lorries. Should a small German force, well equipped with artillery, land in England, it could not be opposed by a force of equivalent strength. In such a case, the civil population would fight with . . . unconquerable resolve." Then, overwhelmed by the image of old men and prepubescent girls with hundred-year-old rifles making desperate last stands in schools, fields, and factories, Churchill said:

It must be realized if Germany defeated either Ally or both, she would give no quarter. They would be reduced to the status of vassals and slaves for ever. It would be far better that the civilization of Western Europe, with all its achievements, should come to a tragic but splendid end than that the two great Democracies should linger on stripped of all that made life worth living.

Spears glanced over at Pétain. The marshal looked "personally insulted." He finds Churchill's rhetoric offensive, Spears thought.

The meeting concluded with a brief discussion of Italy, the third subject on the council agenda. Believing its entry into the war imminent, Churchill proposed that the moment Rome issued a declaration of war, air strikes be launched against its major industrial cities: Turin, Genoa, and Milan. After the meeting adjourned, several of the council principals, including Pétain and Churchill, gathered in front of a bay window near the far end of the conference room. Despite all the setbacks France had endured, Churchill had never given up hope that it would eventually find its man of destiny—its Clemenceau, its Napoleon. Now, watching Pétain, "detached and somber," standing at the bay window, his bent frame silhouetted by the afternoon sun, Churchill realized that France had already found its man of destiny and it was his intention to deliver it a separate peace at the earliest opportunity.

In Britain, Mass Observation's morale index, which had stood at 2.17 on May 29, indicating public optimism, fell to 0.76 on the thirty-first, indicating deep public pessimism. Whatever Churchill might tell the French, the Americans, and the world about British resolve, the reality was, a sizable portion of the British public was distraught and frightened.

CHAPTER TWELVE

END OF THE AFFAIR

Whensoever the last day of the Kingdom of France cometh, it will undoubtedly be the event of the destruction of England.
—Sir Walter Raleigh,
English Voyages of the Sixteenth Century

Later, when men who had been at Dunkirk spoke of their time there, often they spoke first of the nights, of the exploding parachute flares that hung in the night sky like "young moons," of the tracer bullets that cut silvery tracks across the face of Venus and Mars, and of voices singing in the darkness to cheer themselves up. One evening a lone voice sang: "Oh, I do like to be by the seaside. . . . I'll be beside myself with glee" in a thick Yorkshire accent. Then there were the beaches at night: "black with great columns of men, some five miles long and a hundred yards wide," and illuminated by enormous pillars of fire, the front ranks of the column thrusting out into the water, among bomb and shell splashes . . . shoulder deep moving forward . . . heads just above the little waves that rode up to the sand." And behind the front ranks, mile after mile of men passing the Ferris wheel and bandstand near the beaches and stepping down into the sand, their boots making a crunching sound as they crossed the dunes to the water's edge. "Then moving into the water, from ankle deep to knee deep. From knee deep to waist deep, until they . . . came to shoulder depth" and a friendly hand reached out of the darkness and pulled them onto a trawler or schooner, where, shivering, wet, and exhausted, they lay on the deck, looking like sea creatures crawled up to the shore to die.

Saturday, June 1, the day after the Paris meeting, was among the most deadly days of Operation Dynamo. The Luftwaffe was over the beaches early that morning. The destroyer HMS *Keith* was first hit at around seven thirty, and by 10:00 a.m., when the sky cleared, the *Keith* and half a dozen other vessels were underwater and the sea around Dunkirk was filled with corpses in bright yellow life jackets bobbing up and down on the morning tide. One sailor, both arms blown off at the elbows, was simultaneously screaming and attempting to stay afloat in his life jacket. Just before the German attack broke off, the sailor disappeared beneath the sea. If he cried out for help before he died, there is no record of it.

In Paris that morning Churchill had an early breakfast, then was driven out to Villacoublay Aerodrome for his return flight to London. Events in Dunkirk had not yet fully revealed themselves, which left the prime minister free to contemplate the previous day's session of the Supreme War Council. The meeting had provided several particularly striking examples of the new hierarchy of intimidation that had developed among the great democracies of the West. Paris pressured London for military aid with threats of surrender; London pressured Washington for assistance with threats of a German-controlled Royal Navy; and, atop the hierarchy, Washington pressured the Canadians to have the British fleet transferred to North America. The previous day had provided one particularly dramatic example of the first type of intimidation, French-on-British pressure. During the council meeting no one on the French side had played the armistice card, but later, during an informal discussion in the conference room, a high-ranking

French official took Churchill aside and said, in the "polished way" French officialdom spoke of unspeakable things, that "a continuation of military reverses might, in certain eventualities, enforce a modification of the foreign policy on France." Spears, who was standing next to Churchill, immediately calculated the diplomatic etiquette of the situation. It would be better if he, not the prime minister, who spoke for the British nation, responded, and the response should be directed not at the official, who was an impudent functionary, but to the most important Frenchman in the room. Fixing his gaze on Pétain, Spears said, "I suppose you understand, M. le Marechal, that [a French surrender] would mean a British 'blockade' and not only 'blockade' but *bombardment.*'"

When Churchill's car arrived at Villacoublay at about 10:00 a.m., an escort of nine fighter planes was drawn up in a wide semicircle around his Flamingo. "Grinning and waving his stick," Churchill emerged from the backseat and walked toward the pilots, who were standing at attention in front of their planes. Spears, who had come to the airport to see the prime minister off, watched each "handsome young" face light up as Churchill stopped to exchange a word or two. A moment later, the door of the Flamingo slammed shut, a smiling face briefly appeared in one of the windows, and then, like a mother hen gathering up her chicks, the Flamingo led her escorts up into the morning sky. By the time it set down in London around 11:00 a.m., it was apparent that the Luftwaffe was making a supreme effort over Dunkirk that day. The attacks of June 1 sank or disabled thirty-one British vessels, including nine destroyers and personnel ships, cost the RAF several dozen aircraft, and halved the evacuation rate from sixty thousand men on May 31 to thirty-one thousand on June 1.

Though the losses would take a day or so to tabulate fully, briefings by Anthony Eden, the secretary of war, and Lord Gort, who had been evacuated from the beaches the previous night,* left the war cabinet in no doubt that the final extremity had arrived. "Maximum efforts must be made to get as many troops off as possible" that night, said Eden, who was either unaware of or did not care about Churchill's *"Bras dessus, bras dessous"* pledge. The previous day, in a dramatic display of Allied solidarity, the prime minister had shouted *No!* when Reynaud told the Supreme War Council that British troops would receive priority in the evacuation schedule. *"Bras dessus, bras dessous,"* Churchill insisted. Allied troops must leave the beaches arm in arm, French soldiers having equal priority with British.

It was a gallant gesture, but not well thought out. During the morning cabinet, it emerged that tens of thousands of French troops were still making their way up to the beaches and would not arrive until the next day, June 2, or the day after, June 3. The choices confronting Churchill were stark: risk the RAF and the Royal Navy to keep Dunkirk open for the French, or evacuate the BEF and inflict a potentially mortal injury on the Anglo-French alliance. The cabinet transcript gives no hint of indecision. Churchill said that the evacuation must be finished that night. French troops not on or near the evacuation beaches by the end of the night would be left behind. In an urgent cable to Paris that afternoon, General Albert Lelong, the French military attaché, told his superiors, "I have insisted that the question [holding open the beaches] should be discussed by the Chiefs of Staff and the war cabinet. [But] I fear this will not change what I am telling you now." Despite the negative tone of the cable, Lelong, who had been in London long enough to know what British buttons to push, had no intention of giving up. Later that afternoon, he told

---

* Gort's evacuation was ordered by Churchill, who did not want to give the Germans a propaganda victory by capturing or killing the leader of the BEF.

Dill, in that "polished" French way, that it was "one thing to be driven out and forced to evacuate, but it was quite different if an order were issued from London that the evacuation . . . should be completed that night. Such an order would have a disastrous effect on the Alliance, in view of the conclusions reached at the Supreme War Council [on May 31] to the effect that the evacuation should be continued until completed."

When Dill mentioned the conversation at a Chiefs of Staff meeting, it apparently pricked Churchill's conscience. "As long as the front [holds]," he said, "the evacuation should be continued—even at the cost of naval losses." General Harold Alexander, Gort's successor as commander of the BEF, was instructed "to hold on as long as possible in order that the maximum number of French and British be evacuated." The cabinet also gave Alexander final authority on when to end the evacuation. "Impossible from here to judge local situation," his instructions read. "In close cooperation with Admiral Abrial [the French commander at Dunkirk], you must act in this matter on your own judgment."

By the evening of June 1, news of the crushing British losses at Dunkirk had reached Germany, and the Berlin papers were doing a war dance: CATASTROPHE BEFORE THE DOORS OF LONDON AND PARIS. FIVE ARMIES CUT OFF AND DESTROYED. ENGLAND'S EXPEDITIONARY FORCE NO LONGER EXISTS. Scanning the headlines in *B. Z. a.m. Mitag* at a Berlin newsstand that evening, William Shirer wondered where Germany would strike next: "across the Channel against England or roll the French back on Paris and attempt to knock France out of the war?" Shirer's sources in the German High Command were predicting the latter course. For the past few days, German formations had been moving south, toward Paris. The French people were thinking something similar. In the panicked days that followed June 1, France ceased to be a nation and became a noise. "Ten million French people [are] rolling aimlessly along the roads with their mattresses and saucepans, jamming all communications, paralyzing every military movement, smothering like a thick torrent of mud what was left of the country, until the last twitch of life [is] gone," wrote Arthur Koestler, a Hungarian refugee and author of *Darkness at Noon.* In the Lancashire town of Whalley, where the war was still something that people read about in the papers, Nancy Harker, a young nurse, spent the better part of one early June evening on a station platform, awaiting a hospital train carrying Dunkirk casualties. During the wait, Nancy asked a colleague: "Why ever have these poor things had to come all the way to the north of England after all they've been through?" "Because the hospitals in the south are being emptied for the invasion," the colleague replied.

At the end of May, Mass Observation had urged the government "to prepare the people now to the idea of imminent invasion. . . . Make [them] see that it is possible . . . to invade us, [that the Germans] want to invade us, [that] they can invade us. But we just bloody well won't stand for it." Margery Allingham had noticed a few small changes that made her think the government already was making invasion preparations. One was the new habit of previously anonymous wireless announcers to give their names before reading the news. Margery took that as a sly effort by the authorities to get people to recognize the voices of individual broadcasters so that, in the event of an invasion, they would not be taken in by Germans speaking unaccented English. The ban on bell ringing—the other government invasion preparation—was more obvious, and it saddened Margery. In her village, "church bells [were] a great part of normal life." When she was a little girl, field hands would stop work and doff their caps in respect when the bells rang out to mark the passing of a villager; now, the next time they rang, it would be to signal the start of the invasion. Sometimes at night, when Margery's imagination got the better of her, her head would fill with images of the bells "jangling horribly in the night or in the clear air of the dawn," and she would have to cry herself back to sleep.

The North Country woman Nella Last had nights like that, too; but they were offset by days like June 3, when the radio announced that most of the BEF had gotten away safely. "This morning," she wrote in her diary, "I lingered over my breakfast, reading and rereading the account of the Dunkirk evacuation. I felt as if deep inside me was a harp that vibrated and sang—like the feeling on a hillside of gorse in the hot bright sun, or seeing suddenly, as you walk through a park, a bed of clear thin poppies in all their brave splendor. I forgot I was a middle-aged woman who often got up tired and had a backache. The story made me feel part of something undying and never old—like a flame to light . . . warm but strong enough to burn and destroy trash and rubbish. It was a very hot morning and work was slowed a little but somehow I felt everything to be worthwhile, and I was glad I was of the same race as the rescued and the rescuers."

In the British version of Operation Dynamo, the evacuation ended on the night of June 2–3, with General Alexander, microphone in hand, sailing along the Dunkirk shoreline, shouting into the night: "Is anyone there?" In the French version, Dynamo ended the following night, June 3–4, when three thousand French troops were taken off the beaches by British destroyers; and in the German version Dynamo ended on the morning of June 4, when the Oberkommado der Wehrmacht, the Supreme Command of the German Armed Forces, issued a victory proclamation: "Dunkirk has fallen after a furious battle." The bulletin singled out "the brilliant operations of the Luftwaffe" for special praise. This challenged the British version of the battle, which depicted the RAF as the master of the Dunkirk sky. Both versions contained a measure of truth. In terms of the number of planes shot down, the Luftwaffe did prevail over Dunkirk. According to the British Air Historical Branch Narrative, arguably the most authoritative source, the RAF lost 145 planes during the battle (not including the losses sustained by the Royal Navy's Fleet Air Arm, which also fought at Dunkirk); the Luftwaffe, 132. Strategically, though, Dunkirk was a British victory. Under an umbrella of Spitfires and Hurricanes, the Royal Navy, the French Navy, and the small boats were able to evacuate more than 338,000 Allied troops. "The root, branch, and heart" of the British army had been preserved to defend the home island against invasion.

"I have myself, full confidence," Churchill said in a June 4 speech on Dunkirk, "that if all do their duty, if nothing is neglected, and if all the best arrangements are made, as they are being made, we shall prove ourselves once again able to defend our island home, to ride out the storm of war, and to outlive the menace of tyranny, if necessary for years, if necessary alone. At any rate that is what we are going to try to do. That is the resolve of His Majesty's Government, every man of them. . . . We shall go on to the end. We shall fight in France, we shall fight on the seas and oceans, we shall fight with growing confidence and growing strength in the air, we shall defend our island whatever the cost may be. We shall fight on the beaches, we shall fight on the landing grounds, we shall fight in the fields and streets, we shall never surrender and even if, which I do not for a moment believe, this island or a large part of it were subjugated and starving, then our Empire beyond the seas, armed and guarded by the British fleet, would carry on the struggle, until, in God's good time, the new world, in all its power and might, steps forth to the rescue and liberation of the old.

"At any rate that is what we are going to try to do."

Dunkirk was not only a triumph for Britain, it was also a personal triumph for Churchill. The success of the operation solidified the agreement the war cabinet had reached after the last formal discussion of a compromise peace on May 28. Even if France fell, Britain would remain in the war *for now*. The historian Guy Esenough has called this policy "Wait and See," and it represented a compromise between the Churchill wing in the cabinet and House of Commons that was prepared to fight a war of years, continents, and oceans—and figures such as Halifax and Lloyd George, who wanted to save what still could be saved of Britain's wealth and position in the world. For the present, both sides agreed to put aside their differences and allow Churchill to have his battle, the Battle of Britain. Questions about Britain's future role in the war would be held in abeyance until the outcome of that contest was known.

The decision to stake everything on a great air battle was largely dictated by the importance that *British Strategy in a Certain Eventuality* and *British Strategy in the Near Future* attached to airpower; and the special weight both the British *and* the Germans gave it can be explained by a popular fable of the time. It concerned an elephant and a whale who go to war. Though both are formidable creatures, the only way the elephant, who cannot survive in the deep ocean, and the whale, who cannot walk on land, can bring their power to bear in mortal combat is through the medium of the air. Applied to the British skies, this meant that, as long as the RAF maintained air superiority over the home island, Britain could bring its formidable naval power to bear on a German invasion force. Conversely, if Germany dominated the British sky, it could bring its formidable land power to bear. "Supposing Germany gained complete air superiority [over Britain], we consider that the Navy could hold up an invasion for a time, but not for an indefinite period," the Chiefs of Staff noted in *Near*

Future, which devoted seven of its eleven paragraphs to the importance of airpower in a battle of national survival.

In early June, the war cabinet's hopes of keeping the elephant at bay—or perhaps even defeating him—rested on two factors. The first was the setting of the coming contest. Over Dunkirk, where the Germans had enjoyed most of the advantages, the RAF had fought the Luftwaffe almost to a standstill. The next time the two air forces met, it would be over Britain, and in a British sky the RAF could rescue a higher percentage of its downed pilots and fully exploit the advantages of radar—and fuel considerations would limit the flying time of the German fighters to twenty to twenty-five minutes over Britain. The increase in British air production also enhanced confidence. In June 1940, Britain produced 1,163 aircraft; in July, 1,110; and in August, 1,087. However, the aircraft production numbers do not say much about the number of aircraft immediately available for combat operations. And it was this that occasioned Air Marshal Sir Hugh Dowding's visit to Downing Street on the afternoon of June 3.

A tall, thin man with an unconvincing mustache and a lugubrious manner, Dowding, the head of Fighter Command, was singularly lacking in the physical glamour that airmen of his generation were famous for. If he suggested anyone, it was a bachelor uncle, a resemblance his colleagues had taken note of. Behind his back, they called Dowding "Stuffy." In the suave, testosterone-rich environment of the RAF, Dowding's interest in spiritualism, theosophy, and his membership in the Fairy Investigation Society secured his reputation as the oddest of odd ducks. He also had an affectless monotone voice that could make a Dowding briefing excruciating to sit through, though, on June 3, he had no trouble holding the war cabinet's attention. All the charts and statistics Dowding had brought along supported the conclusion he presented to the cabinet. At Fighter Command's present strength level—280 Spitfires and 224 Hurricanes immediately available for combat operations—he could not guarantee air superiority over Britain for more than the first forty-eight hours of the air battle. At the end of the presentation, the cabinet imposed a ban on further transfers of British fighters to France. The six RAF bomber and three fighter squadrons already operating in the country would be brought up to full strength, but there the British commitment ended. No further fighting machines would be allowed to leave the home island.

"We shall go on to the end. We shall fight in France. We shall fight on the seas and oceans." It was the late morning of June 5; the German offensive on the Somme–Aisne line was several hours old; and Spears was reciting Churchill's Dunkirk speech to Pétain (who was staring "down at the floor") and Reynaud, who was becoming annoyed. "It is useless to stress the extreme gravity of the situation . . . if the British air fighter force does not render our army . . . support," he said when Spears finished. Two days later, on June 7, the Germans breached the Somme–Aisne line, the last major French strongpoint before Paris, and on the eighth, a Panzer division was reported to be halfway to Rouen, eighty-two miles northwest of the capital, and a second was said to be approaching Pontoise, eighteen miles from Paris.

Later, when Spears thought of this period, events would often come back to him in a kaleidoscope of images and voices: Anthony Eden telling him that there were only two regular brigades and some territorial units available for home defense. Reynaud saying that if Hitler wins the war, "it will be the Middle Ages again but without the mercy of Christ." General Weygand musing about the nature of fate: in 1918, Weygand had presented the Allied terms to the Germans; now, twenty-two years later, it would fall on him to receive the German terms. Spears also remembered listening to Big Ben chime 1:00 a.m. on the morning of June 10, and thinking Britain and Italy were now at war; and the late-night call from a Frenchwoman of long acquaintance, with two young soldier sons, her voice "sparking with hate and accusation" as she said, "It is the fault of your country. You bear a heavy responsibility, you were a *belliciste* like Churchill. Won't you try to find my sons?" Then "a sob" and the humming sound of a dead phone line in his ear. His other memories of this time included: Hélène de Portes, Reynaud's mistress, in red pajamas and a dressing gown, standing in the courtyard of a château, instructing drivers where to park. The *Daily Telegraph* headline of June 10 proclaiming that the French government would "never" abandon Paris . . . on the day the French government abandoned Paris. A caravan of refugee automobiles in the rain, the sodden mattresses on their roofs hanging over the side like dead animals. Hélène de Portes again, this time interrogating Reynaud after a meeting with his ministers, asking him, "What did he say? What is the sense of going on? Thousands of men are dying. . . . Delay will only mean harsher German terms." And Weygand again, this time issuing an order of the day to the French Army: "For each man, this is a fight without thought of retiring. . . . The German offensive is now launched along the entire front from the sea to Montmédy [a fortress town near the German border]. Tomorrow it will extend to Switzerland. We have reached the last quarter hour. Hold on!" And a final memory: the Allied Supreme Council meeting in Briare on June 11.

A small town of leafy vistas and languorous canals eighty-six miles south of Paris, Briare owed its brief hour of fame to its proximity to the capital, which the Reynaud government had abandoned the previous night, and perhaps also to the fact that General Weygand had a home in the town, La Château du Muguet. Before leaving for France that afternoon, Churchill told a noontime session of the war cabinet that he hoped the meeting would produce a new Anglo-French "Grand Strategy" and that he intended to impress on the French the need to hang on. At some point, Germany's economic vulnerability would slow the pace of the Wehrmacht's advance. (This was a favorite half-truth of British intelligence.) Finally, Churchill got to the paramount reason for the trip. He said he hoped to "discourage any signs of movement towards making a separate peace."

The possibility of a French collapse now loomed so large in Churchill's mind, he had asked Lord Hankey, that most artful and shrewd of civil servants, to prepare a memorandum on the subject. Once his Flamingo was airborne, Churchill removed the memorandum from his valise. It was the kind of document Joe Kennedy would have called "tremendous." Upon capitulation, Hankey urged that the French fleet be sunk immediately, the French air force flown to Britain or to a British territory, and France's gold reserves seized and transferred to the United States. Churchill kept his thoughts on the assumption that underlay the Hankey paper—that the French would help the British implement these measures—to himself. But Spears, who was seated a few rows behind the prime minister on the Flamingo, noticed that for most of the flight, Churchill "brooded in his armchair, his eyes on the horizon."

Spears, who "had no papers to study," also spent the flight brooding. Sometimes he would look up into the sky and imagine a flight of Messerschmitt-109s coming out of the sun. The Flamingo had an escort of twelve Hurricanes, and the Hurricane was the tough little street fighter of the RAF; still, on almost every measure that mattered—speed, dive, power of gun—it was outmatched by the Me 109. At other times, Spears thought of his wife. He had seen her a few days before in Paris, and the image of her "sitting on the edge of a low sofa [in the] long gray cape of her [ambulance] unit . . . looking like a little girl" had stayed with him. Now she and her ambulance were somewhere below in the burning French countryside, "very near to, and perhaps in the conflagration."

The airfield at Briare amounted to a few slabs of concrete thrown over what looked like a deserted cow pasture; the "scattered confusion" of aircraft parts on the runway and tarmac suggested a recent visit by the Luftwaffe. Anthony Eden, who was a member of the British delegation, "felt almost ashamed to be landing in such a desolate, shabby place in the company of a dozen smart-looking Hurricanes; but the fume of danger that the field gave off seemed to stimulate Churchill. While Eden, Generals Dill and Ismay, and the other members of the British delegation deplaned, the prime minister "strolled about the aerodrome, beaming as if he had left all his preoccupations on the plane and had reached the one spot in the world he most wanted to visit at that particular moment." Spears's other vivid memory of the Briare trip was Château du Muguet, Weygand's home and the setting of the Supreme Council meeting. The château's architecture was absolutely "hideous . . . the sort of building the nouveau riche French bourgeoisie delight in, a villa expanded by a successful business in groceries or indifferent champagne into a large monstrosity of red lobster-colored brick and the stone the hue of unripe Camembert." The only notable feature of the château was its name, which Spears thought perfectly suited its kitschy architecture. In English Château du Muguet means Lily of the Valley Castle.

The meeting was scheduled to begin at 7:00 p.m., but a few minutes before its official start, a visibly uncomfortable Reynaud rose from his chair and said he wished to make an announcement. There was an awkward pause. Then, finding his courage, Reynaud said that it was the desire "of the French government that the Anglo-French air strike on Turin and Milan planned for later this evening be canceled." The Italians were sure to retaliate, and Lyon was "completely unprotected," as were "the great petrol depots" near Marseilles.

After a whispered consultation with Ismay, a "beaming" Churchill said that was impossible. The British bombers were already airborne. Reynaud's eyebrows arched upward and Weygand frowned, but they did not challenge the British action. There was another awkward pause, and then Reynaud invited Churchill to address the fourteenth and penultimate session of the Allied Supreme Council. The prime minister began reassuringly. He said his "own impression was that as soon as the Germans had established themselves on a front in France, they would turn on England. He hoped they would. . . . It would give France relief . . . and enable the British to take a fuller and more equal share in the struggle, but, above all, it would give our RAF the opportunity of smashing German airpower." Broadening the survey, Churchill said, "Today we have the battle of France, tomorrow we should have that of Britain, and it is on this field the fate of the war" would be decided. Britain would "never give in," he said. "Never!" She would fight on, of that he was certain, until Germany could "at last be brought to her knees."

This was the first time General Charles de Gaulle, the new French undersecretary for war, had heard Churchill speak; he was impressed by the Englishman's performance. Churchill "appeared imperturbable, full of vitality, yet [he seemed] to be confining himself to a cordial reserve toward the French at bay and to be preoccupied already—not perhaps without an obscure satisfaction—by the terrible and magnificent prospect of an England left alone in her island, waiting for him to lead her in her struggle toward salvation." Later in the meeting, Spears caught Churchill glancing over at de Gaulle and thought "the prime minister . . . was searching for something [in him] he had failed to find in other French faces."

Weygand, who spoke next, was still the impatient mortician. A "deep penetration by enemy tank units might make it impossible to reestablish the [French] line," he said. "If the armies are disarticulated and cut off, it would be impossible to maintain a coordinated defense of the French territory." Later in the meeting, General Georges, commander of the French ground forces, painted an equally black picture of the military situation. Of the 103 divisions the Allied Army possessed on May 10, the day the German offensive began, only 68 were left, Georges said. "In preparation for the new battle . . . the French Command had rushed everything that could be spared from eastern and southeastern France, but the activity had been impeded by the rapidity of the German advance and the activity of the German bombers. . . . Eight to ten divisions had now been reduced to two battalions and a few guns. [A division has ten thousand to fifteen thousand men; a battalion, three hundred to seven hundred.] Half-trained troops had been put in to fill the gaps, but now there was nothing left to put in." Spears glanced over at Churchill, who looked "horrified." Weygand, Churchill could dismiss as a defeatist, but he knew and admired Georges. He was an honest man, and a professional who would not manipulate information to advance his personal views. If he said the situation was desperate, it was desperate. Churchill began "working his mouth." In Spears's experience, this was usually an indication that "he was pouring his ideas into the mould of words." A moment later the prime minister began to speak.

He said he "wished to express Great Britain's immense admiration for the manner in which the French armies were now defending their territory and her grief at finding [he] could give so little help at such a moment. The hard fact [was] that what remained of the BEF had come out of Flanders literally naked and could only resume the struggle once it had been rearmed. . . . If the [French] line could be held for the next few days, [he hoped] it would be possible to organize a counterattack with the help of British forces. . . . If the line held for another three or four weeks, there would be a substantial British force available to attack the enemy's flank."

"It is a question of hours," not days and weeks, Weygand said.

The CIGS, Dill, told the French they could use the British reinforcements currently landing in France for any purpose they wished.

Pétain, who knew how small that number was, dismissed the offer. "At the height of the Verdun battle," he said, "the French still had been able to relieve each unit after a four-day stint in the trenches. Today, the French troops were fighting continuously with no hope of relief within a measurable time."

Eden also couldn't get anywhere with the French. Reynaud dismissed his report about German concern over the high casualty rate as beside the point. "The enemy was now almost at the gates of Paris," Reynaud said. "He had crossed the Seine and the Marne; the French troops were worn out through lack of sleep and shattered by the action of the enemy bombers. There was no hope or relief anywhere."

The British expressions of concern were sincere, but the French delegates could be forgiven for thinking it was all words, and words and a few British reinforcements would not change anything. Only the RAF might—and the British were holding the RAF back for the defense of the home island. It was a poignant moment. The men gathered around Weygand's dining room table had fought two wars together. They had endured the Somme, Ypres, and the 1918 Michael offensive together. They had lost common friends, shared common horrors, and they believed in the same things: honor, duty, freedom, liberty, and the dignity of the individual. Many of the men at the table had risked their lives to defend those values. But national interests, like tectonic plates, are subject to tremendous forces of drift, and French and British interests were now moving in opposite directions. Before leaving Briare the next morning, Churchill encountered an example of how wide the breach had become. He was dressing after his bath when Air Vice Marshal Arthur Barratt burst into his lodgings and reported that the bomber attack on Italy, scheduled for the previous night, had miscarried; the French ground crews at the bombers' base in southern France had blocked the runways and the planes were unable to take off.

In the thirty-six hours between Churchill's visit to Briare and his visit to Tours, site of the fifteenth and ultimate meeting of the Allied Supreme Council, British and French national interests continued to move in opposite directions. At a meeting of the French War Committee on June 12, the day after the Briare conclave, Weygand warned that, failing an immediate armistice, the army would disintegrate and the nation would descend into anarchy and lawlessness. In London that afternoon, British officials examined a new hypothesis. Hankey was wrong. The French would resist attempts to seize their remaining assets and gold reserves.

In between Briare and Tours, Spears had a final conversation with Marshal Pétain.

"Africa?"

Pétain found Spears's suggestion that France should carry on the war from North Africa absurd. "What is the use of sending recruits to Africa? There are no rifles to arm them with. In any case, the disorganization of the Ministry of War is such that they could never get the men to the harbors."

"You cannot leave us to fight on alone," Spears protested.

"You have left us to fight alone. . . . You are withholding the greater part of your air force in this decisive battle."

"Vous verrez, Monsieur le Marechal, vous verrez," Spears said, ("You will see, you will see.")

Pétain was no longer listening. *"C'est la catastrophe, c'est la débandade,"* he was mumbling to himself. ("It is a catastrophe, it is the stampede.")

At Briare, de Gaulle had noticed a new current of alienation in British and French exchanges. The Allies no longer seemed like players playing a common game but rather like negotiators trying to resolve differences. Spears, less subtle of mind, did not notice the current until the Tours meeting, when both sides abandoned the pretense of solidarity and spoke to each other in the language of intimidation and accusation. The French were represented by Reynaud, who arrived at the meeting greatly relieved that a missing secret cable had been found that morning among the sheets in the Comtesse de Portes's bed. Accompanying him was Paul Baudouin, his former chef de cabinet and now undersecretary for foreign affairs. In photographs of the time, Baudouin always stands out. He is taller, handsomer, and younger than anyone else in the photo. The British delegation included Churchill; Spears; Ronald Campbell (the British ambassador); Halifax; Cadogan; Pug Ismay; and the Canadian press magnate and new minister of air production, Lord Beaverbrook, whose untrustworthy face and battered hat brim turned up in the front suggested a London bookmaker of the worst type.

Though historically significant, the Tours meeting possessed none of the pomp and circumstance of a great event. It was just ten men—two French and eight British—gathered on a rainy Thursday afternoon in a smallish, ill-lit first-floor room in a local prefecture. The size of the room produced an atmosphere of intimacy that perhaps made what each man said sound more personal than it might have in a more official setting. Reynaud spoke first, and he began well. He sounded confident and relaxed as he described the French War Committee's rejection of Weygand's demand for an armistice and President Roosevelt's warm reception to his June 10 appeal for assistance. But when it came time to speak of what France would do if Roosevelt denied his request for immediate and large-scale American aid, the authority and ease left his voice; he sounded plaintive and accusatory. France had been "completely sacrificed," he said. It had "nothing left. This being the plain and simple truth, it would come as a shock to the French government and people if Britain failed to understand and did not concede that France was physically incapable of carrying on." Churchill understood what Reynaud could not bring himself to say. France wanted to be released from its no-separate-peace pledge.

"Great Britain realized what France had endured and was still suffering," the prime minister said. That, however, was as empathic as Churchill was prepared to be on this rainy afternoon. "Everything is subordinated to the British determination to destroy Hitler and his gang," he said. "No risk . . . will hinder us. Everything, absolutely everything, will be subordinated to that aim. . . . We must fight, we will fight, and that is why we must ask our friends to fight on. . . . You must give us time. We ask you to fight on as long as possible, if not in Paris, at least behind Paris, in the provinces, down to the sea, then if need be, in North Africa. At all costs, time must be gained." Spears looked over at Baudouin. He was bent over the notepad on his knee, scribbling furiously.

Reynaud was speaking again, and his voice contained a new element—a note of irony. "It is quite natural that Great Britain would want to go on with the war in view of the fact that she has not suffered as we have; in fact, she has suffered little, but we, the French government, do not think we can abandon our people to German domination. . . . If we left, the position would then be that Hitler, in all probability, would set up a puppet government with so-called legal powers, which would at once set about its task of corruption. . . . Would not Great Britain agree that France, having sacrificed what was the finest and best in her youth, could do no more? Would Great Britain not agree that France, having nothing further to contribute to the common cause"—now Reynaud felt agitated enough to say it—should be "release[d] from the agreement concluded three months ago and allow her to conclude a separate peace? Could not this be concluded whilst maintaining Anglo-French solidarity?"

"Under no circumstances will Great Britain waste time in reproaches and recriminations," Churchill said. "But that is a very different matter from becoming a party to a peace made in contravention of an agreement so recently concluded." Then he reiterated the threat that Spears had made to Pétain a few days earlier. "We are fast approaching a universal blockade, a blockade of Europe, which will become increasingly effective. . . . France, if she is occupied by the Germans, cannot hope to be spared." Churchill wandered off in another direction for a moment or two, then made another threat. "If we fight on with success, if we can see the winter through, the struggle will then develop with full fury. France cannot hope to elude the consequence of the duel. As a result, there may well develop a bitter antagonism between the British and French people. There will, in fact, be many questions to be considered if the president's reply is of a negative character."

Reynaud's voice had also acquired an undertone of menace. "If France continued to suffer without England's making a gesture, recognizing what we have endured, I should be very preoccupied for the future. This might result in a new and very grave situation in Europe." There were several more minutes of back and forth in this vein; then the British delegation requested a time-out.

After a consultation in the courtyard of the prefecture, Churchill returned to the meeting room and announced that the British government would not reply to the French request to void the no-separate-peace pledge until President Roosevelt had replied to Reynaud. After the meeting Churchill walked out to the corridor of the prefecture and saw de Gaulle "standing solid and expressionless in a doorway." "*L'homme du destin*" (man of destiny) he whispered as he passed by. De Gaulle "remained impassive."

During the meeting, the courtyard abutting the prefecture had filled with notables, including the son of Georges Clemenceau, who was shaking the prime minister's hand when a female voice shouted, "Mr. Churchill!" Hélène de Portes was standing in the courtyard. "My country is bleeding to death! I have a story to tell you!" Pretending not to hear, Churchill got into his car. Cries of "You must hear me! You must hear me!" followed the prime minister out of the courtyard.

The next day, June 14, Roosevelt's reply to Reynaud's June 10 appeal for assistance produced an embarrassing incident. Though encouraging, the president's response was not the virtual declaration of war that some British officials, including Churchill, took it to be. A British request to publish the reply was flatly denied. June 15 and 16 were dominated by discussions of a proposal to form the Franco-British Union. Mercifully, the scheme, which originated with a French official, René Pleven, and would have made the two nations one, died an unmourned death. On June 16, Marshal Pétain replaced Reynaud as premier. And on June 17, German fighters sunk the British troop ship *Lancastria* while it was evacuating BEF units south of the pocket; five thousand of the six thousand passengers were killed in the attack. A few hours later, Marshal Pétain announced that he had "applied to our adversary to ask if he is prepared to seek with me, soldier to soldier, after the battle, honorably, the means whereby hostilities may cease."

The following day, June 18, William Shirer stood in the place de la Concorde, listening to a loudspeaker announce the French surrender. Shirer had been in Paris for almost forty-eight hours, and this was the first time he had encountered French men and women in any appreciable numbers. Driving into the city the previous day, he had half expected to be greeted by the Paris that had greeted him on half a dozen other June afternoons—the Paris Oscar Hammerstein II wrote about not long after the French surrender:

> The last time I saw Paris
> Her trees were dressed for spring
> And lovers walked beneath those trees
> And birds found songs to sing
>
> I dodged the same old taxicabs
> That I had dodged for years
> The chorus of their squeeky horns
> Was music to my ears.

Instead, Shirer found himself in a German city. Above the Chamber of Deputies flew a "giant" swastika flag; in front of the Ministry of Marine stood a Mark IV Panzer tank. And in the Hôtel Crillon, Woodrow Wilson's residence during the Paris Peace Conference in 1918, German generals spangled with gold braids toasted the Führer and one another. On a walk that morning, Shirer had seen only German Army cars and motorcycles on the streets, and only young German soldiers in the cafés. Where was the "Paris of gay lights, the laughter, the music, the women in the streets? . . . And what was this?" Shirer wondered.

In London that afternoon, Churchill addressed the French surrender in a speech to the House of Commons.

> I do not at all underrate the severity of the ordeal which lies before us, but I believe our countrymen will show themselves capable of standing up to it, like the brave men of Barcelona [a reference to the Republican Army's defense of the city in the Spanish Civil War], and will be able to stand up to it, and carry on in spite of it, at least as well as any other people in the world. Much will depend upon this, and every man and every woman will have the chance to show the finest qualities of their race and render the highest service to their cause. For all of us at this time, whatever our sphere, our station, our occupation, our duties, it will be a help to remember the famous lines, "He nothing common did or mean / Upon that memorable scene."
>
> What General Weygand called the Battle of France is over. I expect that the Battle of Britain is about to begin. Upon it depends the survival of Christian civilization. Upon it depends our own British life and the long continuity of our institutions and our Empire. The whole fury and might of the enemy must very soon be turned on us. Hitler knows that he will have to break us in this island or lose the war. If we can stand up to him, all Europe may be free and the life of the world may move forward into the broad sunlit uplands; but if we fail, then

the whole world, including the United States, and all we have known and care for, will sink into the abyss of a new dark age made more sinister, and perhaps more protracted, by the lights of perverted science.

Let us therefore brace ourselves to our duty and so bear ourselves that if the British Empire and its Commonwealth last for a thousand years men will still say, This was their finest hour.

Three days later, on June 21, Shirer drove up to Compiègne, a town north of Paris, to witness the formal French surrender. The ceremony was even more humiliating than Weygand had feared. The German and French delegates met in the Forest of Compiègne, where Germany had surrendered in 1918, and in the same wagon-lit (railroad sleeping car) where Marshal Foch, the Allied supreme commander, had dictated the Allied terms to the representatives of Imperial Germany. Shirer was standing just outside the wagon-lit when the German delegation entered. He noticed that Hitler took the seat Foch had sat in in 1918. After the ceremony, Shirer and a few other reporters followed Hitler and his party to a granite memorial several hundred feet from the wagon-lit. Hitler stopped in front of it and read the inscription.

HERE ON THE ELEVENTH OF NOVEMBER 1918 SUCCUMBED THE CRIMINAL PRIDE OF THE GERMAN EMPIRE . . . VANQUISHED BY THE FREE PEOPLES WHICH IT TRIED TO ENSLAVE.

Shirer, who was standing some distance away, took out the binoculars he had brought along and scanned Hitler's face. "It [was] afire with scorn, anger, hate, revenge, triumph." After reading the inscription, Hitler began to walk away, then abruptly turned and "glanced back at it: contemptuous, angry. . . . You [could] grasp the depth of his hatred," Shirer wrote later. "But there [was] triumph there, too—revengeful, triumphant hate. Then Hitler "snapped his hands on his hips, arched his shoulders, parted his feet wide apart." Even at a distance of fifty yards, it struck Shirer as "a magnificent gesture of defiance, of burning contempt for this place and all that it had stood for."

CHAPTER THIRTEEN

LAND OF HOPE AND GLORY

Tomorrow, just you wait and see. There'll be love and laughter and peace ever after.

—"The White Cliffs of Dover"

On the afternoon of June 17—a sullen, overcast Monday—two men stood in front of Hanlon's, a clothing store in Bolton, a hard-luck Midlands textile town that had ridden the industrial revolution up to prosperity in the nineteenth century and was now riding it down to penury in the twentieth. Pétain's armistice announcement had come through on the wireless around 1:00 p.m.; it was now a little after three, long enough for the initial shock to wear off. "What can we do?" asked the younger man, an observer from Mass Observation. The older man, the proprietor of Hanlon's, said he had no idea. "We can't stand up to the Italian and French navies combined, that's for sure." The proprietor paused, then added, "You know, I had a fellow in here yesterday and he bought a pair of flannels. [When] I remarked that they were an expensive pair, he told me, 'Oh well, I'll be in a free khaki pair soon, probably. But I'll have these in case I ever come back.' In case I ever come back." The proprietor repeated the words as if he could not quite believe them.

"We chose the wrong age to live in," the observer said.

The proprietor shrugged. "I guess there's nothing we can do about it." Then he went back inside the store.

For the generation of Britons who had come of age during the Great War and thought of the French Army as the greatest military in the world, the fall of France, though unsurprising, still came as a tremendous shock. "From the moment you woke up," said Donald Johnson, an army doctor, "you thought, 'Oh, my God' as you realized [Britain's] position afresh ... It was only after two or three beers at lunch that the situation did not seem quite as bad; but by three thirty in the afternoon it was desperate again— and it was quite time to go back to the mess for another drink. In the evening, the outlook depended entirely on the amount of alcohol you consumed. I use the plural 'you' because everyone was in the same boat." The German bombing raids, which from June 18 became an almost nightly occurrence, put a further strain on morale. In a Midlands chemist's shop, a young woman was over- heard debating whether to get a permanent or get drunk with her friend. After some back-and-forth, the young woman said, "It doesn't encourage you to spend good money on a permanent when you think your head might be blown off tomorrow."

After studying the impact of the French news on civilian morale, the Home Intelligence Committee concluded that, at present, there was a "dogged determination to see the thing through," but warned that, as one inconclusive battle followed another, there was a real possibility the public would grow weary of the struggle and begin agitating for an end to the war. There is, said the Committee, "a feeling not widely expressed but of consid- erable importance, that a negotiated peace with Germany would be preferable to a prolongation of the war."

Churchill was aware of this strain of thought, and, in the days following the French surrender, attempted to counteract it in two speeches that laid out a credible British path to survival and, eventually, victory. The first, the "Finest Hour" speech, was directed at the general public and received a mixed reception. Churchill's words had a "settling" effect on morale, Mass Observation reported the day after the speech, but noted that the effect was "somewhat counteracted by his delivery." Some listeners thought Churchill sounded "drunk"; others, insincere—that "he did not himself feel the confidence he was proclaiming."

The second speech was delivered at a secret session of Parliament on June 21, and its target was the British political class. No copy of the speech survives, but, from Churchill's notes, it is possible to reconstruct his main points. He began with a subject on everyone's mind that afternoon: the "impending" German bombing campaign. Thus far, he said, the Luftwaffe attacks had amounted to little more than nuisance raids, but that was about to change. In the months ahead, the country should prepare for:

> Steady continuous bombing
> Probably rising to great intensity occasionally,
> Must be regular condition of life.

How should civilians respond to the bombing? Churchill's answer was brutally frank:

> Learn to get used to it.
> Eels get used to skinning.

Then, expanding on the point, he said, "The bombing would be a test of our nerves against theirs."

> No one can tell the result.
> The supreme battle depends upon
> the courage of the ordinary man and woman.

Next, Churchill addressed the invasion threat: "Everything depends on attack[ing] the landed enemy at once." We must "leap at his throat and keep the grip until the life runs out of him."

> If Hitler fails to invade
> or destroy Britain,
> He has lost the war . . .

Then Churchill reiterated a point he had made several times during the war cabinet debates:

> If get through next three months
> get through next three years . . .
> But all depends on winning this battle
> Here in Britain, now this summer.

As for the United States, he told the House, "nothing will stir them like fighting in England," which was true. But the suggestion of American assistance in the remark was not. Earlier in the day Churchill had asked his military aide, "Pug" Ismay, for a list of the American aircraft and munitions "which have actually arrived in the country." Ismay told him that nothing had arrived: "Nil." In the secret session speech, "nil" somehow became an American promise of the "fullest aid." Washington did send 250,000 rifles, 130 million rounds of ammunition, and 80,000 machine guns in early June, though not much else since. In a June 27 cable, Lord Lothian, the British ambassador in Washington, warned London that "a wave of pessimism [is] passing over this country to the effect that Great Britain now must inevitably be defeated, and that there is no use in the United States doing anything more to help it. . . . There is some evidence [that the pessimism] is beginning to affect the president." That may have been an understatement. Besides

Roosevelt's obvious reasons for withholding assistance—Britain was probably going to lose anyway; the United States needed what weapons it had to defend itself; and concern about undermining his chances of winning an unprecedented third term—the president had other, less publicized reasons for stepping away from Britain. Through Joe Kennedy, he had learned of the secret war cabinet discussions about a compromise peace, which raised the possibility that any future American aid could end up in a German armory. And, through an unnamed but "good" authority, Roosevelt had been told that Hitler was considering a compromise peace that would allow Britain to remain independent if it agreed to surrender the British fleet and large parts of the empire. This raised an even more ghastly prospect than Kennedy's news: a US Navy confronted by a German-dominated Royal Navy operating from former British territories such as Bermuda.

Independent of Roosevelt, other powerful forces in American life were also working against British interests that summer. On June 22, the day of the official French surrender in the Forest of Compiègne, George Marshall, the Army Chief of Staff, and Admiral Harold Stark, the Chief of Naval Operations, pressed Roosevelt to ban virtually all future arms sales to Britain. The president refused, but plans to sell London twelve B-17s, the US Army Air Corp's new heavy bomber, were abandoned. German documents captured after the Second World War highlighted another, more insidious threat to the Anglo-American relationship. A few weeks before the Republican Convention in the summer of 1940, Hans Thomsen, the German chargé d'affaires in Washington, requested funds from Berlin to finance the visit of fifty Republican congressmen to the convention "so that they may work on the delegates in the Republican Party in favor of an isolationist foreign policy." Thomsen, a seasoned diplomat, knew enough not to name names in a cable, but he did say the fifty guests would be invited by a well-known congressman whom Thomsen said was working with the German embassy in Washington. What is known for certain about this incident is that Hamilton Fish—a prominent New York congressman, bitter opponent of Roosevelt, and leading light of the isolationist movement—did invite fifty of his congressional colleagues to the 1940 convention, and that the congressman did testify before the party's platform committee. Still, if Fish was complicit in a Nazi plot (the fifty congressmen almost certainly were not) he did not have much success. Wendell Willkie, the Republican presidential candidate in 1940, was an international-ist whose views on the war were far closer to Franklin Roosevelt's than to Hamilton Fish's.

During the secret session speech, Churchill made one other point about Anglo-American relations. He said that the most effective way to secure America's help and trust was through bold actions. Britain had to show that it was determined to see the thing through to the end, no matter how far away the end might be or how brutal the passage to it. This was not a new point. In one form or another, Churchill had made it several times since mid-May, but events on the fields of Flanders and northern France had not provided any opportunities for displays of British boldness. The French surrender would.

Late in the afternoon of June 22, a copy of the Germany armi-stice terms was cabled to Chequers, the country residence of Brit-ish prime ministers. The terms filled nine pages of small type, but three articles leaped out at Churchill. The first was the zone of occupation. German domination of the French coast from Dunkirk to the Pyrenees would require a large naval presence along Britain's sea routes to Gibraltar, Malta, and the Suez at a time when every warship was needed in home waters to meet the invasion threat. The second article, which demanded the release of all German prisoners of war, was in itself unremarkable except for one point. Among the released POWs were the four hundred German pilots Reynaud had promised to turn over to Britain before France surrendered and who would now be available for the imminent air war against Britain. The third article—all French warships were to return to home ports immediately to be demobilized and disarmed under German or Italian control—was so alarming it brought Churchill rushing back to London for a 9:30 p.m. session of the war cabinet. More bad news awaited him upon his arrival: the French had agreed to the German terms.

Eleven days later, July 3, Force H, a Royal Navy task force, stood off Mers-el-Kébir, a half moon of sand, sun, and sea along the Algerian coast where the French had a major naval base. When HMS *Hood* took up position a little before 8:00 a.m. that morning, the sights and sounds of a port town in the rising day were unfolding along the shore: sailors swabbing decks, painting hulls, and loading and unloading supplies under a crowded sky of noisy seagulls. Even from a distance, the jaunty pom-pom caps and tight-fitting striped jerseys gave the French sailors a dash lacking in their British counterparts. As the silhouettes of the *Hood*, a battle cruiser, and the HMS *Valiant* and HMS *Resolution*, two battleships, filled the horizon, the French sailors shouted to one another: "The British have arrived. They have come to get us to continue the fight against the Nazis." Watching the scene from the deck of the *Hood*, Vice Admiral James Somerville, commander of Force H, had reason to recall First Sea Lord Dudley Pound's final words to him the previous night: "You are charged with one of the most disagreeable tasks a British admiral has ever been faced with." Operation Catapult, the action that Force H was participating in, arose from Churchill's fear that the French fleet would fall into German hands and the Pétain government's failure to assuage that fear. In addition to attacking Mers-el-Kébir, later in the day Royal Navy units would descend upon French warships at Portsmouth and Plymouth and at the British naval base in Alexandria (Egypt) and offer the ships' captains four choices: fight with Britain; scuttle their ships; neutralize them; or face attack. Operation Catapult went more or less to plan and with minimum loss of life everywhere except at Mers-el-Kébir. Admiral Marcel-Bruno Gensoul, the French commander, assured the British emissaries who visited his office that he would not permit his ships to fall into German hands, but he warned them that any attempt to seize the ships would be met with force. A long, hot July day of frustration, anxiety, and misunderstanding ended at 5:55 that afternoon, when what sounded like a locomotive barreled across the sky. The first salvo of three-quarter-ton British shells sent the seagulls fluttering and produced ear bleeds in the startled French sailors. A moment later, the docks at Mers-el-Kébir disappeared in a ball of flame. André Jaffre, a French sailor who was blown off his ship by a British shell, described the scene in the harbor. The sea was filled "with oil, severed heads, and men with stomachs blown open." The wounded were shouting, "Finish me off, kill me, kill me, please." Some of the French ships returned fire, but, unable to maneuver in the narrow confines of the harbor, they were at the mercy of the British guns. "I swam underwater as far as possible away from the ships," Jaffre recalled sixty years later, but "every time I came up [for air], I came up into this boiling oil. So I'd breathe in the smoke and oil and dive in again for as long as I could." During one visit to the surface, Jaffre saw the battleship *Bretagne* roll onto its side and disappear into the sea, taking a thousand men with it. When Somerville gave the order to cease fire at 6:04, Mers-el-Kébir was enveloped in an enormous plume of black smoke, and Force H had killed 1,250 Frenchmen in the space of nine minutes.

As a military operation, the attack on Mers-el-Kébir was a mixed success. The *Bretagne* was sunk, and its sister ship, the *Provence*, beached; but two 1910-class battleships did not pose a serious threat to British dominance of the Channel, Atlantic, and Mediterranean sea lanes. The two modern battle cruisers at Mers-el-Kébir did, however, and while one, the *Dunkerque*, was run aground during the attack, its sister ship, the *Strasbourg*, escaped, along with its destroyer escort. In psychological and political terms, however, Mers-el-Kébir was an unqualified success. The word "waiting" had floated through the June morale reports like a little black rain cloud. People seemed to be bracing—for what, they were unsure; but in the meantime they seemed unwilling to look up, down, or sideways for fear of a "smashup." Mers-el-Kébir changed the national mood overnight. On July 4, Home Intelligence reported: "News about the French fleet has been received in all regions with satisfaction and relief. . . . There is considerable regret that we had to take the actions against some elements of the French fleet . . . [But] it is felt that this strong action gives welcome evidence of government vigor and decision." The next day, July 5, the British public liked the Mers-el-Kébir attack even more. "All regions express widespread approval of our action against the French fleet. The public feel that no other course was possible and they welcome this evidence of our initiative." The boldness of the attack also made a deep impression on America. "Fair-minded opinion will agree. The British were right in what they did," the *New York Times* noted in a July 5 editorial. *The Boston Globe*, like a number of other papers, singled out Churchill for special praise: "This latest decision shows he still possesses the courage and audacity for needed decisions." The White House was also impressed. During a visit to London in January 1941, Harry Hopkins, a Roosevelt confidant, told John Colville it was Mers-el-Kébir that convinced the president that Joe Kennedy was wrong;

Britain would remain in the war, if necessary for years, if necessary alone. Churchill reiterated his no-surrender policy in a speech to the House of Commons on July 4, the day after the attack.

> The action we have already taken [at Mers-el-Kébir] should be, in itself, sufficient to dispose once and for all of the lies and rumors which have been so industriously spread by German propagandists and fifth columnists' activities that we have the slightest intention of entering negotiations in any form and in any channel with the German and Italian governments. We shall, on the contrary, prosecute the war with the utmost vigor by all the means that are open to us until the righteous purposes for which we have entered upon it have been fulfilled.

The moment Churchill finished speaking, the entire House, including the previously cool Conservative MPs, leaped to their feet and cheered and shouted for a "full two minutes." "What it was all about, I still don't know," Eric Seal, Churchill's private secretary, told his wife a few days later. Churchill knew what it was about. In his memoirs, he wrote: "The elimination of the French Navy as an important factor almost in a single stroke by violent action produced a profound impression in every country. Here was the Britain which so many had counted down and out, which strangers supposed to be quivering on the brink of surrender . . . striking ruthlessly at her dearest friends of yesterday and securing . . . to herself the undisputed control of the sea."

Mers-el-Kébir also had another important consequence. After it, talk of a compromise peace became less frequent, and, as national resolve stiffened, the two leading advocates of a negotiated settlement were put on their back foot. Lord Halifax's last foray into peace diplomacy occurred on June 17, the day France fell. That morning Rab Butler, a Halifax confidant, ran into Björn Prytz, the

Swedish ambassador, in St. James's Park and invited him back to the Foreign Office for a talk. In 1965, after a quarter of a century of rumor, innuendo, and speculation, Prytz published the account of the talk he sent to Stockholm on the night of the seventeenth. In it, he has Butler making a number of incriminating statements, including "the official attitude [of the British government] will for the present be that the war should continue but . . . no opportunity should be missed [for] a compromise if reasonable conditions could be agreed on." He also has Butler saying that "no diehards [likely a reference to Churchill] would be allowed to stand in the way." The report also included a quote from Halifax, who summoned Butler to his office during Prytz's visit and asked him to convey a message to the Swedish ambassador: "Common sense and not bravado would dictate the British government's policy."

When Churchill learned of this episode a few days later, Halifax assured him that Butler "had been completely loyal to the government policy." But two pieces of evidence suggest that the official explanation for Halifax's and Butler's incriminating statements—Prytz misconstrued their words—may not be the whole truth. On June 18, the day after the Swede's visit to the Foreign Office, Alex Cadogan noted cryptically in his diary: "No reply from Germans." The cable the Italian ambassador in Sweden sent to Rome that day is also suggestive: "The British representative [Victor Mallet, the British ambassador in Stockholm] requested an interview with the Swedish foreign minister and notified him that the British government is inclined to enter into peace negotiations with Germany and Italy. The secretary general of the Foreign Ministry here . . . informed me . . . that this declaration by the British representatives is of an official character." Churchill never commented publicly on this episode. But it may be indicative of his feelings toward Halifax that when Lord Lothian, the British ambassador in Washington, died unexpectedly in late 1940, the foreign secretary was shipped off to America as ambassador over his vigorous protests and the even more vigorous protests of Lady Halifax.

Lloyd George, who placed a close second to Halifax in the shadow contest to replace Churchill and who was the most famous public figure to advocate a compromise peace, also began to fade from the scene. He continued to refuse invitations to join the Churchill government and to advocate for a negotiated end to the war; but he refused an offer to become spokesman for the Stokes Group, thirty antiwar MPs who had gathered around the Labor MP Richard Stokes. The position would have given Lloyd George a larger megaphone for his views, but by July he had come halfway to Churchill's position. In an article in the *Sunday Pictorial*, he said the predicate for a negotiation with Germany should be a British battlefield victory. He was also approaching seventy-eight, and at that point in his life he probably found it easier and more fun to remain in the backbenches, make mischief, and wait for "Winston to go bust."

By mid-July Britain, in all its divisions and branches, creeds and constituencies, had united behind Churchill, but, until tested in the battle, it was impossible to tell how strong this unity was.

A little after one in the afternoon on July 14, 1940, Charles Gardner, an enterprising young BBC reporter, stood on a bluff above the Dover Straits watching a convoy of freighters embroider frothy white patterns in the sea with their propellers. Above the ships a half dozen Hurricanes, the convoy's escort, were making lazy circles in the gray-blue sky while waiting for their charges to clear the straits. The people who lived in this tidy little corner of southeast England knew that sooner or later the war would come to them. Suffolk, Norfolk, Lincoln—all the towns and villages, factories, and military installations along the east coast of England

and Scotland—were supplied through the Dover Straits. But the Luftwaffe's first attacks on the straits in June had been surprisingly modest: just a flight or two of light bombers, whose bombs rarely hit anything except the water. Then, abruptly and for no apparent reason, on July 10 the attacks escalated sharply, and with the escalation came a new name for the straits—Hellfire Corner—and the attention of dozens of reporters, including Gardner, who had decided to record a broadcast from the straits for the BBC's evening news program. At around 1:30 p.m. Gardner took out the script he had prepared. The sound man nodded, and Gardner began to read. He was a few sentences in when the drone of plane engines broke his train of thought. When he looked up, what seemed to be the entire Luftwaffe—forty Junkers 87 dive-bombers and too many Me 109 fighters to count—was flying straight at him from a dot in the Channel sky. Behind him Gardner heard the familiar throb of British engines. The Chain Home radar system had picked up the German flight over Calais and scrambled several Hurricane squadrons to reinforce the convoy's escort.

Gardner threw away his script and began to narrate extemporaneously. "There's one coming down in flames—there somebody's hit, a German—and he's coming down—there's a long streak—he's coming down completely out of control—a long streak of smoke— ah, the man's bailed out by parachute—he's a Junkers 87 and he's going slap into the sea and there he goes *sma-a-a-sh*. Oh boy! I've never seen anything so good as this—the RAF fighters really have these boys taped." Thus was the British public introduced to what would later be called the Battle of Britain.

In 1980, the British historian A. J. P. Taylor called the battle a "decisive" contest, and it *was* decisive—but only for one side. Between mid-May, when an unenthusiastic Grand Admiral Erich Raeder first raised the question of invading Britain, and August 13, the date the German calendar marks as the beginning of the

Battle of Britain, Hitler's enthusiasm for an invasion waxed and waned; mostly, though, it waned. The conquest of London and Leeds would not get Germany a mile closer to Kiev or Moscow, to the creation of the new German Empire in the east that would keep the name Adolf Hitler alive for a thousand generations. True, subduing Britain before striking east would enhance Germany's security, but not enough to make invasion a necessity. At the end of the French campaign invasion was only one of several options available to Hitler, and the evidence suggests it was not an option he was giving much thought to. Expecting the British to seek terms, on June 15 Hitler ordered the German Army reduced in size. Eight days later, on June 23, Joseph Goebbels, the Minister of Propaganda and a Hitler intimate, told a gathering of fellow ministers: "We are very close to the end of the war." The Churchill government would fall soon and a "compromise government [would be] formed." After Mers-el-Kébir, Hitler ordered an invasion plan drawn up but told his commanders, "If the results of the air war are unsatisfactory, invasion preparations will be stopped."

On the British side of the Channel, the question that commanded attention in the early summer of 1940 was not whether the Germans would invade; the intelligence seemed clear on that point. In late June, maps of Britain had been distributed to German antiaircraft units; the Luftwaffe's long-range bomber force would finish refitting on July 8; and what appeared to be invasion rafts were under construction in Kiel harbor. In July, London's attention was focused on a second question: can an invasion be repelled? There were not enough fully trained and equipped divisions in Britain to mount a credible defense of the east coast from Dover to the Tyne, 318 miles to the north, and many of the brigades in Kent—among the most likely landing sites—had no more than three or four thousand men to defend a four- to five-mile front. Like nearly everyone else in Britain that summer, the senior soldiers and War Office officials were quoting Shake-speare's "Come the three corners of the world in arms, and we shall shock them," but only in public and not to one another. Toward the beginning of July, Sir John Dill, the CIGS, told Chamberlain: "The troops are not trained and may not be steady when the test comes." "Dill sounded like all the other soldiers," Chamberlain wrote in his diary that night. General Edmund Ironside, who as commander of Home Forces was responsible for repelling the invasion, quietly sent his diaries to Canada, just in case. Even General Alan Brooke, who replaced Ironside in July and was famously resolute, took up his new post with a heavy heart. "I knew well enough the dangers we were exposed to," Brooke wrote later. "The probability of an attempt to invade these islands, the unpreparedness of our defense, the appalling lack of equipment, the deficiencies of training and battle-worthiness in the majority of our formations. The idea of failure was . . . enough to render the responsibility almost unbearable. Perhaps the hardest part of it all was the absolute necessity to submerge all one's innermost feelings and maintain a confident exterior."

The senior naval officers were visited by similar doubts and fears. Eight hundred destroyers, corvettes, and other small, nimble warships had been assembled in the waters of southern England to meet an invasion; but should the Luftwaffe overwhelm this force in the battle for air superiority, the battleships and battle cruisers of the Home Fleet, currently safely out of harm's way in northern Scotland, would be called south to meet the invaders. In the view of many senior naval officers, that would be tantamount to a suicide mission. The big ships would be well within the range of German bombers and fighters based in France and Holland, and, unable to maneuver in the narrow seas of the south, would make easy targets. During a visit to Downing Street in July, Admiral Charles Forbes, Commander of the Home Fleet, told Churchill that under no circumstances would he risk his capital ships south of the Wash, a bay and estuary roughly midway up the east coast of England. Pug Ismay, who was present at the meeting, waited for Churchill to explode. Instead, the prime minister smiled "indulgently" at Forbes and said he "never took much notice of what the Royal Navy said they would or would not do in advance, since they invariably . . . undertook the impossible without a moment's hesitation. [He] had not a shadow of a doubt that if the Germans invaded the south coast of Britain, we would see every available battleship storming through the Straits of Dover."

As the summer days passed and the strength and frequency of the German air attacks increased, it became evident to the officials studying the invasion threat that the fate of the Home Fleet, and of the small, underequipped British Army defending the coast of Suffolk, Essex, and Kent, would be determined by the contest between the elephant and the whale.

On July 5, eight months before his sixtieth birthday and nine days before his retirement, Air Marshal Sir Hugh Dowding received a letter from the Air Ministry requesting him to defer his retirement until October. Archibald Sinclair, the Air Minister, was not happy about the extension. Dowding was a difficult subordinate, but Sinclair had no choice. Fighter Command was built around the Dowding System, and the only person who knew how to operate the system was "Stuffy" Dowding. An elderly Victorian gentleman with an enthusiasm for communicating with the dead, Dowding hardly seemed an avatar of the future; yet the Dowding System—a combination of radar, radio monitoring, intelligence transcripts, and operation-room tracking—amounted to a first edition of the modern command and control system. With it, Fighter Command could respond earlier and more accurately to German attacks. Hitler's dithering about an invasion also worked to Fighter Command's advantage by providing time to replace the almost five hundred Hurricanes and Spitfires lost in the French campaign. On July 10, the first day of the Battle of Britain on the British calendar, Dowding had 664 operational aircraft, most of them modern Spitfires and Hurricanes. The Germans had 760 Me 109s and 220 Me 110s, twin-engine heavy fighters. The odds against the British were not as formidable as these numbers suggest, however. Big and ungainly, the Me 110's lack of maneuverability made it an easy target; and while the Me 109 was superior to every British fighter, its pilots would be facing an enemy who often knew when they were coming and what corner of the sky they would come from, an important advantage in a battle where the margin of victory for either side was likely to be inches.

The British people were also prepared for the coming battle. The sharp improvement in the July morale numbers owed something to good leadership, but the uptick also reflected an important change in public perception of the war. The arrival of the Luftwaffe over Britain, the experience of sharing the dangers and hardship of combat, had instilled in ordinary men and women a sense that they were fighting what some were already calling a "People's War." The public anger heaped on the Home Office for infringing on civil liberties, on the Ministry of Information for—allegedly—using morale interviews to collect personal data, and on wealthy Britons for sending their children abroad was a manifestation of an empowered public's view that, as frontline fighters, they were entitled to a voice in how the war was conducted.

Given the invasion rumors and the growing intensity of the air war, it would have been odd if the July morale reports had been uniformly positive. Some people were still avoiding news or conversation about the war, or were engaging in other forms of distancing; and there were still pockets of real despair in the country. A London society doctor reported that more of his wealthy patients were requesting poison capsules. Still, the general picture that emerged from the July data was that of a united nation calmly gathering itself for battle, an impression strengthened by the reaction to Hitler's July 19 peace offer to Britain. "People laughed and jeered," Home Intelligence reported.

From the offices in the American embassy on Grosvenor Square, Ambassador Joseph Kennedy and General Raymond Lee, the military attaché and head of US intelligence in London, had followed Britain's progress over the summer and had come to different conclusions about its prospects. In early August, the ambassador told a visiting American military delegation that Britain's "absolutely only chance" of avoiding defeat was to hold on until Roosevelt won a third term and then try to get the United States to "pull them out." Lee, an affable midwesterner who looked like a movie-star version of an American general—he bore a remarkable resemblance to the modern-day actor Tom Selleck—was more optimistic. Some of the optimism can be put down to the Anglophilia of a Missouri boy dazzled by the sophistication of London, but only a small portion. Lee had witnessed the discipline of the British public under fire; had inspected the beaches of southern England and found them better defended than the London rumor mill had it; had met Brooke and Ismay and been impressed by their resolve and skill; and had stood in the twilight in Victoria Station, piercing air-raid sirens throbbing in his ears, watching Winston Churchill gruffly refuse to put out his cigar or take cover. Yet if anyone had asked Lee, "Why do you think Britain will avoid defeat?" the first thing he would have mentioned was the Dowding System, which he inspected during a visit to Fighter Command on August 7. The warren of passageways below Dowding's office led to "two great rooms" where Lee was introduced to "two of the most intricate and modern organizations [in] the world. . . . In one room [was] the huge map on which moment by moment the reports of enemy locations [were] plotted and enemy air and sea movement exposed; in another room, an even greater chart where actions [were] followed [second] by second. "The great rooms [were] almost silent," Lee wrote that night—"only a soft murmur of voices as messages come and go over headsets and . . . operators [move] counters and markers from point to point and others tend electric bulletins and switchboards. The whole establishment watches the slightest movements of both sides day and night. . . . I had no idea the British could evolve and operate so intricate, so scientific, and [so] rapid an organization."

Six days after Lee's visit to Fighter Command came Adler Tag, Eagle Day: August 13, the beginning of the Battle of Britain on the German calendar. In July, the Luftwaffe had concentrated on coastal shipping, making occasional forays inland to strike industrial targets. In August, it had a new mission: knock the sword from the Whale's hand so the invasion could proceed. On the eve of battle, the leader of the Luftwaffe told his air crews the target was Fighter Command and its supporting infrastructure, airfields, airplane factories, and so forth.

> FROM REICHSMARSCHALL GÖRING TO ALL UNITS
> OF AIRFLEET 2, 3 AND 5. OPERATION EAGLE. WITHIN A
> SHORT PERIOD YOU WILL WIPE THE BRITISH AIR FORCE
> FROM THE SKY
>   HEIL HITLER

It was still dark when the bomber crews at the German air base in Arras began revving up their engines on the morning of August 13. A moment later lights flickered on in the farmhouses abutting the airfield, and cursing, half-dressed French farmers tumbled out into the early morning darkness to soothe their frightened livestock. The area around Arras had seen a lot of fighting in May, and on a clear day the bomber crews flying to England could see the point where a BEF attack had been repulsed on May 24. This morning the marking point—the hulks of a few scorched Cruiser tanks—was shrouded by a two-thousand-foot cloud bank. At first light, the Arras unit and two other bomber groups were circling above the clouds, looking for the fighters that would escort them to their target, Eastchurch, a British air base fifty-eight miles south of London. At a little after 6:00 a.m. a single escort, an Me 110 heavy fighter, emerged out of a cloud, dived several times on the lead bomber, then was swallowed up by the cloud again. Oblivious to the malfunction in his radio, and unaware that the fighter pilot had been signaling him to turn back, Adler Tag had been postponed until the afternoon—due to the cloud cover—Oberst Johannes Fink, the flight commander, led his eighty-four Dorniers out over the Channel. As the Thames estuary came into view, the clouds briefly parted and the pencil-shaped shadows of the Dorniers raced across the white-capped sea. The radar stations at Dover, Foreness, and Whitstable picked up the flight, but, uncertain of the bombers' direction, failed to issue a warning. Just before seven, the Dorniers were approaching Eastchurch when a squadron of Spitfires swept out of the sky and pounced on the bombers at the rear of the formation. The first burst of machine-gun fire made the interior of the Dorniers glow red; short tongues of flame licked their fuselages, followed by plumes of black smoke; the sequence concluded with the piercing drone of a mortally wounded bomber falling into a death spiral, its burning undercarriage silhouetted against the summer sea. It is unclear how many bombers the Spitfires shot down, but British historian Richard Collier says that after the attack "more than fifty Dorniers sped on to their target," which suggests heavy German losses. Despite the Spitfire strike, continuing confusion at the Chain Home radar stations kept Eastchurch innocent of the menace descending upon it until the last moment. At a little after 7:00 a.m. a young RAF pilot having breakfast in the mess hall looked out the window and shouted, "They're dropping bombs, they're dropping bombs on us!" just as the first of a hundred high-explosive bombs fell on the runways. That was the last piece of good fortune Oberst Fink enjoyed on Adler Tag. Flying home, the Dorniers were savaged again by marauding Spitfires and Hurricanes. Five more planes fell from the sky. Thirteen others were badly damaged. It was only a little after eight in the morning.

"Pile, it's a miracle."

Normally, Air Marshal Dowding was the most undemonstrative of men, but on the morning of August 14 he was so excited by the previous day's events that he did a very un-Dowding-like thing. He began dive-bombing the office wastebasket with his folded spectacles to demonstrate to General Frederick Pile, the Chief of Antiaircraft Command, how his pilots had fallen on the German bombers. The Luftwaffe report on Adler Tag correctly identified the number of sorties German pilots flew on August 13: 1,485, the most thus far in the battle; however, almost every other important statistic in the report was either incorrect or misleading. The RAF had lost fifteen planes on the thirteenth, not eighty-eight as the report claimed (the Germans lost thirty-nine planes on the thirteenth), and, while nine air bases were attacked on Adler Tag, only a few belonged to Fighter Command. Eastchurch and Detling, its sister base, were part of Coastal Command, and Andover, another frontline base, was part of the Army Co-operation Command.

"Morale high in all reports. News of air battles stimulating," Home Intelligence noted in its morale report for August 14. Dowding's impromptu attack on his office wastebasket said all that needed to be said about morale in Fighter Command, but, as that uneventful Wednesday passed from morning to afternoon, exhilaration gave way to puzzlement. The Luftwaffe was in the air that day, but not in very large numbers. An Enigma transcript resolved the mystery. Reichsmarschall Göring's goal was to "wipe" the RAF from the sky in a week, and, to ensure the deadline—August 15, the third day of its air offensive—was met, the Luftwaffe would deploy 2,119 planes against Britain, far more than on Eagle Day; and, to stretch Fighter Command to the breaking point, major attacks would be launched against northern England as well as Kent and the other countries along the southeast coast.

The fifteenth, a sunny Thursday, began peacefully enough. At nine that morning, there were only a few German reconnaissance planes poking about between the Bristol Channel and East Anglia. Then, a little before eleven, radar stations picked up a flight of thirty-plus German planes crossing the Channel. The flight passed the lighthouse in Dungeness on the English side of the Channel coast, sending the soldiers on the beaches below diving for cover; then the Germans swung northeast toward the village of Hawkinge, where Fighter Command had a base. The local men were in the fields taking in the wheat crop when almost two dozen Ju 87 dive-bombers and six Me 109 fighters arrived overhead. The work in the fields stopped and the men looked up. Thirty seconds of the "metallic pang panging of the airfield's Bofors gun" and the high-pitched scream of the diving Ju 87s was sufficient to satisfy everyone's curiosity; the fieldhands dropped their implements and fled through rows of unharvested wheat toward "the shelter of a distant elm grove." One of the older fieldhands pulled his shirt over his head as he ran, as if trying to protect himself from rain, not bombs. The man behind him found the gesture so absurd he was "chok[ing] with laughter" when he reached the elm grove.

An hour after the Hawkinge attack, radar picked up a flight of a hundred German bombers and seventy fighters approaching the Farne Islands, a bleak collection of windswept rocks off the coast of Northern England. This morning Luftflotte 5, a Luftwaffe unit based in Norway, was using the islands as a navigational point. As they came into view, half the flight peeled away and turned south toward the county of Yorkshire, while the other half continued westward toward Tyneside, an industrial center that straddles the northeast counties of Northumberland and Durham. The attacks were a feint designed to pull Fighter Command's southern squadrons northward, but Luftflotte 5 was picked up by radar while it was still well out to sea. In both Yorkshire and Tyneside, British fighters were waiting when the bombers and their escorts arrived. In the ensuing mêlée, Luftflotte 5 lost 20 percent of its planes and played no further role in the Battle of Britain.

The main German effort of the day was made along the Channel coast. At 2:14 p.m., radar picked up a flight of thirty planes assembling over Calais, and another fifty planes over Saint-Omer. At 2:28 p.m. a hundred planes were identified assembling to the north of Saint-Omer; and at three o'clock, a further eighty planes were tracked crossing the Channel. Shouts of "Many, many bandits" crackled through the radios of the 130 Spitfires and Hurricanes scrambled to meet the onslaught. Below the crowded sky, groups of onlookers gathered to watch the battle. To one man, the "thundering phalanx of planes" overhead "seemed to make an aluminum ceiling of the sky." To another, the contrails that embroidered the flawless afternoon sky brought to mind an ice-skating rink. As the afternoon progressed, "blazing planes, parachutes, shrapnel, bombs," and body parts began to rain down on the

Channel counties of Kent, Sussex, and Hampshire. Between dog-fights, one wealthy Kent family sent their butler out to sweep the lawn. All afternoon the battle swung back and forth. A little after three, a flight of twenty-four German bombers broke through a screen of Spitfires and bombed the Fighter Command base at Martlesham Heath unopposed for five long minutes. The base at Hawkinge, which had been bombed on August 13, was bombed again on the fifteenth, this time so intensely that the antiaircraft crews defending the base developed blood clots in their ears from the pom-pomming of their guns. The Coastal Command base at Eastchurch also received a second visit on the fifteenth. After an attack on Short Brothers, an aircraft works in Kent, just before four, the August sky abruptly emptied and remained so until 5:00 p.m., when radar picked up a flight of two to three hundred German planes approaching Portsmouth and Portland, two important naval centers on the Channel coast.

All day, in twos and threes, fours and fives, and then in sixes and sevens, the British pilots in reserve—the men on thirty minutes' notice, lounging on the grass, and those on instant notice, sitting in their cockpits—were called into battle. By the time Churchill and Pug Ismay visited Fighter Command's operations room early in the evening of August 15, every red light but one was lit up on the wall panel that tracked the number of squadrons in the air. Then a report came in that Croydon, a town ten miles to the south of London, was being bombed—and the last red light blinked on. The attack was a mistake; Hitler had banned air strikes in the London area in hopes of encouraging the British to accept a compromise peace. But even if Ismay had known the attack was the result of a navigational error, it would not have eased his anxiety. Every squadron in southern England was now either engaged or out of action. What would happen if the Germans launched an evening attack? The thought of it made Ismay "sick with fear." Croydon, though, proved to be the last of it. After the attack the sky emptied out again, and one by one the Spitfires and Hurricanes returned to their bases in the August twilight. On the drive back to Chequers, Churchill was unusually quiet. Ismay attempted to start a conversation, but was cut off. "Don't speak to me—I never have been so moved," Churchill said. The two men drove on in silence for a few minutes; then Churchill said, more to himself than to Ismay, "Never in the field of human conflict was so much owed by so many to so few."

The generation that lived through the Battle of Britain has largely passed from the scene, but the story of their everyday heroism during the fateful summer of 1940 lives on in the morale reports of Mass Observation and Home Intelligence. August 20 (as the German air attacks escalate): "Morale remains high. There is confidence and cheerfulness." August 27: "Air raids dominate thought and conversation. Determination has not weakened." September 9 (two days after the first big German attack on London): "In areas which have been most heavily raided there has been little sign of panic and none of defeatism, but rather of . . . increased 'determination to see it through.'" September 16 (the day after the second German attack on London): "Yesterday's aerial successes have produced enthusiastic praise for the RAF. . . . Many people anticipate an invasion within the next few days and are very confident that it will be a failure."

The courage and steadiness of the British public in the face of invasion and daily bombing owed something to their growing ownership of the war, their sense that they were fighting a People's War. But it also owed a great deal to the leadership of Winston Churchill.

It was Churchill's unique achievement that, in the midst of

mortal danger, he was able to fashion a new national narrative out of the gray, sordid business of modern war—out of the ration cards, the food shortages, the queues, the air-raid drills, and the death notices—and make the plumber and the shopgirl feel like participants in a great historical pageant. There have been many theories about why ordinary people found the Churchillian narrative so compelling. Margery Allingham thought it was because the prime minister "brought you up to his level"; Ernst Kris, a psychoanalyst and student of wartime propaganda, thought it was because Churchill helped the British people understand the crisis they were facing. There is a measure of truth in both theories. But only the British historian Isaiah Berlin has captured the music in Churchill's achievement:

> Mr. Churchill is not a sensitive lens which absorbs and concentrates and reflects and amplifies the sentiments of others.... He does not play on public opinion like an instrument. In 1940, he assumed an indomitable stoutness and unsurrendering quality on the part of his people and carried on. If he did not represent the quintessence and epitome of what his fellow citizens feared and hoped in their hour of danger, this was because he idealized them with such intensity that in the end they approached the ideal and began to see themselves as they saw him: the buoyant and imperturbable temper of Britain "which I have the honor to express"—it was, indeed, but he had a lion's share in creating it. So hypnotic was the force of his words, so strong his faith, that by the sheer intensity of his eloquence he bound his spell upon them until it seemed to them that he was indeed speaking what was in their hearts and minds. If it was there, it was largely dormant until he had awoken it in them.

After he had spoken to them in the summer of 1940 as no one had ever before or since, they conceived a new idea of themselves, which their own prowess and the admiration of the world has since established as a heroic image in the history of mankind, like Thermopylae or the defeat of the Spanish Armada. They went into battle transformed by his words. The spirit they found within them, he had created within himself from his inner resources and [he] poured it into his nation.

It needs to be said that many of the Britons who embraced Churchill's heroic narrative knew, in most cases probably subconsciously, that they were playacting—that when the war ended they would take off their costumes and return to ordinary life. Nonetheless, the British public recognized Churchill's achievement. The narrative he wove in the summer of 1940 carried the nation through the Battle of Britain and the Blitz, and then, later in the war, through the hill towns of Italy and the *bocage* of Normandy; through the V1 and V2 attacks; through almost six years of death, deprivation, sorrow, and loss—and, at the end, it delivered Britain into a world where "love and laughter and peace ever after" had become possible again.

ACKNOWLEDGMENTS

For their assistance, I would like to thank Christopher Hill, Cambridge University; Richard Overy, University of Exeter; John Charmley, University of East Anglia; David Kaiser, professor emeritus, US Naval War College; and John Tofanelli, Columbia University. I also owe a debt of gratitude to Nigel Hamilton, senior fellow, John McCormick Graduate School of Policy Studies, for pointing me in the right direction, and to the staffs at the British National Archive, London, and the Churchill Archive Centre, Churchill College, Cambridge.

NOTES

CHAPTER ONE: NEVER AGAIN

1   *foul English weather*: *Times of London*, July 19, 1919.

1   *Victory Day Parade*: Hyde Park Review: *Times of London*, July 20, 1919, *Manchester Guardian, Morning Post* [London], July 20, 1919; British celebrations: *Fielding Star* [New Zealand], July 21, 1919; Peace March for Glorious Dead, http://www.royalmunsterfusiliers.org/zllapece.htm.

2   *Great War casualties*: http://pbs.org/greatwar/resources/casdeath_pop.html.

5   *Unknown Soldier*: Ronald Blythe, *The Age of Illusion* (London: Faber and Faber, 1964), 7–10.

6   *death ship*, The Dying Creeds, *etc.*: Richard Overy, *The Morbid Age: Britain and the Crisis of Civilization, 1919–1939* (London: Penguin, 2010), 18.

6   *"Oh God, Our Help in Ages Past"*: Michael Howard, *The Continental Commitment* (London: Temple Smith, Ltd., 1972), 75.

6   *"This is not a peace"*: Brian Bond, *British Military Policy Between the Two World Wars* (New York: Oxford University Press, 1980), 79.

7   *"There will be no serious direct consequences"*: Overy, *The Morbid Age*, 68.

8   *British Chiefs of Staff*: "Chiefs of Staff Annual Review of Defense Policy," COS Cab 310, Cab 53/23, 1933.

8   *East Fulham*: Winston Churchill, *The Gathering Storm* (New York: Bantam Books, 1961), 100; C. T. Stannage, "The East Fulham By-Election, 25 October 1933," *The Historical Journal* 14, no. 1 (March 1971): 165–200.

9   *"Our cities will be rendered uninhabitable"*: Chiefs of Staff, "The Potential Air Menace To This Country From Germany," 335, Cab 52/23, June 1934.

9   Things to Come: Michael Korda, *With Wings Like Eagles* (New York: Harper-Collins, 2009), 20.

10 *Baldwin, Churchill, and Fighter versus Bomber Controversy*: Ibid., 20–28; John Terraine, *A Time For Courage* (New York: Macmillian, 1985), 15–30.

10 *"I dread the day"*: Churchill, *The Gathering Storm*, 101.

11 *"When Winston was born"*: Andrew Roberts, *The Holy Fox: A Life of Lord Halifax* (London: Weidenfeld & Nicolson, 1991).

11 *Expected casualties at beginning of new war*: Angus Calder, *The People's War* (New York: Pantheon Books, 1969), 22.

NOTES

11 *Peace Ballot*: Martin Ceadel, "The First British Referendum: The Peace Ballot," *English Historical Review* 95, no. 377: 810–39.

11 *"Two thousand years after"*: Korda, *With Wings Like Eagles*, 28.

12 *"Altogether, he looks entirely"*: Robert Self, ed., *The Neville Chamberlain Diary Letters*, vol. 4, *The Downing Street Years, 1934–1940* (Burlington, VT: Ashgate Publishing Co., 2005), 346.

13 *"Men of the German Reichstag"*: William Shirer, *Berlin Diary* (New York: Knopf, 1941), 149–53.

13 *Articles of Versailles Treaty*: Churchill, *The Gathering Storm*, 172.

13 *"The country was never told the truth"*: Lynn Olson, *Troublesome Young Men* (New York: Farrar, Straus and Giroux, 2007), 102.

14 *"What is honor"*: William Shakespeare, *Henry IV Part 1*, 5.1.

14 *"Public opinion . . . and certainly the Labour Party"*: Robert Rhodes James, *Anthony Eden: A Biography* (New York: McGraw-Hill, 1987), 165.

16 *Profile of Chamberlain*: Self, *The Neville Chamberlain Diary Letters*, vol. 4, 30–48; Ernest R. May, *Strange Victory: Hitler's Conquest of France* (New York: Hill & Wang, 2001), 170–73.

17 *"This year has seen"*: Self, *The Neville Chamberlain Diary Letters*, 232.

17 *"The Queen . . . remarked"*: Ibid., 252.

17 *Decline of British power*: Ibid., 1–15.

18 *"We cannot foresee the time when"*: "Comparison of the Strength of Great Britain with that of Certain Other Nations as [of] January 1938," CID paper, 1366-B.

19 *Halifax visits Hitler*: James, *Anthony Eden*, 184.

20 *"Those d—d Germans"*: Self, *The Neville Chamberlain Diary Letters*, 323–24.

20 *Blame Czechs*: Viscount Halifax to Sir Neville Henderson, No. 169 Telegraphic, May 21, 1938.

21 *Chiefs of Staff's warning*: *Documents on British Foreign Policy 1919–1939*, Third series, vol. 1, 220.

21 *"appeasement of the world"*: Keith Feiling, *The Life of Neville Chamberlain* (London: Macmillan, 1946), 355; Margery Allingham, *The Oaken Heart* (London: Michael Joseph Ltd., 1941), 20–23.

22 *Reminders of 1914 during Munich Crisis*: Overy, *The Morbid Age*, 345; Feiling, *The Life of Neville Chamberlain*, 361.

22 *fresh bouquets on Cenotaph*: Alec Douglas Home, *The Way the Wind Blows* (London: HarperCollins, 1976), 78.

22 *"Well, it's been a pretty awful week"*: Self, *The Neville Chamberlain Diary Letters*, 344.

22 *flight to Germany*: Ibid., 346.

23 *"It is you who have big rooms in England"*: Ibid., 347.

23 *"I'd rather be beat"*: David Dilks, ed., *The Diaries of Sir Alexander Cadogan, 1938–1945* (New York: G.P., Putnam, 1972), 104.

23 *"I approve wholeheartedly"*: Feiling, *The Life of Neville Chamberlain*, 349.

24 *"Hitler has given Chamberlain the double cross"*: Shirer, *Berlin Diary*, 138.

24 *"Like a nightmare"*: Olson, *Troublesome Young Men*, 135.

24 *"Hitler has cast a spell over Neville"*: Alfred Duff Cooper, *Old Men Forget* (London: Faber and Faber, 2011), 235.

24 *Warning of General Hastings Ismay*: Cab 21/544, September 23, 1938.

24 *Five days later the Chiefs of Staff issued a similar warning*: COS 772, September 28, 1938.

26 *Public reaction to Munich Agreement*: German reaction: Shirer, *Berlin Diary*, 145–49; French reaction: Cooper, *Old Men Forget*, 243; British reaction: Olson, *Troublesome Young Men*, 158.

26 *Antiappeasement feeling rises sharply*: Olson, *Troublesome Young Men*, 348.

27 *test the strength of Never Again*: October Gallup poll, *News Chronicle*, October 28, 1938.

27 *Substratum of antiwar feeling in Britain*: Cooper, *Old Men Forget*, 244.

CHAPTER TWO: AGAIN

29 *"We seemed to go to war as a duty"*: Allingham, *The Oaken Heart*, 85.

30 *Defense preparations*: Cab 24/288/cabinet paper 188, August 31, 1939.

30 *Greta Garbo–like cartoon character*: Calder, *The People's War*, 32.

30 *Countdown to war*: Chamberlain speaks of "gravest possible conditions" and Halifax describes talks with Theo Kordt and Count Ciano and of Mussolini's desire to play role of peacemaker, Cab 47 (39) September 1, 1939.

31 *"The big thing was a European settlement"*: David Nasaw, *The Patriarch: The Remarkable Life and Turbulent Times of Joseph P. Kennedy* (New York: Penguin, 2012), 405.

32 *Evacuation and other war precautions*: David Cameron Watt, *How War Came* (New York: Pantheon, 1989), 591–95; Calder, *The People's War*, 35–37.

32 *"The road [was] alive"*: Vera Brittain, *England's Hour* (London: Continuum, 2005), 3.

33 *Halifax and Cadogan in palace garden*: Dilks, *The Diaries of Sir Alexander Cadogan*, 212.

33 *The day before the day of the dead*: Halifax gave a brief description of the last-minute efforts to save the peace at the afternoon cabinet on September 2. A more comprehensive description of the final day of negotiations can be found in two cables Halifax sent Sir Eric Phipps, the British ambassador in France, on September 11, 1939: *British Documents on Foreign Affairs*: Viscount Halifax to Sir E. Phipps, Document 271, C13081/G, and Document 272, C13088.

34 *Description of events in House of Commons Smoking Room, September 2*: Sir Edward Spears, *Assignment to Catastrophe*, vol. 1, *July 1939–May 1940* (London: William Heinmann, Ltd., 1954), 11–22.

35 *"All those bands of sturdy Teutonic youths"*: Winston Churchill, Hansard, House of Commons debate, November 23, 1932, vol. 272, 221.

35 *"fine true thing"*: Jon Meacham, *Franklin and Winston* (New York: Random House, 2003), 51.

35 *"Mr. Churchill constantly prefers"*: R. A. C. Parker, *Churchill and Appeasement* (London: Macmillan, 2000), 13.

36 *"When he was wrong, well, my God"*: Meacham, *Franklin and Winston*, 13.

36 *Biography of Henry Channon*: Robert Rhodes James, ed., *Chips: The Diaries of Sir Henry Channon* (London: Penguin, 1970), 7–22.

36 *Channon's observations*: James, *Chips*, 261–62.

NOTES

38 *"I am speaking under very difficult circumstances"*: Arthur Greenwood, Hansard, House of Commons debate, September 2, 1939, vol. 351, 280–86.

38 *"Speak for England"*: Leo Amery, *My Political Life*, vol. 3 (London: Hutchinson, 1955), 324.

38 *Channon's observation about House debate of September, 2, 1939*: James, *Chips.*

38 *"all the old Munich rage"*: Ibid., 261.

39 *"It must be war, Chip, old boy"*: Ibid., 263–64.

39 *Cruise up Amazon*: *Times of London*, September 4, 1939.

40 *"strength of feeling"*: Cab 49/39, September 2, 1939, 11:30 p.m.

40 *Chamberlain declares war*: Spears, *Assignment to Catastrophe*, 23–24.

40 *Air raid sirens*: Ibid., 25.

41 *"Thus we tumbled into Armageddon"*: Robert Boothby, *I Fight to Live* (London: Gollanez, 1947), 190.

41 *Pace of rearmament*: M. M. Postan, *British War Production* (London: H. M. Stationary Office and Longmans, Green & Co., 1952), 53–54.

41 Hitler and the Working Man: Ian McLaine, *The Ministry of Morale* (London: Allen & Unwin, 1979), 141.

42 *British and German production*: Adam Tooze, *The Wages of Destruction: The Making and Breaking of the Nazi Economy* (New York: Penguin, 2008), 310–12.

42 *Antagonism between Lloyd George and Chamberlain*: Anthony Lentin, *Lloyd George and the Lost Peace* (New York: Palgrave Macmillan, 2001), 108.

43 *Profile of Lloyd George*: Paul Addison, "Lloyd George and Compromise Peace in the Second World War," in A. J. P. Taylor, ed., *Lloyd George: Twelve Essays* (New York: Athenaeum, 1971), 361–84.

43 *"Artful as a cartload of monkeys"*: Colin Cross, ed., *Life with Lloyd George: The Diary of A. J. Sylvester, 1931–1945* (London: Macmillan, 1975), 244.

44 *Lloyd George speaks to All Party Group*: Taylor, *Lloyd George*, 367.

44 *Lloyd George's speech on a compromise peace*: Hansard, House of Commons, October 3, 1939, vol. 351, 1875–79.

45 *Attack on Lloyd George's speech*: Cooper, *Old Men Forget*, 267.

45 *Public reaction to Lloyd George's speech*: Self, *The Neville Chamberlain Diary Letters*, 455; Lentin, *Lloyd George and the Lost Peace*, 115–16.

46 *"Peacock with his tail in full show"*: Cross, ed. *Life With Lloyd George*, 242.

46 *Dominions complain Chamberlain's reaction to Hitler's speech is too harsh*: Lentin, *Lloyd George and the Lost Peace*, 120.

46 *Chamberlain's war aims*: "Conversation with Sumner Welles," March 7, 1940, *Foreign Relations of the United States, 1940*, vol. 1, 87; Guy Nicholas Esnouf, *British Government War Aims and Attitudes Toward a Negotiated Peace, September 1939 to July 1940*, unpublished PhD thesis, King's College London, 76, 77, 100–101.

47 *"Don't believe [the war] will go beyond spring"*: November 8, 1939, *Foreign Relations of the United States, 1940*, vol. 1, 526–27.

48 *"Put in some war regulation"*: Nasaw, *The Patriarch*, 404–5.

48 *"They [the British] have no intention of fighting"*: Joseph Kennedy to Secretary of State Cordell Hull, September 25, 1939, *Foreign Relations of the United States*, vol. 1, 454.

49 *"Tweak the lion's tail"*: Nasaw, *The Patriarch*, 404–5, 418.

49 *"Keep the US out of War" sign*: Olson, *Troublesome Young Men*, 54.

49 *a 95 to 5 percent margin*: Meacham, *Franklin and Winston*, 50.

50   *"consistent in his inconsistencies"*: Watt, *How War Came*, 125.

50   *Background of Spears*: Max Egremont, *Under Two Flags: The Life of Major General Sir Edward Spears* (London: Weidenfeld and Nicolson, 1997), 10–50.

52   *Only two Union Jacks on map*: Eleanor M. Gates, *End of the Affair: The Collapse of the Anglo-French Alliance, 1939–40* (Oakland: University of California Press, 1981), 27.

52   *Bastille Day Parade*: May, *Strange Victory*, 288.

53   *Maginot Line*: Alastair Horne, *To Lose a Battle: France 1940* (Boston: Little, Brown and Company, 1969), 25–30.

54   *French political class*: Spears, *Assignment to Catastrophe*, 43–46, 56–72.

54   *Paris in autumn*: Horne, *To Lose a Battle*, 102.

55   *Spears told Jean Giraudoux*: Ibid., 62–63.

55   *Disparity in sacrifice between British and French*: Gates, *End of the Affair*, 28–31.

56   *Mandel's joke*: Spears, *Assignment to Catastrophe*, 59–60.

56   *"Ever seen the French monument to the dead"*: Brittain, *England's Hour*, 19.

CHAPTER THREE: EUROPE IN WINTER

57   *Origins of Finnish war*: Churchill, *The Gathering Storm*, 480–85.

57   *Soviet invasion of Finland*: Tom Shachtman, *The Phony War* (New York: Universe, 2001), 121–22.

58   *"A real war, a man's war" and maps of Finland*: Horne, *To Lose a Battle*, 134.

58   *Western Front*: Hugh Sebag-Montefiore, *Dunkirk: Fight to the Last Man* (London: Penguin, 2006), 17–20; Horne, *To Lose a Battle*, 101–2.

59   *Profile of Gort*: Arthur Bryant, *The Turn of the Tide: A History of the War Years Based on the Diaries of Field-Marshal Lord Alanbrooke, Chief of the Imperial General Staff* (New York: Doubleday & Co., 1957), 59–60; John Colville, *Man of Valour: The Life of Field Marshal The Viscount Gort* (London: Collins, 1972), 20–40.

59   *"Queer kind of war"*: Shirer, *Berlin Diary*, 224.

60   *"War of nerves"*: Susan Briggs, *The Home Front: The War Years in Britain 1939–1945* (New York: American Heritage Publishing Co., 1975), 28.

60   *"The British people are"*: Ibid., 39.

60   *Nanny state*: Peter Lewis, *A People's War* (York, UK: Methuen, 1986), 16–21.

61   *"Galaxy of footmen"*: John Colville, *The Fringes of Power: 10 Downing Street Diaries 1939–1955* (New York: W. W. Norton, 1985), 42.

61   *In the East End*: Olson, *Troublesome Young Men*, 243.

61   *Reclaiming their evacuated children*: Calder, *The People's War*. 35–50.

61   *"Don't do it, mother"*: Wartime Posters, Pinterest, htt

61   *Bitter winter weather*: Monthly weather report of the uary 1940, His Majesty's Stationary Office, Londo

62   *"An elderly statesman with gout"*: Max Hastings, *Wi* tage, 2011), 319.

62   *Nearly a third of the public favors immediate discussion War Aims*, 127.

63   *"People call me defeatist"*: Cecil King, *With Malice To* don: Sidgwick & Jackson, 1970), 13.

64   *Belgians capture German plan*: Sebag-Montefiore,

64   *"Telegram from Brussels"*: Dilks, *The Diaries of Sir Alexander Cadogan*, 245.

65   *Generals meet Hitler, description of Führer's office*: May, *Strange Victory*, 16–20.

65   *German steel production*: Harold Deutsch, *The Conspiracy against Hitler in the Twilight War* (Minneapolis: The University of Minnesota Press, 1968), 190.

66   *Germany would be incapable of launching a decisive offensive*: Horne, *To Lose a Battle*, 140.

66   *Four hundred thousand dead*: Deutsch, *The Conspiracy against Hitler*, 191.

66   *Aim of Allies to obliterate Germany*: Ibid., 193–94.

66   *German offensive plan develops*: May, *Strange Victory*, 225–30; Horne, *To Lose a Battle*, 139–41.

68   *German plot to unseat Hitler*: May, *Strange Victory*, 218–23; Deutsch, *The Conspiracy against Hitler*, 222, 228–29.

68   *Gestapo cable to London after Venlo incident*: Shachtman, *The Phony War*, 108.

69   *Indefinite postponement of Case Yellow*: Ibid., 133.

70   *Allied Supreme Council meeting*: J. R. M. Butler, *Grand Strategy*, vol. 2 (London: Stationary Office Books, 1957), 108.

71   *Sumner Welles fact-finding trip to Europe*: *Foreign Relations of the United States, 1940*, vol. 1.

71   *Opposition to the Welles mission*: Christopher O'Sullivan, *Sumner Welles, Postwar Planning, and the Quest for a New World Order, 1937–1943* (New York: Columbia University Press, 2008), 110–30.

72   *Welles visits Mussolini, February 28, 1940*: Ibid., 27–33.

73   *Welles visit with Hitler, March 2, 1940*: Ibid., 43–50.

74   *Welles exchanges views with French politicians, March 7–9*: Ibid., 58–72.

75   *Welles meets with Chamberlain, Churchill, Halifax, and other leading politicians, March 11–13, 1940*: Ibid., 72–91.

76   *Welles profile of Churchill*: Ibid., 83–84.

76   *Welles returns to Rome for talk with Mussolini, March 16, 1940*: Ibid., 100–106.

CHAPTER FOUR: SEARCHING FOR SOMETHING SPECTACULAR

79   *Hélène de Portes and Madame de Crussol*: Spears, *Assignment to Catastrophe*, 90–92.

79   *"du Barry of France"*: Clare Boothe, *Europe in the Spring* (New York: Alfred A. Knopf, 1940), 148.

80   *Reynaud*: Horne, *To Lose a Battle*, 176–78; Spears, *Assignment to Catastrophe*, 89–91.

80   *Welles's assessment of Reynaud*: *Foreign Relations of the United States, 1940*, vol. 1, 70–72.

81   *drôle de guerre*: May, *Strange Victory*, 328.

82   *Simone de Beauvior on Phony War*: Horne, *To Lose a Battle*, 102–3.

82   *Chamberlain was also feeling the need to do something spectacular*: Colville, *The Fringes of Power*, 96–97; Robert Mackay, *Half the Battle: Civilian Morale in Britain During the Second World War* (Manchester, UK: Manchester University Press, 2003), 55.

      Reynaud proposal for allied action: "Note by the French Prime Minister on the ⌐⌐ch Government's Views on the Future Conduct of the War," March 26, ⌐ W.P. (40) 109; Martin Gilbert, *Finest Hour* (Boston: Houghton Mifflin ⌐ 198–99.

NOTES

83 *Reynaud's war aims*: Esnouf, *British Government War Aims*, 140–50.

83 *Chamberlain "went through the ceiling"*: Roderick Macleod and Denis Kelly, eds., *Time Unguarded: The Ironside Diaries, 1937–1940* (New York: David Mackay, 1963), 234–35.

84 *"The lack of spectacular military events"*: Report by Chiefs of Staff on Certain Aspects of the Present Situation, March 26, 1940, W.P. (40) 111.

86 *War cabinet criticizes Reynaud plan*: Cab, March 27, 1940, 65/6 W.C. 76 (40).

87 *the new French Premier arrived in London amid a swirl of rumor*: Nick Smart, *British Strategy and Politics During the Phony War* (Westport, CT: Praeger, 2003), 195.

87 *"Little Reynaud sat there"*: Macleod and Kelly, *Time Unguarded*, 237.

88 *Reynaud speaks of French morale at Allied Supreme Council*: Churchill, *The Gathering Storm*, 514–15.

88 *Allied plan of attack in Norway*: Butler, *Grand Strategy*, vol. 2, 109–11.

88 *Warnings Germans eyeing Norway*: Gilbert, *Finest Hour*, 197; Churchill, *The Gathering Storm*, 520.

89 *Animosity between Reynaud and Daladier*: Smart, *British Strategy and Politics During the Phony War*, 198; Gates, *End of the Affair*, 47.

89 *Daladier refused to dine with him*: Spears, *Assignment to Catastrophe*, 99–100.

90 *Growth of antiappeasement political block*: Olson, *Troublesome Young Men*, 263–74.

90 *In the March Gallup poll*: British Institute of Public Opinion, *British Institute of Public Opinion Polls 1938–1946*, March 1940 (Storrs, CT: Roper Center, University of Connecticut, 1984). Significantly, the March Gallup poll also showed that nearly a quarter of the British public favored talks with Germany.

91 *Cabinet reshuffle*: Spears, *Assignment to Catastrophe*, 202; Smart, *British Strategy and Politics During the Phony War*, 202.

92 *"Hitler missed the bus"*: *Times of London*, April 5, 1940.

92 *Letter to Hilda Chamberlain*: Self, *The Neville Chamberlain Diary Letters*, 516.

93 *Churchill believes German government will take no retaliatory actions*: Confidential Annex, Cab, April 3, 1940, 65/12 W.M. (40).

93 *Chamberlain also says Germans will take no retaliatory action*: Cab, April 3, 1940, 65/6, W.C. (80) 40.

94 *German attack in Norway and British response*: Gilbert, *Finest Hour*, 213–14; Colville, *The Fringes of Power*, 96–98; David Reynolds, *In Command of History* (New York: Basic Books, 2005), 122–23; Churchill, *The Gathering Storm*, 525–30.

95 *Attack on Glowworm*: J. L. Moulton, *The Norwegian Campaign of 1940* (Athens: Ohio University Press, 1967), 74–78.

95 *"Demoralizing effect of surprises"*: Hastings Ismay, *The Memoirs of General Lord Hastings Ismay* (New York: Viking, 1960), 119.

95 *Oslo, Bergen, Trondheim captured*: Cab, April 9, 1940, 65/6 W.C. 85 (40).

96 *Warned that due to "acute differences . . . on private and personal matters"*: Ronald Campbell, British ambassador to France, to Confidential Annex, Cab, April 8, 1940, 65/12 W.M. (40) 84; Spears, *Assignment to Catastrophe*, 110.

96 *"Will it be Holland or Belgium [next]?"*: Colville, *The Fringes of Power*, 101–2.

96 *"These will be fateful days"*: Macleod and Kelly, *Time Unguarded*, 249.

97 *Press and public reaction to Norway news*: Olson, *Troublesome Young Men*, 281.

97 *"Tales of victory and triumph" . . . "A cold wave of disappointment"*: Harold Nicolson, *Diaries and Letters 1939–1945* (London: Faber, 2009), 70.

NOTES

97   *Many people expected*: Mass Observation, *Morale Now*, April 30, 1940. (Mass Observation was a social research organization that tracked public opinion daily during the spring and early summer of 1940.)

98   *General Mackesy, Admiral Cork, and the confusion of command*: Macleod and Kelly, *Time Unguarded*, 254; Gilbert, *Finest Hour*, 224–25.

98   *Churchill visits General Ironside*: Macleod and Kelly, *Time Unguarded*, 253, 257–58.

100   *Almost immediately*: Gilbert, *Finest Hour*, 242–43.

101   *"For God's sake, tell them"*: Olson, *Troublesome Young Men*, 280.

101   *Plight of 146th and 148th brigades*: David Fraser, *And We Shall Shock Them* (London: Bloomsbury Academic, 2012), 50–52.

102   *"We had always thought"*: Allingham, *The Oaken Heart*, 165–66.

102   *For the first time*: Mass Observation, *Morale Now*, April 30, 1940; Mass Observation, *The Norway Crisis*, May 15, 1940.

104   *"An expedition against the Zulus"*: Gates, *End of the Affair*, 50.

104   *"Considering the prominent part I played"*: Churchill, *The Gathering Storm*, 579.

104   *In the unedited version of that sentence*: Reynolds, *In Command of History*, 125.

104   *"Norway might well have ruined you"*: Ibid. See also Gilbert, *Finest Hour*, 287.

104   *"I don't think my enemies will get me this time"*: Self, *The Neville Chamberlain Diary Letters*, 524.

CHAPTER FIVE: CHAMBERLAIN MISSES THE BUS

106   *March of Old Contemptible*: Manchester Guardian, *Times of London*, *Daily Mirror*, May 5, 1940.

107   *"All the boys felt"*: Machester Guardian, May 6, 1940.

107   *"There was never a break in the [bombing] attacks"*: Daily Mail, May 6, 1940.

107   *Chronic shortage of tanks, munitions, etc.*: Gilbert, *Finest Hour*, 288.

107   *Warning about effect of bombing, Turkey, attack from Norway, mining Thames, Tyne River*: Cab, May 1, 1940, 65/7, (40) 109.

107   *"If I were the first of May"*: Colville, *The Fringes of Power*, 115.

108   Review of the Strategical Situation: Cab, May 4, 1940, 65/7 (40) 145.

110   *Lord Salisbury demands more vigorous pursuit of war*: Larry Witherell, "Lord Salisbury's Watching Committee and the Fall of Chamberlain, May 1940, *English Historical Review* 115, no. 469 (November 2001): 1134–46.

110   *Salisbury warns Halifax*: Foreign Office Papers, 800/236.

110   *"Oh! The excitement"*: James, *Chips*, 299.

110   *Origins of Norway debate*: Harold Macmillan, *The Blast of War, 1939–1945* (New York: HarperCollins, 1968), 54; Amery, *My Political Life*, 358.

110   *Lobbying for Norway debate*: James, *Chips*, 297; Nicolson, *Diaries and Letters*, 74–75.

111   *Nancy Dugdale*: Andrew Roberts, *Eminent Churchillians* (London: Weidenfeld & Nicolson, 1994), 141–42.

111   *More lobbying for Norway debate*: Nicolson, *Diaries and Letters*. 297.

112   *Winston "is too apt to look the other way"*: Self, *The Neville Chamberlain Diary Letters*, 527.

112   *"Winston was being loyal"*: Colville, *The Fringes of Power*, 118–19.

112   *Churchill offers Lloyd George post in his government*: Taylor, *Lloyd George*, 372; A. J. Sylvester, *The Real Lloyd George* (London: Cassell and Company, 1947), 243.

NOTES

112 *"People call me a defeatist"*: King, *With Malice Toward None*, 25.

113 *"We have no chance of avoiding defeat"*: Julian Jackson, *The Fall of France: The Nazi Invasion of 1940* (Oxford, UK: Oxford University Press, 2004), 204.

113 *Press barons pledge to support pro-peace Lloyd George*: Taylor, *Lloyd George*, 371–72.

113 *Meeting with Nancy Astor*: Tom Jones, *Lloyd George* (Cambridge, MA: Harvard University Press, 1951), 253–55.

115 *Profile of David Margesson*: *Daily Mail*, May 7, 1940.

115 *"You utterly contemptible"*: Olson, *Troublesome Young Men*, 305.

116 *One of the few journalists*: *Manchester Guardian*, May 7, 1940.

117 *"We chatted for a moment"*: James, *Chips*, 300.

118 *Chamberlain's speech at Norway debate*: Hansard, *Conduct of the War*, vol. 360, 1073–85.

118 *He "spoke haltingly"*: James, *Chips*, 300.

119 *"The earlier Chamberlain"*: *Manchester Guardian*, May 8, 1940.

119 *Attlee's speech Norway debate*: Hansard, *Conduct of the War*, vol. 360, 1086–94.

120 *Roger Keyes speech*: Ibid., 1125–30.

121 *Description of Amery's thoughts and feelings as he prepares to speak*: Amel7/34, Churchill Archive Center, Cambridge University, Cambridge, UK: Amery, *My Political Life*, vol. 3, 366.

121 *Amery's address at Norway debate*: Hansard, *Conduct of the War*, vol. 360, 1140–51.

123 *Reactions to* Conduct of War *debate*: Channon "most uneasy about tomorrow," James, *Chips*, 300; "The efficacy of the Government": Nicolson, *Diaries and Letters*, 78; Chief Whip Margesson warned: "nadir of gloom": Colville, *The Fringes of Power*, 118.

124 *"I ask that the vote"*: Herbert Morrison, Hansard, *Conduct of the War*, vol. 360, 1251–54.

124 *"I have friends in the House"*: Chamberlain, ibid., 1266.

125 *"Little Neville"*: James, *Chips*, 301.

125 *"The right honorable gentleman"*: Lloyd George, Hansard, *Conduct of the War*, vol. 360, 1283.

125 *Churchill's speech at Norway debate*: Ibid., 1348–61.

125 *Reaction to Churchill speech*: Nicolson, *Diaries and Letters*, 79.

126 *Violet Bonham Carter, Dingle Foot, Lady Alexandra Metcalfe*: Roberts, *Eminent Churchillians*, 139.

126 *Description of atmosphere in House during division (vote)*: Spears, *Assignment to Catastrophe*, vol. 1, 127–30.

128 *Kennedy . . . looked "haggard and shaken"*: Nasaw, *The Patriarch*, 439; Amery, *My Political Life*, 369.

CHAPTER SIX: THE ROGUE ELEPHANT

129 *Public complain about Chamberlain*: Mass Observation, *Political Crisis Report*, May 5, 1940.

129 *Disparaging remarks about George VI and his test scores*: Roberts, *Eminent Churchillians*, 7–8.

130 *King's relationship with Chamberlain*: Ibid., 11.

NOTES

131 *"A little defeatist" after a talk with Ambassador Kennedy*: Dilks, *The Diaries of Sir Alexander Cadogan*, 215.

131 *Queen disapproves of Churchill*: Roberts, *Eminent Churchillians*, 24–25.

131 *King offers to speak to Labour Party*: Ibid., 36.

132 *Whips mount Iron Man defense*: John Barnes and David Nicholson, eds., *The Empire at Bay: The Leo Amery Diaries, 1929–1945* (London: Hutchinson, 1987), 612.

132 *Whips attempt to woo rebel Torys*: Amery, *My Political Life*, vol. 3, 370.

132 *The Whips are putting it about*: Nicolson, *Diaries and Letters*, 80.

132 *Churchill and the Tonypandy Raids*: Anthony Mór-O'Brien, "Churchill and the Tonypandy Riots," *Welsh History Review* 17, no. 1 (1994): 67–78.

132 *Labour Party supports Halifax*: Roberts, *The Holy Fox*, 199–200.

132 *"bitterly opposed to Winston"*: Ibid., 39.

133 *"Don't agree and don't say anything"*: Anthony Eden, *The Reckoning: The Memoirs of Anthony Eden* (Boston: Houghton Mifflin Co., 1965), 111.

134 *German merchant fleet had switched to the frequency*: David Irving, *Churchill's War* (New York: Avon Books, 1991), 261–62.

134 *"When the history [of this period] comes to be written"*: Lloyd George, Hansard, May 9, 1940, vol. 360, 1496.

134 *Lloyd George is "stak[ing] out a position"*: Self, *The Neville Chamberlain Diary Letters*, 530.

134 *"Unable to distinguish between the P.M. and Halifax"*: Gilbert, *Finest Hour*, 302–3.

134 *"Our party won't have you"*: Kenneth Harris, *Attlee* (London: Weidenfeld & Nicolson, 1995), 174.

135 *Halifax's reservations about becoming Prime Minister*: Roberts, *Holy Fox*, 195–205.

136 *Churchill's version of how he became Prime Minister*: Churchill, *The Gathering Storm*, 592.

137 *Halifax's version of how Churchill became Prime Minister*: Roberts, *Holy Fox*, 204–5.

138 *Halifax goes to the dentist*: Ibid., 207–8.

138 *Profile of General Gamelin*: May, *Strange Victory*, 129–32; Horne, *To Lose a Battle*, 116–22.

139 *Reynaud disillusioned with Gamelin*: Paul Reynaud, *In the Thick of the Fight, 1930–1945* (London: Cassell and Company, 1955), 284–85.

139 *"That nerveless man"*: May, *Strange Victory*, 379.

139 *Reynaud's miraculous recovery on the ninth*: Ibid., 378–79.

139 *Description of Paris on afternoon of May 9, 1940*: Boothe, *Europe in the Spring*, 127.

140 *"If [Gamelin] is guilty, I am,"*: Ibid., 379.

140 *London learned of the German offensive*: Cab, May 10, 1940, 65/7 117 (40).

140 *"How crazy . . . Children playing by the stream"*: Horne, *To Lose a Battle*, 211.

140 *The general had dismissed a warning*: Reynaud, *In the Thick of the Fight*, 294.

140 *in Downing Street*: Cab, morning cabinet, May 10, 1940, 65/7 117 (40).

141 *"Perhaps the darkest day in English history"*: James, *Chips*, 306.

141 *General Gamelin "strode up and down the corridor"*: André Beaufre, *1940: The Fall of France* (London: Cassell, 1967), 388.

142 *"Oh, I don't know about that"*: Gilbert, *Finest Hour*, 306.

142 *Chamberlain had announced that he intended to stay in office*: Eden, *The Reckoning*, 111; Hugh Dalton, *The Fateful Years: Memoirs 1931–1945* (London: Frederick Muller, Ltd, 1957), 344.

NOTES

142 *Alec Douglas-Home addresses Watching Committee*: Nicolson, *Diaries and Letters*, 80.

142 *Brendan Bracken mobilizes votes for Churchill*: Gilbert, *Finest Hour*, 308.

143 *Labour Party refuses to back Chamberlain*: Cab, afternoon cabinet, May 10, 1940, 65/7 119 (40).

143 *"all my past life"*: Churchill, *The Gathering Storm*, 596.

144 *"I have met a genius"*: Paul Addison, *Churchill: The Unexpected Hero* (Oxford, UK: Oxford University Press, 2005), 3.

145 *"If I had to spend my whole life"*: Nella Last, *Nella Last's War: The Second World War Diaries of Housewife, 49* (London Profile Books, 2006), 46–47.

145 *"Old men forget"*: Roberts, *Eminent Churchillians*, 137.

145 *"True blue" Tory*: Ibid., 145.

145 *"The crooks are on top"*: John Charmley, *Churchill: The End of Glory* (New York: Harcourt, 1993), 396.

145 *"King over water"*: James, *Chips*, 307.

146 *Cabinet appointments*: Charmley, *Churchill*, 397.

146 *"The only hope lies in"*: Roberts, *The Holy Fox*, 209.

147 *"Victory, victory at all costs"*: Churchill inaugural speech as prime minister, May 13, 1940, Hansard, *Conduct of the War*, vol. 360, 1501–25.

CHAPTER SEVEN: "THERE FADED AWAY THIS NOISE WHICH WAS A GREAT ARMY"

149 *"There faded away this noise which was a great army"*: Victor Hugo, "Waterloo! Waterloo! Waterloo! Morne plaine!"

149 *"It went too damn well"*: Drew Middleton, *Our Share of Night: A Personal Narrative of the War Years* (New York: Viking, 1946), 40.

149 *Schlieffen plan*: May, *Strange Victory*, 260, 294–95.

150 *"Everything so far has been running like clockwork"*: Alex Danchev and Dan Todman, eds., *War Diaries 1939–1945: Field Marshal Lord Alanbrooke* (London: Weidenfeld & Nicolson, 2001), 59–60.

150 *"In towns and villages"*: Sebag-Montefiore, *Dunkirk*, 61.

151 *"Retracing steps taken in a dream"*: Middleton, *Our Share of Night*, 40.

151 *"When we took the decision to go into Belgium"*: Sebag-Montefiore, *Dunkirk*, 66.

151 *"I could have wept with joy"*: Jackson, *The Fall of France*, 28.

152 *"It's a miracle! It's a miracle!"*: Ronald Atkin, *Pillar of Fire: Dunkirk 1940* (Edinburgh: Birlinn, Ltd., 2001), 40.

152 *General Irwin Rommel began May 13*: Horne, *To Lose a Battle*, 272–74.

152 *French strategic errors at Meuse*: May, *Strange Victory*, 426–31.

153 *"Beat it!"*: Reynaud, *In the Thick of the Fight*, 302.

153 *French despair at German breakthrough*: Beaufre, *1940*, 185.

153 *Reynaud requests ten RAF squadrons immediately*: Cab, May 14, 1940, 65/7 122 (40).

154 *twenty-nine . . . fighter squadrons currently available*: Cab, evening cabinet, May 16, 1940, 65/7 25 (40).

154 *Churchill sends Reynaud an ambiguous reply*: Premier papers, 3/188.

155 *Conversation with Joe Kennedy*: Nasaw, *The Patriarch*, 441.

155 *Reynaud makes second desperate request for RAF squadrons*: Cab, May 15, 1940, 65/7 123 (40).

NOTES

155   *Description of mood on Paris streets, May 15 to 18*: Horne, *To Lose a Battle*, 385–89.

156   *"The road to Paris is open"*: Reynaud, *In the Thick of the Fight*, 319–20.

157   *Convenes emergency meeting to discuss defense of Paris*: Ibid., 322.

157   *London receives grave news on morning of May 16*: Cab, May 16, 1940, 65/7 124 (20).

158   *Paris could fall within the next few days*: Hastings Ismay, *The Memoirs of General Lord Hastings Ismay* (New York: Viking, 1960), 127.

158   *"The French High Command is already beaten"*: Gilbert, *Finest Hour*, 349; Supreme War Council minutes May 16, 1940, 99/3.

158   *Conflicting accounts of Anglo-French meeting of May 16*: Churchill, *Their Finest Hour*, 38–44; Reynaud, *In the Thick of the Fight*, 323–30.

159   *Paul Baudouin's observations about Daladier*: Ibid., 392–93.

159   *Venerable officials burning documents*: Churchill, *Their Finest Hour*, 39.

160   *"I assure you that in this bulge"*: Horne, *To Lose a Battle*, 394.

160   *"Inferiority of numbers, inferiority of equipment"*: Churchill, *Their Finest Hour*, 43.

160   *walked over to the window again*: Ibid., 42.

160   *"Churchill is still thinking of his books"*: Colville, *The Fringes of Power*, 132.

161   *May 14 . . . lost seventy-one planes*: Terraine, *A Time for Courage*, 34.

161   *Ismay sends message in Hindustani*: Ismay, *The Memoirs of General Lord Hastings Ismay*, 130.

161   *Description of meeting at Reynaud's apartment*: Gates, *End of the Affair*, 125–26.

162   *"Don't fuss and budget, dearie"*: Ismay, *The Memoirs of General Lord Hastings Ismay*, 130.

162   *"We are living in a new phase of history"*: MacLeod and Kelly, *Time Unguarded*, 310.

163   *"I think they are going to beat us"*: Sandra Koa Wong, ed., *Our Longest Days* (London: Profile Books, 2008), 23.

163   *Developments in public opinion in second half of May, including changing perception of Hitler*: Mass Observation, *The General Morale: Background Situations*, May 30, 1940.

165   *Roosevelt's skepticism about Churchill*: David Reynolds, *The Creation of the Anglo-American Alliance 1937–1941* (Chapel Hill: University of North Carolina Press, 1982), 112–14.

166   *Chamberlain was claiming that "everything [was] finished"*: Esnouf, *British Government War Aims*, 189.

166   *"Could we maintain the Air Struggle?"*: MacLeod and Kelly, *Time Unguarded*, 313.

166   *"A miracle may save us"*: Dilks, *The Diaries of Sir Alexander Cadogan*, 288.

166   *"If the Germans received fair peace terms"*: Hastings, *Winston's War*, 32.

167   *Basil Liddel Hart, Montagu Norman, John Gielgud, Sybil Throndike, George Bernard Shaw, etc.*: Jackson, *The Fall of France*, 204; Hastings, *Winston's War*, 32–33.

CHAPTER EIGHT: *A CERTAIN EVENTUALITY*

169   *General Pownall's visit to Dunkirk*: Colville, *Man of Valour*, 203.

170   *"You ought to have cried, 'Shame'"*: Gilbert, *Finest Hour*, 362–63.

170   *Cabinet debates whether Gort should retreat to sea*: Cab, Confidential Annex, May 19, 1940, 65/13 W.M. (40) 140.

172 *"be ye men of valour"*: Churchill's first broadcast to British people as prime minister, May 19, 1940.

172 *"A withdrawal south"*: Gates, *End of the Affair*, 86.

173 *"last alternative"*: Horne, *To Lose a Battle*, 492.

173 *Reynaud appoints Pétain and Weygand to his government*: Spears, *Assignment to Catastrophe*, 151–52.

174 *"Instead of ectoplasm, we [have] a man!"*: Beaufre, *1940*, 190; Gilbert, *Finest Hour*, 56–57.

174 *Design and object of Weygand offensive*: Reynaud, *In the Thick of the Fight*, 364–67.

175 *Weygand offensive miscarries*: Gilbert, *Finest Hour*, 384–87; Colville, *Man of Valour*, 212–15.

175 *Churchill tells King a seaborne evacuation still might be necessary*: John Wheeler Bennett, *King George VI: His Life and Reign* (New York: St. Martin's Press, 1958), 458.

175 *German pressure on Channel ports of Calais and Boulogne threatens BEF*: Cab, Confidential Annex, May 23, 1940, 65/13 W.M. (40).

175 *"Not many sailing"*: Sebag-Montefiore, *Dunkirk*, 223.

175 *Situation in Calais*: Ibid., 230.

175 *Calais to be defended to last round*: MacLeod and Kelly, *Time Unguarded*, 331–32.

175 *"The final debacle cannot be long delayed"*: Ibid., 332.

176 *Chamberlain study group organized to examine the effect the fall of France would have on Britain*: P. M. H. Bell, *A Certain Eventuality: Britain and the Fall of France* (London: Saxon House, 1974), 32.

176 *Could Britain continue the war alone? The Chiefs of Staff view*: Chiefs of Staff, *British Strategy in a Certain Eventuality*, May 25, 1940, Cab 66/7, W.P. (40) 168.

178 *Henry Channon buries his diaries*: James, *Chips*, 312.

178 *Vera Brittain imagined herself at a requiem for "European civilization"*: Brittain, *England's Hour*, 34.

179 *"The appalling size of the smash up"*: Allingham, *The Oaken Heart*, 181.

180 *Spears flight to Paris May 25*: Spears, *Assignment to Catastrophe*, 176–77.

181 *Paris and London blame each other*: Gates, *End of the Affair*, 133.

181 *"Many people now quite openly blame"*: Boothe, *Europe in the Spring*, 265.

182 *Description of Reynaud and Spears's meeting at Ministry of Defense*: Spears, *Assignment to Catastrophe*, 180–81.

182 *Reynaud's telephone annoys Spears*: Ibid., 187–88.

182 *meeting with Major Fauvelle*: Ibid., 189–91.

183 *"Gort's only hope is to get to the coast"*: Oliver Harvey, *The Diplomatic Diaries of Oliver Harvey, 1937–1940* (New York: St. Martin's Press, 1971), 368.

183 *Italian embassy suggests Anglo-Italian talks*: Cab, May 25, 1940, 65/7 W.M. (40) 138; Andrew Roberts's *The Holy Fox* provides more detail about the invitation on page 214.

184 *he drafted a cable to Roosevelt in Churchill's name*: Reynolds, *The Creation of the Anglo-American Alliance*, 103.

184 *Churchill said he had "no objections" to talking to the Italians*: Cab, May 25, 1940, 65/7 W.M. (40) 138.

185 *Halifax describes his talk with Bastianini in a cable to Percy Lorraine, the British ambassador in Rome*: Cab, May 26, 1940, 66/7 W.P. (40) 170.

185 *Paresci complains meeting had miscarried*: Roberts, *The Holy Fox*, 214–16.

NOTES

185 *"Black as black"*: Dilks, *The Diaries of Sir Alexander Cadogan*, 289–90.

186 *Captured German map*: Bryant, *The Turn of the Tide*, 96.

186 *Weygand describes how France will fall*: Reynaud, *In the Thick of the Fight*, 389.

187 *Albert Lebrun urges that France initiate talks with Germany immediately*: Gates, *End of the Affair*, 140–41.

188 *Pétain and Campinchi offer their views to committee*: John Lukacs, *Five Days in London: May 1940* (New Haven, CT: Yale University Press, 2001), 88.

189 *"If I ever have to go through another war"*: Charles Ritchie, *The Siren Years: A Canadian Diplomat Abroad, 1937–1945* (Toronto: McClelland & Stewart, 2001), 54.

189 *The "pipe will go on passing water through"*: Bryant, *The Turn of the Tide*, 98.

190 *"lunatics . . . were the last straw"*: Ibid., 98.

190 *"lame women suffering"*: Ibid., 89.

190 *"March north to the coast in battle order"*: Defense Committee, May 25, 1940, Cab papers 69/1.

191 *Young woman crying at bus stop*: Edward Bliss, ed., *In Search of Light: The Broadcasts of Edward R. Murrow, 1938–1961* (New York: Da Capo Press, 1997), 25.

191 *"Horrifying sense of living the same old nightmare"*: Mollie Panter Downes, *London War Notes, 1939–1945* (New York: Farrar, Straus and Giroux, 1971), 62.

CHAPTER NINE: THE ITALIAN APPROACH

195 *"Morale of German troops fantastically good"*: Shirer, *Berlin Diary*, 380.

195 *"You ought to have a 'bare bodkin'"*: Nicolson, *Diaries and Letters*, 90.

196 *National Prayer Day*: Manchester Guardian, May 27, 1940.

196 *Description of cabinet room*: Ian Colvin, *The Chamberlain Cabinet* (West Sussex, UK: Littlehampton Book Service, 1971), 18–21.

197 *Halifax proposes Britain examine a compromise peace*: Cabinet, Confidential Annex, May 26, 1940, 65/13 W.M. (40) 139.

199 *Description of National Prayer Day*: Times of London, Daily Mail, Daily Express, May 27, 1940; David Baldwin, *Royal Prayer: A Surprising History* (London: Bloomsbury Academic, 2010), 88–90.

200 *"In Westminster Abbey"*: John Betjeman, *Collected Poems* (New York: Farrar, Straus & Giroux, 2006), 74.

201 *Three versions of Reynaud's visit to London*: French War Committee's version, Esnouf, *British Government War Aims*, 211; Reynaud's version, *In the Thick of the Fight*, 404; Colonel de Villelume's version, Gates, *End of the Affair*, 145.

202 *Reynaud and Churchill's lunchtime conversation*: At the afternoon cabinet, Churchill described the topics he and Reynaud discussed; Confidential Annex, May 26, 1940, Cab 65/13 W.M. (40) 140.

204 *Reynaud sounded remarkably like Halifax*: Esnouf, *British Government War Aims*, 212–13.

204 *British Strategy in the Near Future*: May 26, 1940, Cab 66/7 W.P. (40) 169.

204 *German GDP greater than that of Britain or the United States*: Tooze, *The Wages of Destruction*, 383.

205 *Churchill's manipulation of Chiefs of Staff to produce a more optimistic assessment of Britain's ability to fight on alone*: Private communication to the author; also see

Christopher Hill, *Cabinet Decisions on Foreign Policy* (Cambridge, UK: Cambridge University Press, 1991), 154–55.

206 *"We [are] in a different position from France"*: notes on the third and last cabinet of May 26 can be found in the concluding paragraphs of Confidential Annex, Cab 65/13 W.M. (40) 140.

208 *Halifax's disadvantages in compromise peace debate*: Hill, *Cabinet Decisions on Foreign Policy*, 159–61.

208 *Churchill's advantages in debate*: Ibid., 147–54.

208 *Role of Chamberlain, Attlee, Greenwood in debate*: Ibid., 156–57.

209 *"The Duce . . . plans to write a letter to Hitler"*: Hugh Gibson, ed., *The Ciano Diaries 1939–1943* (New York: Simon Publications, 1945), 255.

212 *Fall of Calais*: Sebag-Montefiore, *Dunkirk*, 228–38; Charles Whiting, *The Poor Bloody Infantry* (London: Hutchinson, 1987), 44–45.

212 *"Operation Dynamo is to commence"*: Gilbert, *Finest Hour*, 405.

212 *"Fear not the result"*: Ibid., 406.

CHAPTER TEN: "GOOD MORNING, DEATH"

213 *"Any ideas how we shall win?"*: Nigel Balchin, *Darkness Falls From the Air* (London: Cassel Military, 2002), 40.

213 *Visiting the pediatric ward*: Calder, *The People's War*, 107.

214 *"Every time we meet now"*: Nicolson, *Diaries and Letters*, 90.

214 *"In the last war"*: Boothe, *Europe in the Spring*, 284–85.

214 *Johnny Churchill's arrival from France*: Gilbert, *Finest Hour*, 429–30.

215 *Every road was packed*: Whiting, *The Poor Bloody Infantry*, 46.

216 *"I have never felt greater serenity"*: Colville, *The Fringes of Power*, 140.

216 *"A timely miracle would be acceptable"*: Ibid., 141.

217 *Keyes says he is not optimistic about Belgium*: Gilbert, *Finest Hour*, 414–15.

217 *Dill's mistaken belief that Calais is still holding and cabinet debate about air estimates*: Confidential Annex, Cab, May 27, 1940, 65/13 W.M. (40) 141.

219 *"I trust you realize, Mr. President"*: Warren F. Kimball, ed., *Churchill and Roosevelt: The Complete Correspondence*, vol. 1 (Princeton, NJ: Princeton University Press, 1984), 37.

219 *"If members of the present administration"*: Ibid., 40.

220 *"The United States has given us practically"*: Cab, May 27, 1940, 65/7 W.M. (40) 141.

220 *"This statement would apply"*: Confidential Annex Cab, May 27, 1940, 65/13 W.M. (40) 141.

221 *Australian prime minister favors peace conference*: Clive Ponting, *1940: Myth and Reality* (Lanham, MD: Ivan R. Dee Publisher, 1993), 111, 116.

222 *Events in Rome, May 27, 1940*: Reynaud, *In the Thick of the Fight*, 407–15.

225 *Events in Paris, May 27, 1940*: Spears, *Assignment to Catastrophe*, 239–43.

226 *"Good morning, death"*: Boothe, *Europe in the Spring*, 270–71.

226 *Patrick Turnbull's flight to Dunkirk*: Patrick Turnbull, *Dunkirk: Anatomy of Disaster* (Des Moines, IA: Home Publishing Co., 1978), 160–70.

227 *French not told about Dunkirk evacuation*: Gates, *End of the Affair*, 106–8.

228 *"Who shot him"*: Bryant, *The Turn of the Tide*, 108.

229   *"Things [are] as bad as that, are they?"*: Allingham, *The Oaken Heart*, 197.

230   *Churchill and Halifax clash at afternoon cabinet of May 27, 1940*: Confidential Annex, May 27, 1940, 65/13 W.M. (40) 141.

231   *Colville hears rumors of dischord after cabinet ends*: Colville, *The Fringes of Power*, 141.

231   *"I can't work with Winston any longer"*: Dilks, *The Diaries of Sir Alexander Cadogan*, 291.

231   *"I thought Winston talked the most frightful rot"*: Gilbert, *Finest Hour*, 413.

232   *Churchill was too restless to go to sleep*: Colville, *The Fringes of Power*, 141.

232   *"My impression of the situation"*: Nasaw, *The Patriarch*, 448.

CHAPTER ELEVEN: "WE WERE NO LONGER ONE"

233   *Strength of Belgian army*: John Keegan, *The Second World War* (New York: Penguin Books, 2005), 324.

234   *"Spring came late this year"*: The woman I call Jane Pratt is one of several hundred people who kept a wartime diary for Mass Observation. In MO's files she is listed as J. L. Pratt, subject 5041; I've turned the *J* into "Jane" in order to clarify her gender. And as indicated in the text, the diary entry was made at some point during late morning or early afternoon of May 28, 1940.

236   *"All this day of the twenty-eighth"*: Churchill, *Their Finest Hour*, 84–85.

236   The German Triumph in the West: Shirer, *Berlin Diary*, 383–84.

237   *"I have no intention of suggesting"*: Churchill, Hansard, May 28, 1940, vol. 361, 421–22.

237   *"A deed without precedent"*: Jacques Benoist-Méchin, *Sixty Days that Shook the West: The Fall of France, 1940* (New York: Putnam, 1963), 179.

237   *French hostility to Belgian refugees*: Horne, *To Lose a Battle*, 541.

237   *"Polyphonic symphony"*: Arthur Koestler, *Scum of the Earth* (London: Eland Books, 2007), 186.

237   *Spears visits Reynaud, morning of May 28*: Spears, *Assignment to Catastrophe*, 253–54.

238   *Gort and Blanchard meet*: Henry Pownall, *Chief of Staff: The Diaries of Lieutenant-General Sir Henry Pownall* (London: L. Cooper, 1972), 347–50; Gates, *End of the Affair*, 107; Sebag-Montefiore, *Dunkirk*, 337.

239   *Churchill's tribute to defenders of Lille*: Churchill, *Their Finest Hour*, 85.

239   *Number of British ships involved in Dunkirk evacuation*: Churchill, *Their Finest Hour*, 88.

240   *Evacuation numbers as of midday, May 28; warning of Air Marshal Sir Hugh Dowding*: A description of the situation at Hazebrouck can be found in Cab 65/7 W.M. (40) 144.

240   *Defense of Cassel and biography of Brigadier Nigel Somerset*: Sebag-Montefiore, *Dunkirk*, 368–69.

242   *Lloyd George discusses past with Churchill*: Sylvester, *Life With Lloyd George*, 263–65.

242   *Lloyd George believes war is unwinnable*: Memo, September 12, 1940, Lloyd George Papers, G/81; David Reynolds, "Churchill and the British decision to fight on in 1940," in Richard Langhorne, ed., *Diplomacy and Intelligence in the Second World War* (Cambridge, UK: Cambridge University Press, 2004), 154–55.

242   *Rationing ends in 1954*: www.primaryhomeworkhelp.co.uk/war/rationing.htm.

244 *Churchill tests Lloyd George*: Taylor, *Lloyd George*, 586.

245 *Ashford hosts Dunkirk evacuees*: Mass Observation, *Dover*, June 6, 1940.

246 *Discussion in afternoon cabinet, May 28*: Confidential Annex, May 28, 1940, 65/13. W.M. (40) 140.

249 *"People are calm but exceedingly anxious"*: Mass Observation, *Morale Today*, May 28, 1940.

250 *"He was quite magnificent"*: Hugh Dalton, *The Fateful Years: Memoirs 1931–1945* (London: Cape, 1957), 335–37. The evening meeting of the war cabinet that followed Churchill's speech to the outer cabinet was a continuation of 65/13 W.M. (40) 140.

252 *The cabinet agreed to reject it*: Cypher telegram from Prime Minister to M. Reynaud, May 28, 1940, no. 235 DIPP.

253 *"Now we have the Allies in both pockets"*: Shirer, *Berlin Diary*, 384.

253 *"In these dark days"*: Gilbert, *Finest Hour*, 80.

253 *"A gallant man"*: Macleod and Kelly, *Time Unguarded*, 344.

253 *"I wonder as I gaze out"*: James, *Chips*, 313.

254 *Dill and Pound wobbly*: Esnouf, *British Government War Aims*, 265.

254 *Ignorance is bliss*: Mass Observation, *Morale Today*, May 29, 1940.

255 *"The English were stiffening themselves for the coming struggle"*: Boothe, *Europe in the Spring*, 276.

255 *Foreign diplomats impressed by British morale*: Lukacs, *Five Days in London*, 173.

255 *Trancelike state of British*: Bliss, *In Search of Light*, 25.

255 *George Orwell lists latest rumors*: George Orwell, *A Patriot After All: 1940–1941* (London: Secker & Warburg, 1999), 168.

257 *"waxen immobility" of the dead*: Ritchie, *The Siren Years*, 55–59.

257 *A little before 4:00 a.m. on Thursday, May 30*: Spears, *Assignment to Catastrophe*, 277–80.

258 *Churchill's instructions for Spears*: Premier papers, 3/175.

259 *At the morning meeting of the French War Committee*: Spears, *Assignment to Catastrophe*, 281–84.

260 *Rumors about why compromise peace debate had ended*: James, *Chips*, 312–13; Dilks, *The Diaries of Sir Alexander Cadogan*, 292.

260 *Fighter Command puts fewer patrols over Dunkirk*: John Terraine, *A Time for Courage: The Royal Air Force in the European War, 1939–1945* (New York: Macmillan, 1985), 156.

260 *request for continuous fighter action in the air*: Gilbert, *Finest Hour*, 430.

260 *J. B. Priestley's broadcasts on the "little boats"*: Calder, *The People's War*, 108.

261 *"For all the good you chaps seem to be doing"*: Terraine, *A Time for Courage*, 156–57.

261 *Number of troops evacuated and discussion of invasion threat*: Evening war cabinet, May 30, 1940, 65/7, (40) 148.

262 *British party arrives at Villacoublay Aerodrome*: Spears, *Assignment to Catastrophe*, vol. 2, 292–93.

264 *Churchill opened the . . . Supreme War Council with an announcement*: Supreme War Council Minutes, May 31, 1940, 99/3. See also Gilbert, *Finest Hour*, 95–96; Spears, *Assignment to Catastrophe*, 296–310; Ismay, *The Memoirs of General Lord Hastings Ismay*, 133; Reynaud, *In the Thick of the Fight*, 449–51.

NOTES

269   *The evacuation at Dunkirk*: Eyewitness to History, www.eyewitnesstohistory.com.

270   *Destroyer* Keith *attacked, armless sailor*: Sebag-Montefiore, *Dunkirk*, 416–17.

271   *"polished way"*: Gilbert, *Their Finest Hour*, 98.

271   *Spears threatens Pétain*: Spears, *Assignment to Catastrophe*, 316.

271   *Number of men evacuated June 1, 1940*: Churchill, *Their Finest Hour*, 47.

272   *"Maximum efforts must be made"*: War Cab 65/7 (40) 151; Gilbert, *Finest Hour*, 99.

272   *"Bras dessus" pledge*: Churchill, *Finest Hour*, 96–97.

272   *Lelong's urgent cable to Paris*: Montefiore, *Dunkirk*, 421.

273   *Churchill changes his mind about shutting down evacuation*: Gilbert, *Finest Hour*, 448.

273   *Headlines in Berlin papers*: Shirer, *Berlin Diary*, 390–91.

273   *"Ten million French people"*: Koestler, *The Scum of the Earth*, 167.

274   *"Why ever have these poor things"*: Sebag-Montefiore, *Dunkirk*, 419.

274   *"prepare the people"*: Mass Observation, *Some Notes for the Weekend*, June 3, 1940.

274   *Invasion preparations*: Allingham, *The Oaken Heart*, 208–9.

275   *"I forgot I was a middle-aged woman"*: Last, *Nella Last's War*, 54.

276   *German and British air losses over Dunkirk*: Terraine, *A Time for Courage*, 157.

277   *"Wait and See"*: Esnouf, *British Government War Aims*, 244–45.

277   *Elephant and whale*: Colville, *The Fringes of Power*, 157.

278   *British aircraft production in the summer of 1940*: Terraine, *A Time for Courage*, 191.

279   *Dowding can't guarantee air superiority for more than forty-eight hours*: Confidential Annex, June 3, 1940, 65/13, W.M. (40) 153.

279   *"We shall go on to the end"*: Spears, *Assignment to Catastrophe*, vol 2, 56.

279   *Anthony Eden warns Britain has only two brigades of regular troops and a few territorial units for home defense*: Spears, *Assignment to Catastrophe*, vol. 2, 146.

279   *"it will be the middle ages all over again"*: Ibid., 165.

280   *listening to Big Ben chime*: Ibid., 65.

280   *"It is the fault of your country"*: Ibid., 100.

280   *Hélène de Portes directing traffic*: Ibid., 190.

280   *French government abandoned Paris*: Ibid., 202.

280   *Hélène de Portes again*: Ibid., 196.

280   *Weygand again*: Ibid., 124.

281   *Churchill on flight to Briare*: Spears, *Assignment to Catastrophe*, vol. 2, 139–41.

282   *Meeting at Briare*: Supreme War Council minutes, June 11, 1940, 99/3; Ismay, *The Memoirs of General Lord Hastings Ismay*, 136–41; Eden, *The Reckoning*, 114–17; Spears, *Assignment to Catastrophe*, 140–71; Churchill, *Their Finest Hour*, 130–36; Reynaud, *In the Thick of the Fight*, 493–99.

286   *Spears and Pétain have a second talk*: Spears, *Assignment to Catastrophe*, vol. 2, 83.

287   *De Gaulle had noticed a new current*: Charles de Gaulle, *The Complete War Memoirs of Charles de Gaulle* (New York: Da Capo, 1967), 64.

287   *Secret cable found in Hélène de Portes's bed*: Spears, *Assignment to Catastrophe*, vol. 2, 195.

288   *Meeting at Tours*: Supreme War Council Minutes, June 13, 1940, 99/3; Reynaud, *In the Thick of the Fight*, 494–500; De Gaulle, *The Complete War Memoirs of Charles de Gaulle*, 68; Spears, *Assignment to Catastrophe*, vol. 2, 202–10; Ismay,

The Memoirs of General Lord Hastings Ismay, 143–45; Churchill, *Their Finest Hour*, 154–58.

290   "My country is bleeding to death": Gilbert, *Finest Hour*, 535–36.

291   *A visit to occupied Paris*: Shirer, *Berlin Diary*, 412–18.

293   *Shirer drove up to Compiègne*: Ibid., 419–24.

CHAPTER THIRTEEN: LAND OF HOPE AND GLORY

295   *Discussion outside Hanlon's*: Mass Observation, *Capitulation Talk in Worktown* (code name for Bolton), June 18, 1940.

296   *"From the moment you woke up"*: Calder, *The People's War*, 111.

296   *Visit to a chemist's shop*: Mass Observation, *Capitulation Talk in Worktown*, June 18, 1940.

296   *Home Intelligence Committee*: Esnouf, *British Government War Aims*, 273–74.

297   *Churchill sounded "drunk"*: Mass Observation, *Morale Today*, June 19, 1940.

297   *Churchill's secret session speech*: Gilbert, *Finest Hour*, 378–80.

298   *"Nil"*: Premier Papers, June 21, 1940, 3/179.

298   *American aid as of June 1940*: Reynolds, *The Creation of the Anglo-American Alliance*, 109. The figures Ismay presented to Churchill—192,600 rifles and 89 million rounds of ammunition—are somewhat smaller than those cited by Reynolds, but the difference between the two figures may be because they count American aid from different periods in the summer of 1940.

298   *American skepticism about Britain's survival*: Ibid., 111–15.

299   *Hans Thomsen and Hamilton Fish*: Chargé d'affaires, German embassy, Washington to German Foreign Ministry, Most Urgent, Top Secret, Telegram no. 1150, June 12, 1940.

300   *British reaction to articles of French surrender*: Gilbert, *Finest Hour*, 398.

302   *British attack on Mers-el-Kébir*: P. M. H. Bell, *France and Britain, 1940–1994: The Long Separation* (London: Longmans, 1997), 19–25; Martin Thomas, "After Mers-el-Kébir: The Armed Neutrality of the Vichy French Navy, 1940–43," *English Historical Review* 112, no. 447 (1997): 642–70; "Mers-el-Kébir: A Battle Between Friends," 2003, www.militaryhistoryonline.com/; Churchill, *Their Finest Hour*, 201–5.

302   *Interview with André Jaffre, survivor of Mers-el-Kébir attack*: *Daily Mail*, February 5, 2010.

303   *Reaction to attack on the French Fleet*: Home Intelligence, July 4, 1940.

303   *"All regions express widespread approval"*: Ibid., July 5, 1940.

303   *Mers-el-Kébir impresses Roosevelt*: Gilbert, *Finest Hour*, 643–44.

304   *"The elimination of the French Navy"*: Churchill, *Their Finest Hour*, 205.

305   *Halifax and the Swedish approach*: Ponting, *1940*, 113–16.

306   *he had come halfway to Churchill's position*: In an article in the July 28, 1940, *Sunday Pictorial*, the former prime minister wrote: "We first have to prove to Hitler's satisfaction that this combination [of air, sea, and ground defenses] is invincible." See also Taylor, *Lloyd George*, 378.

307   *Report of Charles Gardner*: Calder, *The People's War*, 143; Home Intelligence, July 15, 1940.

308 *Hitler reduces size of army*: Paul Addison and Jeremy A. Crang, *The Burning Blue: A New History of the Battle of Britain* (London: Faber and Faber, 2011), 16.

308 *Hitler leaves invasion option open*: Ibid., 268–69.

309 *Senior British military officials express doubts*: Esnouf, *British Government War Aims*, 265; Churchill, *Their Finest Hour*, 283; Macleod and Kelly, *Time Unguarded*, 365; Bryant, *The Turn of the Tide*, 155.

310 *Profile of Dowding*: Korda, *With Wings Like Eagles*, 132, 151–52; *The Herald* (Scotland), September 8, 2000.

310 *Commander of the Home Fleet refuses to take his ships south*: Ismay, *The Memoirs of General Lord Hastings Ismay*, 188–89.

311 *Number of German and British fighters*: Terraine, *A Time for Courage*, 170–81.

311 *Public ownership and views*: The public's growing ownership of the war and views on how it should be fought begins to become apparent in the mid-July morale reports of Home Intelligence. July 16: "Evidence suggests that . . . the public in raided areas are becoming acclimatized to air raids. Damage is accepted philosophically." July 17: "Growing criticism of lack of details published about air raid casualties. General agreement that raid warnings should not be sounded for lone raiders. Widespread view that many local authorities are not providing facilities for collecting and separating waste."

312 *"People laughed and jeered"*: Home Intelligence, July 20, 1940.

312 *Lee and his view of Britain's prospects*: James Leutze, ed., *The London Journal of General Raymond E. Lee, 1940–1941* (Boston: Little Brown, 1971), 36–38.

312 *Kennedy's briefing to visiting military dignitaries*: Ibid., 36–38.

312 *Lee visits Dowding at Fighter Command*: Ibid., 30.

313 *First German attack of Eagle Day*: Richard Collier, *Eagle Day: The Battle of Britain* (New York: Dutton, 1966), 81–83.

315 *August 14, 1940, Eagle Day plus one*: Ibid., 75; Terraine, *A Time for Courage*, 186.

316 *"Wipe" the RAF from the sky*: Addison and Crang, *The Burning Blue*, 59.

316 *Attack of August 15, 1940*: T. D. C. James, *The Battle of Britain*, vol. 2, *The Air Defense of Britain* (New York: Routledge, 2000), 85.

317 *attack on Tyneside*: Collier, *Eagle Day*, 83–85.

318 *Second attack on Eastchurch*: James, *The Battle of Britain*, 61, 86–87; Collier, *Eagle Day*, 86.

318 *attack on Croyden*: James, *The Battle of Britain*, 91.

319 *Churchill and Ismay visit Fighter Command*: Ismay, *The Memoirs of General Lord Hastings Ismay*, 180–83.

319 *Air war in late August and early September*: James, *The Battle of Britain*, 100–130.

320 *Isaiah Berlin on Churchill*: Isaiah Berlin, "Mr. Churchill," *The Atlantic*, September 1949.

PHOTO CREDITS

INDEX

INDEX

INDEX

Chamberlain, Neville (*cont.*)
  criticisms of, 42–43, 90–92
  declaration of war, 40
  defeatism of, 166
  desire to delay war, 24, 83–84
  ego and vanity of, 17, 24
  fall of, 108–28
  foreign policy of, 19
  the French and, 85–86
  German Anschluss, reaction to, 20
  German coup attempts and, 68
  on German occupation of Norway,
    96–97
  Germany's invasion of Poland and,
    30–31, 37
  "gravest possible conditions"
    statement, 30, 326n
  guarantee to Poland, 27, 88
  hailed as hero, 25–26
  Hitler and, 17
  Hitler meets with, at Berchtesgaden,
    September 1938, 22–23
  Hitler peace offer, October 12, 1939,
    rejection of, 66
  indecision of, 31–32
  invasion threat and, 309
  "Iron Man defense" of, 124, 132
  Kennedy and, 47, 48
  the king and, 46, 129, 130, 131
  Lloyd George and, 243
  on Lloyd George's evisceration in the
    House of Commons, 45
  military budget cuts and, 18
  "missed the bus" phrase and, 92, 118,
    123, 126, 127
  Munich Conference and, 24–25
  Mussolini and, 17
  "In the Name of God, go" phrase
    and, 123, 126
  negotiated peace settlement and,
    46–47, 198
  Norwegian campaign and, 98, 117
  opinions about, 16–17, 129
  "peace in our time," 25, 30, 68
  pessimism and morale, 254
  political climb of, 16

  political family of, 16
  popularity of, 90, 104, 129
  RAF squadrons pledged to France by,
    160–61
  rearmament plan, 83–84
  resignation, 136–37, 142–43
  Reynaud and, 87–88
  Reynaud's three-point plan memo
    and, 83–84
  Roosevelt and, 72
  speech to House of Commons after
    invasion of Poland, 37–38
  study group on French surrender,
    176
  Sudeten crisis and, 22–24
  terminal cancer of, 198
  United States and, 50
  war leadership of, 31, 42, 91
  warning sent to Germany, 31–32
  war plan of, 41–42, 47, 85–86, 88
  war policy and, 85, 167
  Welles's meeting with, 75
  Whitsun debate, 115, 117–19, 128
Channon, Henry, 36–37, 38, 141
  appearance, 36
  as Chamberlain supporter, 37, 38–39,
    117, 123, 125, 145, 259
  on Churchill, 111–12
  egotism of, 36
  on London in May 1940, 110
  pessimism of, 253
  on Whitsun debate, 118
Chaplin, Charlie, 73–74
"Charge of the Light Brigade"
  (Tennyson), 241
Charmley, John, 250
Chiefs of Staff, 83–84
  British Strategy in a Certain Eventuality,
    176–78, 183, 197, 204, 217, 277
  British Strategy in the Near Future, 197,
    204–5, 217, 277
  first warning about new European
    war, 8
  importance of airpower, 277
  memorandum of 1937, 18
  Norwegian expedition and, 100

352

INDEX

INDEX

INDEX

Mers-el-Kébir undermines influence on Roosevelt, 303
  Roosevelt and, 165
  self-promotion by, 47–48
Kent, England, 308, 310
Keyes, Sir Roger, 119–20, 217
Keynes, John Maynard, 7
King, Cecil, 112
King, Mackenzie, 22–23, 220
Kitchener, Horatio Herbert, 3
Koestler, Arthur, 274
Kordt, Theo, 31, 326n
Kris, Ernst, 320

Labour Party, 90, 131
  anti-Churchill sentiment in, 132
  antiwar position and, 14, 27
  Bournemouth conference, 134–35, 141
  Chamberlain confidence vote and, 124, 126, 132, 134
  Chamberlain not supported by, 142, 143
  Churchill as PM and, 138
  Churchill's appointments from, 146
  East Fulham by-election on disarmament platform, 8
  Greenwood's speech for war, 38
  Tonypandy, 132, 138
Last, Nella, 144, 275
"Last Time I Saw Paris, The" (song), 139, 291
Laval, Pierre, 54, 75, 89
Lavelle, Major, 197
Law, Dick, 92
League of Nations, 7
  Germany and Japan walk out, 8
  Rhineland coup and, 15
Lebrun, Albert, 74–75, 187
Lee, Raymond, 312–13
Left Book Club, 115
Lelong, Albert, 272–73
Leopold, King of Belgium, 150, 217, 233, 235, 237, 259
Liberal Party, 126
Liddell Hart, Basil, 112–13, 167

Life magazine, 65
Lille, France, 238–39, 252–53
Limoges, France, 237
Lindbergh, Charles, 49
Lloyd George, David, 28, 42–46, 62–63, 123, 126, 189
  ambitions to be PM, 243, 306
  Chamberlain and, 243–44
  as Chamberlain's primary critic, 43
  Churchill's meetings with, 241–44
  compromise by, 277
  on Hitler, 43
  memorandum of May 1940, 242, 242n
  negotiated peace settlement and, 44–46, 112–13, 134, 167, 243, 243n, 244, 306
  posed as Chamberlain successor, 112–14
  Whitsun debate, 125
London
  air defenses, 30, 32, 39, 248
  Cenotaph (empty tomb) in, 4, 201
  Finsbury Square, 105
  first air raid alert, 40–41
  German air attacks on, September 9 and September 15, 1940, 319
  morale in, 162–63, 190–92, 195, 210, 319
  National Prayer Day in, May 26, 1940, 196–97, 199–201
  preparation for war, 30, 39–40, 199
  public fear, 255
  relocations and evacuations, 30, 61, 178
  Victory Day Parade (1919), 1–4
  warning about German air strikes, 39
  war rumors, 255
Londonderry, Lord, 28, 45
London Evening Standard, 28
London Illustrated News, Never Again and, 7
Lothian, Lord, 298
Luftwaffe (German Air Force), 9n, 33, 63, 65, 66, 281
  Adler Tag (Eagle Day) attack on Britain, August 13, 1940, 313–15

361

INDEX

INDEX

INDEX

INDEX

About the Author

John Kelly is a talented popular historian who specializes in narrative history. He is the author of *The Graves Are Walking: The Great Famine and the Saga of the Irish People*; *The Great Mortality: An Intimate History of the Black Death, the Most Devastating Plague of All Time*; *Three on the Edge*; and more. Kelly lives in New York City and Sandisfield, Massachusetts.